First World War

and Army of Occupation

War Diary

France, Belgium and Germany

63 (ROYAL NAVAL) DIVISION
Divisional Troops
Royal Army Medical Corps
150 Field Ambulance
14 May 1916 - 28 May 1919

WO95/3106/3

The Naval & Military Press Ltd
www.nmarchive.com
Published in association with The National Archives

Published by

The Naval & Military Press Ltd

Unit 10 Ridgewood Industrial Park,

Uckfield, East Sussex,

TN22 5QE England

Tel: +44 (0) 1825 749494

www.naval-military-press.com

www.nmarchive.com

This diary has been reprinted in facsimile from the original. Any imperfections are inevitably reproduced and the quality may fall short of modern type and cartographic standards.

Contents

Document type	Place/Title	Date From	Date To
Heading	WO95/3106/3		
Heading	63rd Division 3rd Fld Ambulance R.N.D May 1916-Jun 1917 (became 150th (RN) Fld Amb. Jly 1917)		
Heading	War Diary of 3rd Field Ambulance R.N.D From 14th May 1916 To 31st May 1916 Vol 1		
War Diary	Mudros West	14/05/1916	16/05/1916
War Diary	Mudros	18/05/1916	18/05/1916
War Diary	At Sea	19/05/1916	23/05/1916
War Diary	In Train	24/05/1916	25/05/1916
War Diary	Wanel	26/05/1916	31/05/1916
Heading	War Diary 3rd Field Ambulance R.N. Division From 1st June 1916 To 30th June 1916		
War Diary	Wanel	01/06/1916	01/06/1916
War Diary	La Somme	01/06/1916	12/06/1916
War Diary	Wanel	13/06/1916	16/06/1916
War Diary	Abbeville	16/06/1916	16/06/1916
War Diary	Bruay	17/06/1916	17/06/1916
War Diary	La Thieuloye	18/06/1916	30/06/1916
Heading	War Diary of 3rd Field Ambulance 63rd (RN) Division From July 1st 1916 To July 31st 1916		
War Diary	La Thieuloye	01/07/1916	16/07/1916
War Diary	Left La Thieuloye arrived	17/07/1916	17/07/1916
War Diary	Barlin	17/07/1916	31/07/1916
Heading	War Diary of 3rd Field Ambulance 63rd (RN) Division From August 1st 1916 To August 31st 1916		
War Diary	Barlin	01/08/1916	31/08/1916
Heading	War Diary of 3rd F.A From September 1st 1916 To September 30 1916		
War Diary	Barlin	01/09/1916	17/09/1916
War Diary	Bruay	18/09/1916	30/09/1916
Heading	War Diary of 3rd Field Ambce 63rd (R.N.) Division From 1st October To 31st October 16		
War Diary	Bruay	01/10/1916	03/10/1916
War Diary	On The March	04/10/1916	04/10/1916
War Diary	En Route	05/10/1916	05/10/1916
War Diary	On The March	05/10/1916	06/10/1916
War Diary	O.36.c.9.3 In Camp Rr of Verennes-Harponville Road	07/10/1916	10/10/1916
War Diary	O.36.c.9.3	10/10/1916	25/10/1916
War Diary	Q.31.b.7.7 On Rt Of Englebelmer-Martinsart Road	26/10/1916	27/10/1916
War Diary	Q.31.b.7.7	27/10/1916	31/10/1916
Heading	War Diary of 3rd Field Ambce 63rd (R.N.) Division From November 1st 1916 To November 30th 1916		
Heading	63rd Div 3rd R.N.D Field Ambulance Nov 1916		
War Diary	In The Field	01/11/1916	30/11/1916
Heading	War Diary of 3rd Field Ambce 63rd (R.N.) Division From December 1st 16 To December 31st 16		
War Diary	In The Field	01/12/1916	31/12/1916
Heading	War Diary of 3rd Field Ambce 63rd (R.N.) Division From Jan 1st 1917 To Jan 31st 1917 Vol 9		
War Diary	In The Field	01/01/1917	21/01/1917

War Diary	Clairfaye	21/01/1917	02/02/1917
Heading	War Diary of 3rd Field Ambulance 63rd (R.N.) Division From February 1st 1917 To February 28th 1917 Vol 10		
War Diary	Clairfaye	03/02/1917	12/02/1917
War Diary	In The Field	12/02/1917	28/02/1917
Heading	War Diary of 3rd Field Ambulance 63rd (R.N.) Division From March 1st 1917 To March 31st 1917 Vol XI		
War Diary	Clairfaye	01/03/1917	20/03/1917
War Diary	Beauval	21/03/1917	21/03/1917
War Diary	Bonniers	22/03/1917	22/03/1917
War Diary	Blangermont	23/03/1917	24/03/1917
War Diary	Hestrus	25/03/1917	25/03/1917
War Diary	Livossart	25/03/1917	26/03/1917
War Diary	La Flandrie	27/03/1917	31/03/1917
Heading	War Diary of 3rd Field Ambce 63rd (R.N.) Division From April 1st 1917 To April 30th 1917		
Miscellaneous	Summary Of Medical War Diaries For 3rd R.N F.A. 63rd Div 13th Corps	11/04/1917	11/04/1917
Miscellaneous	3rd R.N F.A 63rd Divn. 13th Corps		
War Diary	La Flandrie O.36.c.4.7 Map 36a Edition 6 France	01/04/1917	03/04/1917
War Diary	La Flandrie	03/04/1917	08/04/1917
War Diary	Bruay J.16.c.8.2	09/04/1917	10/04/1917
War Diary	Bruay	11/04/1917	11/04/1917
War Diary	Bajus	12/04/1917	14/04/1917
War Diary	St. Catherine Arras	15/04/1917	17/04/1917
War Diary	St Catherine	18/04/1917	30/04/1917
Heading	War Diary of 3rd (R.N.) Field Ambulance From May 1st 1915 To May 31st 1915		
Miscellaneous	Summary Of Medical War Diaries For 3rd R.N. F.A 63rd Div. 13th Corps		
Miscellaneous	3rd R.N F.A 63rd Div. 13th Corps		
War Diary	St Catharine	01/05/1917	03/05/1917
War Diary	Guestreville	03/05/1917	11/05/1917
War Diary	Cambligneul	12/05/1917	21/05/1917
War Diary	Anzin St Aubin	21/05/1917	31/05/1917
Heading	War Diary of 3rd (R.N.) Field Amb From June 1st 1917 To June 30th 1917		
War Diary	Anzin St Aubin	01/06/1917	11/06/1917
War Diary	Garubligueul	11/06/1917	16/06/1917
War Diary	Maroeuil	17/06/1917	30/06/1917
Heading	63rd Division 150th (R.N.) Field Ambulance 1916 May-1919 May		
Heading	War Diary of 150th (R.N.) Field Ambulance From July 1st 1917 To July 31st 1917		
War Diary	Maroeuil	01/07/1917	03/07/1917
War Diary	Anzin-St. Aubin	04/07/1917	31/07/1917
Heading	War Diary of 150 (R.N.) Field Ambulance From 1st August 1917 To 31st August 1917		
War Diary	Anzin St. Aubin	01/08/1917	31/08/1917
Heading	No.150 F.A Sept 1917		
Heading	War Diary of 150th (R.N.) Field Ambulance From 1st September 1917 To 30th September 1917		
War Diary	Anzin St. Aubin Map 51 B.G.7.c.7.8	12/09/1917	24/09/1917
War Diary	Beugin Map 36 B.P.1.d.0.2	24/09/1917	29/09/1917

Heading	War Diary of 150th (R.N.) Field Ambulance From October 1st To October 31st 1917 Vol 18		
War Diary	Beugin Map 36 B P.1.d.0.2	01/10/1917	03/10/1917
War Diary	Zermezeele I.27.d.4.6 Map Belgium And France Sheet 27	07/10/1917	07/10/1917
War Diary	Houtkerque Map Belgium d 18.6.6.3 France Sheet 27	11/10/1917	21/10/1917
War Diary	Duhallow C.25.d.3.0 Sheet 28 Belgium & France	24/10/1916	30/10/1916
Heading	War Diary of 150th (R.N.) Field Ambulance From 1st November 1917 To 30th November 1917		
Heading	No.150 F.A. Nov 1917		
War Diary	Duhallow C.25.d.3.0 Sheet Belgium & France	04/11/1917	18/11/1917
Heading	No.150 F.A. Dec 1917		
Heading	War Diary of 150th (R.N.) Field Ambulance From 1st December 1917 To 31st December 1917		
War Diary	Duhallow C.25.d.3.0 Sheet 28 Belgium & France	01/12/1917	06/12/1917
War Diary	Godewaersvelde Q.23.a.3.5 Sheet 27 Belgium & France	10/12/1917	10/12/1917
War Diary	Rocquiny O.27.d.4.8 Sheet 57c	11/12/1917	13/12/1917
War Diary	Etricourt V.13.a.3.9 Sheet 57c	14/12/1917	14/12/1917
War Diary	Nurlu V.28.d Sheet 57c	16/12/1917	16/12/1917
War Diary	Lechelle P.25.c Map 57c	30/12/1917	30/12/1917
Heading	No.150 F.A Jan 1918		
War Diary	Metz Q.19.b.9.1 Sheet 57c	02/01/1918	24/01/1918
War Diary	Rocquigny O.27.d.O.4. Sheet 57 c	25/01/1918	30/01/1918
Heading	No.150 F.A. Feb 1918		
War Diary	Rocquigny O.27.d.0.4 Sheet 57c	09/02/1918	09/02/1918
War Diary	Barastre O.15.b.5.4 Sheet 57c	14/02/1918	14/02/1918
Heading	150 F.A March 1918		
War Diary	Barastre O.15.b.5.4 Sheet 57c	01/03/1918	15/03/1918
War Diary	Barastre	16/03/1918	23/03/1918
War Diary	Les Boeufs	24/03/1918	24/03/1918
War Diary	Meaulte	24/03/1918	24/03/1918
War Diary	Bouzincourt	25/03/1918	25/03/1918
War Diary	Lealvillers	25/03/1918	31/03/1918
Heading	150th Field Ambulance April 1918		
Heading	War Diary of 150th (R.N.) Field Ambulance From 1st April 1918 To 30th April 1918 Volume XXIII		
War Diary	Lealvillers	01/04/1918	02/04/1918
War Diary	Clairfaye	03/04/1918	22/04/1918
War Diary	On Line of March	22/04/1918	22/04/1918
War Diary	La Vicogne	23/04/1918	30/04/1918
Heading	No.150 (R.N.) F.A May 1918		
Heading	War Diary of 150th (R.N.) Field Ambulance From 1st May 1918 To 31st May 1918		
War Diary	La Vicogne	01/05/1918	05/05/1918
War Diary	Le Menage	06/05/1918	31/05/1918
Heading	150th F.A June 1918		
Heading	War Diary of 150th (R.N.) Field Ambulance From 1st June 1918 To 30th June 1918		
War Diary	La Meaage (Cramont)	01/06/1918	05/06/1918
War Diary	Toutencourt	06/06/1918	22/06/1918
War Diary	Raincheval	23/06/1918	30/06/1918
Heading	150th F.A July 1918		
Heading	War Diary of 150th (R.N.) Field Ambulance From 1st July 1918 To 31st July 1918		
War Diary	Raincheval	01/07/1918	28/07/1918
War Diary	H.24.d.9.7 Sheet 57 D	29/07/1918	31/07/1918

Heading	War Diary of 150th (R.N.) Field Ambulance From 1st August 1918 To 31st August 1918		
War Diary	Marieux	01/08/1918	04/08/1918
War Diary	Beauquesne	04/08/1918	08/08/1918
War Diary	Beaucourt Sur L'Hallue	09/08/1918	09/08/1918
War Diary	Beaucourt	10/08/1918	14/08/1918
War Diary	Famechon	15/08/1918	15/08/1918
War Diary	Thievres	15/08/1918	20/08/1918
War Diary	Pas	20/08/1918	20/08/1918
War Diary	Fonquevillers	21/08/1918	24/08/1918
War Diary	Achiet Le Petit	25/08/1918	30/08/1918
War Diary	Boiry Ste Rictrude	31/08/1918	31/08/1918
Miscellaneous	Appendix to 150th (R.N.) Field Ambulance Order No.0811	19/08/1918	19/08/1918
Heading	Sept 1918		
Heading	War Diary of 150th (R.N.) Field Ambulance From 1st September 1918 To 30th September 1918		
War Diary	Boiry Ste Rictrude	01/09/1918	01/09/1918
War Diary	Nr Henin Sur Cojeul	02/09/1918	02/09/1918
War Diary	Hendecourt	02/09/1918	03/09/1918
War Diary	Cagnicourt	03/09/1918	07/09/1918
War Diary	Croisilles	08/09/1918	09/09/1918
War Diary	Boyelles	09/09/1918	09/09/1918
War Diary	Laherliere	09/09/1918	09/09/1918
War Diary	Bailleuval	09/09/1918	10/09/1918
War Diary	Blaireville	10/09/1918	12/09/1918
War Diary	St Leger	21/09/1918	26/09/1918
War Diary	Louverval	26/09/1918	27/09/1918
War Diary	Blaireville	13/09/1918	16/09/1918
War Diary	St Leger	16/09/1918	20/09/1918
War Diary	Louverval	27/09/1918	29/09/1918
War Diary	Bapaume-Cambrai Rd	30/09/1918	30/09/1918
Heading	150th F.A Oct 1918		
War Diary	Bapaume-Cambrai Rd	01/10/1918	01/10/1918
War Diary	57.c. S.E.28.c.7.7	01/10/1918	07/10/1918
War Diary	Anneux	07/10/1918	09/10/1918
War Diary	Morchies	09/10/1918	11/10/1918
War Diary	Belval	12/10/1918	22/10/1918
War Diary	Villers-Sir-Simon	23/10/1918	31/10/1918
Heading	150th F.A Nov 1918		
War Diary	Villers-Sir-Simon	01/11/1918	01/11/1918
War Diary	Le Forest	01/11/1918	05/11/1918
War Diary	Thiant	05/11/1918	06/11/1918
War Diary	Saultain	06/11/1918	07/11/1918
War Diary	Sebouquiaux	07/11/1918	09/11/1918
War Diary	Audregnies	09/11/1918	10/11/1918
War Diary	Sars La Bruyiere	10/11/1918	10/11/1918
War Diary	Bougnies	10/11/1918	26/11/1918
War Diary	Erquennes	26/11/1918	30/11/1918
Miscellaneous	List Of Instructions		
Miscellaneous	Time Table		
Heading	No.150 F.A. Dec 1918		
War Diary	Erquennes	01/12/1918	23/12/1918
War Diary	In The Field	24/12/1918	31/12/1918
Heading	63rd Div Box 2985 No.150 F.A Jan 1919		
War Diary	In The Field	01/01/1919	31/01/1919

Heading	War Diary of 150 (Royal Naval) Field Ambulance For Period 1st February 1919 To 28th February 1919		
War Diary	In The Field	12/01/1919	28/02/1919
Heading	War Diary of the 150th (R.N.) Field Ambulance From 1st March 1919 To 31st March 1919		
War Diary	In The Field	01/03/1919	31/03/1919
Heading	War Diary of 150th (R.N.) Field Ambulance For Period 1st April 1919 To 30th April 1919		
War Diary	In The Field	01/04/1919	30/04/1919
Heading	No.150 Field Ambulance May 1919		
War Diary	In The Field	01/05/1919	10/05/1919
War Diary	St Ghislain Belgium	10/05/1919	21/05/1919
War Diary	Dunkirk	22/05/1919	24/05/1919
War Diary	At Sea	25/05/1919	25/05/1919
War Diary	Southampton	25/05/1919	26/05/1919
War Diary	Aldershot	26/05/1919	28/05/1919
War Diary	London	28/05/1919	28/05/1919

63RD DIVISION

3RD FLD AMBULANCE R.N.D.
MAY 1916-JUN 1917
(BECAME 150TH(RN)FLD AMB.JLY 1917)

3 F. Amb
May
Vol I

May/16

War Diary
of
3rd Field Ambulance
R.N.D.

From
14th May 1916.
to
31st May 1916.

To/
The A G's Office
3rd Echelon

Will A Sewell
Surg. RNVR
O.C. 3rd F.A.

Med. E. F.

May/16

Army Form C. 2118.

Instructions regarding War Diaries and Intelligence Summaries are contained in F. S. Regs., Part II. and the Staff Manual respectively. Title pages will be prepared in manuscript.

WAR DIARY
or
~~INTELLIGENCE SUMMARY~~
(Erase heading not required.)

Hour, Date, Place	Summary of Events and Information	Remarks and references to Appendices
14th May 1916 Mudros West.	Instructed by Staff Surgeon Stanford R.N. O.C. 2nd Field Amb. R.N.D to take charge temporarily of 3rd F.A. R.N.D, which had been reformed. The personnel only are available ~~&~~ no officers ~~&~~ no stores.	
15th & 16th May 1916. Mudros West	Standing by to embark	
18th May 1916. Mudros	Embarked with 2nd F.A. on board H.M.T Franconia for France.	
17th May to 23rd May at Sea.	Voyage good - arrived Marseilles 23rd and embarked in train for Railhead at ~~S~~ 1738	
24th May to 25th May in train	Passed through Lyons, Versailles & disembarked at Pont Remy about 1800. ~~to~~ Left Pont Remy at 2000 & arrived Wanel where ambulance was billeted.	
26th May to 31st May Wanel.	Men have been employed cleaning up billets, squad & stretcher drill route marches & physical drill. No stores so ambulance not available for patients. Stores, horse & motor transport, have been indented for, also clothing for personnel	W.A. Sewell Surgeon R.N.V.R.

1247 W 3299 200,000 (E) 8/14 J.B.C. & A. Forms/C. 2118/11.

No 3 June Vol 2

June/16

War Diary

3rd Field Ambulance
R.N. Division

From.
1st June 1916
to
30th June 1916

To A-G's Office
3rd Echelon

Will A. Sewell
Surgeon. R.N.V.R.
O.C. 3rd F.A.
R.N.D.

Instructions regarding War Diaries and Intelligence Summaries are contained in F. S. Regs., Part II. and the Staff Manual respectively. Title pages will be prepared in manuscript.

WAR DIARY
or
~~INTELLIGENCE SUMMARY~~

(Erase heading not required.)

(1.)

Army Form C. 2118.

Hour, Date, Place	Summary of Events and Information	Remarks and references to Appendices
1st June 1916. WANEL LA SOMME.	Men have been exercised in stretcher & squad drill & route marching no complaints from villagers.	
2nd June 1916 } 3rd June 1916 } →	Signalling – physical drill route march.	2nd June 1916 Surgeon Gow rejoined 2nd F.A. R.N.D.
4th June 1916	Physical drill & lecture on 1st aid & use of Field dressings – afternoon make & mend for all hands.	
5th June 1916	Gas helmets have arrived – ~~drill~~ helmets issued and men instructed in there use – short lecture on measures against gas for sections A & B. Medical equipment – panniers etc drawn from Abbeville No. 2. Stationary hospital. Riding horses arrived 12 in number.	
6th June 1916.	Drew 3 ambulance wagons, 3 water carts, horse transport / 8 horses [6 G S limbered & 6 G S wagons & one maltese cart] today at ABBEVILLE from advanced Horse Transport depot.	
7th June – 11th June 1916	Routine as usual, gas helmet drill, stretcher drill route marching. ~~[illegible]~~ June 10th discharged C.F Chapman to 1st F.A. R.N.D suffering from abdominal colic – appendix? June 11th detailed Sergt Bagley to proceed to AIRES for gas instruction.	
12th June. 1916.	Order by the King referring to loss of Lord Kitchener in H.M.S Hampshire 7th June – Routine Order 62 relating to cameras read to all hands – cameras have all been sent home. One section had route march taking their gear & wagons with them. Signal from No. 2. Stationary Hospital Abbeville stating that Pte Chapman has died of acute intestinal obstruction ~~[illegible]~~ operation performed. Glanders test applied to Horses by A.D.V.S. Major Williams.	W. A. Sewell Surgeon RNVR

1247 W 3299 200,000 (E) 8/14 J.B.C. & A. Forms/C. 2118/11.

Instructions regarding War Diaries and Intelligence Summaries are contained in F. S. Regs., Part II. and the Staff Manual respectively. Title pages will be prepared in manuscript.

WAR DIARY
or
INTELLIGENCE SUMMARY.
(Erase heading not required.)

(2)

Army Form C. 2118.

Place	Date	Hour	Summary of Events and Information	Remarks and references to Appendices
WANEL ~~13 June 1916~~	13.6.16		Mallein test on horses negative. Surgeons Mayne & Sparrow with 33 other ratings arrived from MUDROS via MARSEILLES.	
WANEL	14.6.16.		Surgeons Mayne & Sparrow with two men left to report at ABBEVILLE at 2100 to proceed to join 2nd F.A. they sent off base kit today. Pte Cleves S.3577 to be acting lance corporal unpaid for packstore duties. Surgeon Cox from 1st F.A R.N.D. joined up for duty temporarily	
ditto.	15.6.16		Proceeded to 1st Brigade Head Quarters CITERNE where instructions received that Ambulance was to pack up & proceed to BRUAY where instructions as to eventual destination would be received. 3rd F.A. were to send 2 N.C.O.S & 2 men to TRIAGE ABBEVILLE to report to R.T.O. at 13.15 main body to arrive at 13.30 finishing loading ~~at~~ 16.45 and train to leave at 17.25. Journey to take about 6 hours in train. Men to have two days rations. All gear except cooks gear packed in wagons by 1800.	
WANEL	16.6.15	08.30	All billets cleaned up - latrines filled in. Men & transport fell in 08.30 & ~~and~~ column moved off. After 6 kilometers halted to water horses about 10.30 again halted 11.30 for dinner arrived TRIAGE at 13.10 and as station was clear parked wagons beside line where train was expected. Train was late & did not come alongside till 14.40 instead of 13.30. Men worked well & loading finished at 16.42. Men had	W. A. Sewell Surg RNVR

T.134. Wt. W708-776. 500000. 4/15. Sir J. C. & S.

Instructions regarding War Diaries and Intelligence Summaries are contained in F. S. Regs., Part II. and the Staff Manual respectively. Title pages will be prepared in manuscript.

WAR DIARY
or
~~INTELLIGENCE SUMMARY.~~
(Erase heading not required.)

(3)

Army Form C. 2118.

Place	Date	Hour	Summary of Events and Information	Remarks and references to Appendices
ABBEVILLE.	16 June 1916	–	tea and were embarked at 17.15 train left about 17 25 & arrived BRUAY 10.30. where we were instructed to disembark & proceed to LA THIEULOYE. By 11.30 train unloaded. Horses were watered & men served with tea.	
BRUAY	17.6.16	00.10	left BRUAY proceeding by HOUDAIN - BEUGIN - LA COMTÉ - BAJUS arrived at LA THIEULOYE at 04.00. no men fell out & all were present at the end of the march. Weather was excellent & not too hot. Billets were ready & after parking transport men piped down for about four hours. Horses were parked in field & picketed out.	
LA THIEULOYE	18.6.16.		Moved horses & drivers into an empty farm were good accommodation & undercover field was very wet & muddy. men were moved into billets which were more convenient & closer together.	
La Thieuloye	19.6.16 to 21-6.16		Routine - drill physical - gas helmet - stretcher. men warned about agricultural machines being moved out of barns etc - Fires - passing through cultivated ~~ground~~ fields - damage to crops. - spies. Helmets inspected & marked with date of issue. On 21st sent 1 Sergt 2 corporals & 47 men by motor bus to work under officer in charge forest control in forest of ~~R~~ DE NIEPPE - these left at 08.00 About 11.00 Lieut Rowley R.M. arrived to take charge his orders being to report A.M. sent him a/by car. Motor Ambulances five Siddley Deasy large cars & two small Fords arrived this morning 1 Sergt 1 lance copl and	W.A. Sewell Surg RNVR

T. 131. Wt. W708–776. 500000. 4/15. Sir J. C. & S.

Instructions regarding War Diaries and Intelligence Summaries are contained in F. S. Regs., Part II. and the Staff Manual respectively. Title pages will be prepared in manuscript.

WAR DIARY
or
~~INTELLIGENCE SUMMARY.~~

(Erase heading not required.)

(4.)

Army Form C. 2118.

Place	Date	Hour	Summary of Events and Information	Remarks and references to Appendices
LA THIEULOYE	22.6.16.		Routine gas helmet drill, stretcher, wagon, & physical drill. Tent pitching.	
	23.6.16.		Surgeon Cox rejoined 1st F.A. Surgeon Low attached to 3rd F.A. from 2nd F.A. to assist in routine.	
	24.6.16.		Route march with all gear weather very bad. Horses inoculated to test for glanders by Captn Massey.	
	25.6.16		Sunday routine make & mend in afternoon. 50 men & 1 officer proceeded to presentation of Croix de Guerre by General Wilson to Lieut Corkey, Surgeon Schlessinger & Medaille Militaire to Lieut Quartermaster Wilson.	
	26.6.16		1. N.C.O. & 20 ratings detailed to proceed to HOUDAIN to report to O.C. 25th Coy. R.E. routine as usual route march packs, gas helmet stretcher & physical drill.	
	27.6.16.		All horses seem healthy no trace of glanders. Have been instructed to take over a Chateau & prepare it for sick wounded & rest cases. All hands took over and washed place down which was in filthy state now looks much better.	
	28.6.16.		Sent "A" section to do duty at Chateau, Staff Sergt Booth to be senior N.C.O. Inoculation "C" section	
	29.6.16.		Gas helmet drill etc as usual. Order to be read out re saluting. Inoculation "B" section	
	30.6.16.		Physical drill stretcher drill. Lieut Quartermaster J. Wilson joined up last night for duty.	

W. H. A. Sewell
Surgeon RNVR

T.134. Wt. W768-776. 500000. 4/15. Sir J. C. & S.

July/16

Headquarters.
3rd Field Ambulance
63rd (R N) Division
July 31st 1916

"Confidential."

War Diary
of
3rd Field Ambulance.
63rd (R N) Division
from
July 1st 1916
to
July 31st 1916.

To/
The A.G.'s Office
3rd Echelon

William Bradbury
Surgeon R N
O.C. 3rd F.A.

63 July
3 F. Amb
Vol 3

Instructions regarding War Diaries and Intelligence Summaries are contained in F. S. Regs., Part II. and the Staff Manual respectively. Title pages will be prepared in manuscript.

WAR DIARY
or
~~INTELLIGENCE SUMMARY.~~
(Erase heading not required.)

July (1)

Army Form C. 2118.

Place	Date	Hour	Summary of Events and Information	Remarks and references to Appendices
LA THIEULOYE	1st July 1916		Routine wagon, stretcher drill with 1st Aid. Route march. 40 men sent as working party to O.C. Forest control De Meppe to replace 40 men supernumerary to F.A. establishment who were to be returned to base. Attack by French & British began this morning 07.30.	
" "	2nd July 1916		Sunday routine - ~~church~~ church Service by Padré Fleming 16.30. Attack to the South said to be progressing. Two riding horses received today.	
" "	3rd July 1916		Sent 40 men to base depot ETAPLES today marched to BRUAY ~~this~~ this morning - 10 minutes halt every hour - distance covered 15 Kilometres in 3 hours and 10 minutes. Handed 40 men & 5. P.B. men to Surgeon Crooke R.N.V.R at BRUAY station as he was in charge of party proceeding to base.	
" "	4th July 1916		Captn Massy inspected horses today and found all correct. Work at chateau proceeding and sick quarters much improved in consequence. Received new code words tonight from the 4th Corps. Very heavy rain during afternoon with thunder storm. Order S/361 from D.M.S. re slight cases loafing about entrances to dressing ~~station~~ stations of FAs this is forbidden. 793. Defective Vision cases to be sent any day of the week to NO. IV. Stationary Hospital ARQUES.	
" "	5th July 1916		Continuing work at Chateau cases are beginning to arrive. Captains Hutcheson & Lewis	Willa Sewell

T.134. Wt. W708–776. 500000. 4/15. Sir J. C. & S.

Instructions regarding War Diaries and Intelligence Summaries are contained in F. S. Regs., Part II. and the Staff Manual respectively. Title pages will be prepared in manuscript.

WAR DIARY
or
~~INTELLIGENCE SUMMARY.~~

(Erase heading not required.)

July (2.)

Army Form C. 2118.

Place	Date	Hour	Summary of Events and Information	Remarks and references to Appendices
LA THIEULOYE.	5th July 1916.		R.A.M.C. reported today for duty in ambulance and were taken on strength of unit. Surgeon Bradbury R.N. to be in command.	
	6th July 1916		Captains Davys & Lieuts Walker, Guthrie, & Aspinall reported for duty & were taken on strength of unit. Routine general fatigues & improvement at chateau.	
	7th July 1916.		Surgeon Bradbury visited ambulance prior to taking over tomorrow. Six tubs are now available with two Sawyer's stoves for washing purposes at the chateau.	W. L. A. Sewell
	8 July 1916.		Surgeon W. Bradbury arrived & took over Command from Surgeon Sewell R.N.V.R. Routine fatigues & improvements continued at Chateau.	
	9th July 1916.		Officers told off for their duties at Chateau for week ending July 16. Officer in charge of sick Captain Hatchem R.A.M.C to sleep there. Divine service by Padre Fleming 16.30. Order received from D.M.S 1st Army re speed of Motor Ambulance cars not to exceed 10 miles per hour.	
	10th July 1916.		Officers detailed for their Sections. Improvements continued at Chateau. Gas helmet drill and inspection of helmets.	
	11th July. 1916		Routine and work continued. Order re closing of Estaminets except during certain hours read on Parade.	W. Bradbury.

T.2134. Wt. W708-776. 500000. 4/15. Sir J. C. & S.

Instructions regarding War Diaries and Intelligence Summaries are contained in F. S. Regs., Part II. and the Staff Manual respectively. Title pages will be prepared in manuscript.

WAR DIARY
or
~~INTELLIGENCE SUMMARY.~~
(Erase heading not required.)

July (3)

Army Form C. 2118.

Place	Date	Hour	Summary of Events and Information	Remarks and references to Appendices
LATHIEULOYE	12 July	1916.	Routine continues the same, work continued on Chateau. The following order given to Officers 'As scabies is prevalent in this Division special care is to be taken in examination of patients; all cases of Scabies to be discharged to 1st F.A. R.N.D.'	
	13 July.	1916	Routine and work continued; instructions on Gas helmets and First Aid given. Lecture on the War given by Padre Fleming 1800.	
	14 July.	1916.	Holy Communion administered by Padre Fleming 07.00 Trial loading of a sections gear, B's sections gear loaded in 30 minutes. Bathing of personnel commenced.	
	15 July	1916	Lieut. Guthrie struck off strength; detailed for service with King Edwards Horse. Captain Forester R.A.M.C. taken on strength, but detached for service with IV Corps school of Instruction at Pernes.	
	16 July	1916	Divine Service held by Rev. Fleming 16.30. Preparations made to move, Stores loaded at 16.00 with exception of those at Chateau. Medical Comfort Panniers kept completely equipped. Men completely equipped with First Field dressings, Iron rations and water bottles thoroughly cleansed.	W Bradbury

T.134. Wt. W708–776. 500000. 4/15. Sir J. C. & S.

Instructions regarding War Diaries and Intelligence Summaries are contained in F. S. Regs., Part II. and the Staff Manual respectively. Title pages will be prepared in manuscript.

WAR DIARY
or
~~INTELLIGENCE SUMMARY.~~
(Erase heading not required.)

July (4)

Army Form C. 2118.

Place	Date	Hour	Summary of Events and Information	Remarks and references to Appendices
Left LA-THIEULOYE	17 July	1916	Reveille 0500. Men paraded 0745. Billets inspected 0715. Advance party	
	"	0815	consisting of Surgeon Gow 1 NCO + 2 men moved off at 0800. Captain Hutcheson	
arrived			also moved off at same time with Ambulance convoy containing patients	
BARLIN	"	14:30	who had to be taken with Unit. Unit moved off 08.15 and arrived	
			Q2 A62 by 14:30. Accomodation for patients consists of two wooden huts	
			capable of holding 60 men in each. Officers and men of Unit	
			billeted in houses in the vicinity.	
Barlin	18 July	1916	All available men employed on Sanitation, whitewashing wards, cookhouses	
			etc. digging of deep latrines (fly proof).	
	19 July	"	Work on Sanitation continued by all available men.	
	20 July		Ordinary routine continued and sanitation of which there remains much to	
			be done.	
	21 July		Ambulance inspected in morning by D.D.M.S and in afternoon by	
			D.M.S and D.A.D.M.S	
	22 July		Unit inspected for Scabies. Surgeon Sewell placed in charge of Surgical	
			ward. Surgeon Gow of Medical, and Lieut Walker R.A.M.C. of rest cases for	W Bradbury,
			week commencing July 22.	

Instructions regarding War Diaries and Intelligence Summaries are contained in F. S. Regs., Part II. and the Staff Manual respectively. Title pages will be prepared in manuscript.

WAR DIARY
or
~~INTELLIGENCE SUMMARY.~~
(Erase heading not required.)

July (5).

Army Form C. 2118.

Place	Date	Hour	Summary of Events and Information	Remarks and references to Appendices
BARLIN	23 July		All available men attended Divine service at Barlin 10.00; Mass for Roman Catholics in Barlin Church 09.00.	
	24 July		Ordinary Routine with necessary Sanitary work continued. B section stood off duty from 12.00; all this section's kit being packed and billets thoroughly cleaned preparatory to moving off at short notice.	
	25 July		Surgeon Sewell with 28 men proceeded to Advanced Dressing Station Bully Grenay for one weeks instruction + Lieut Aspinall RAMC with 28 men to Aix Noulette for same purpose; both parties moved off at 09.00. Captain Hutcheson RAMC gave lecture on Hygiene at School of Instruction Pernes. Surgeon Gow placed in charge of Medical + Surgical Cases + Lieut Walker RAMC of Sick cases for week commencing July 25th.	
	26 July		Captain Hutcheson proceeded to Aix Noulette to join his section there for weeks instruction. Sanitary work continues, road leading past Ambulance + Transport lines thoroughly cleaned.	
	27 July		Surgeon Gow + myself visited Dressing Stations at Bully Grenay + Aix Noulette, where	W Bradbury

T.131. Wt. W708–776. 500000. 4/15. Sir J. C. & S.

...uctions regarding War Diaries and Intelligence ...maries are contained in F. S. Regs., Part II. ...d the Staff Manual respectively. Title pages ...ll be prepared in manuscript.

WAR DIARY
or
~~INTELLIGENCE SUMMARY.~~
(*Erase heading not required.*)

July 1916

Place	Date	Hour	Summary of Events and Information	Remarks and references to Appendices
BARLIN	21 July 1916		B section are doing their week's course of Instruction	
	28 July 1916		Routine continues the same. Typhoid and Paratyphoid inoculation of C section completed.	
	29 July 1916		Typhoid and Paratyphoid inoculation of A section completed	
	30 July 1916		Men paraded 0915 for C of E service and marched to Marie Barlin where Divine Service was held 1000 Captain Lewis RAMC took the Parade. Mass for Roman Catholics Barlin Church 0900 Unit inspected for Scabies 13·30	
	31 July 1916		Routine continues the same. A section struck off duty for 1200 cleaning billets and packing gear preparatory to relieving B section at Advanced Dressing Stations of 1st & 2nd Field Ambulances. Ambulance inspected by Colonel Meeks DDMS expressed himself satisfied but suggested a few improvements e.g. food receptacles in wards cooks to wear aprons. These suggestions I am having carried out.	W Meadh

63

Confidential

Headquarters.
3rd F.A.
63rd (R N) Division
Sept 1. 1916.

Vol

War Diary
of
3rd Field Ambulance
63rd (R N) Division
from
August 1st 1916
to
August 31st 1916.

To/
The A G's Office
3rd Echelon

William Bradbury
Surgeon. R.N.
O.C. 3rd F.A.

August 1916

Instructions regarding War Diaries and Intelligence Summaries are contained in F. S. Regs., Part II. and the Staff Manual respectively. Title pages will be prepared in manuscript.

WAR DIARY
or
~~INTELLIGENCE SUMMARY~~.
(Erase heading not required.)

Army Form C. 2118.

August (1)

Place	Date	Hour	Summary of Events and Information	Remarks and references to Appendices
BARLIN.	Aug 1	1916.	Lieut Walker + 24 O.R. proceeded to A.D.S. 1st F.A. at Aix Noulette and relieved section of this Unit there who returned to Camp. Captain Davys + 24 O.R. proceeded to Bully Grenay 2nd F.A. and relieved section there. Gas helmets were inspected before party moved off at 0900. Board of Survey consisting of Surgeon Bradbury, Surgeon Gow, + Capt Lewis, held on A. Bainbridge Div. Train private found fit for duty.	
	Aug 2	1916.	Unit medically inspected for Scabies; no one found to be effected. Routine continues the same.	
	Aug 3	1916.	Improvements in Camp being continued.	
	Aug 4	1916.	Ten N.C.O.s + men arrived here from the Base; majority of these were those who had been sent there from this Unit as being bark suitable for work with a F.A.; according to orders these men were taken on strength, and ten from this Unit despatched to Base in their place.	
	Aug 5	1916.	All men in Camp medically examined, no disease found. Gas helmets inspected.	W. Bradbury
	Aug 6	1916	Captain Lewis R.A.M.C. took Church Parade Service 1000. Make + mend.	

Instructions regarding War Diaries and Intelligence Summaries are contained in F. S. Regs., Part II. and the Staff Manual respectively. Title pages will be prepared in manuscript.

WAR DIARY
or
~~INTELLIGENCE SUMMARY.~~
(Erase heading not required.)

August (2)

Army Form C. 2118.

Place	Date	Hour	Summary of Events and Information	Remarks and references to Appendices
BARLIN.	Aug. 6 1916.		for everyone except duty section from 1200.	
	Aug 7. 1916		Drainage at Transport lines being continued, Routine continues the same.	
	Aug 8. 1916		C section paraded 08.45 gas helmets inspected. Surgeon Gow with C Tent section moved off at 0900 for Bully Grenay to relieve section there. Captain Lewis with C Bearer Section moved off at same time for Aix Noulette; Sections relieved, returned to Unit.	
	Aug 9 1916.		The following have been put in orders "As an accurate account of drugs, dressings etc used for treatment of civilians, must be kept; Officers in future on using any materiel for this purpose, will indent on Quartermaster for amount supplied." also "In future all lights must be extinguished one hour after sunset"	
	Aug 10 1916		Extracts from daily Orders, "Officers in charge of Wards to give daily instruction to their Ward Orderlies in Ward duties + Sanitation.	
	Aug 11 1916		Extract from D.R.O. 418 dated 9.8.16 posted in Daily orders of this Unit. "Documents Captured from the Enemy to be forwarded at once to nearest General Staff Officer"	W. Bradbury

T.131. Wt. W708–776. 500000. 4/15. Sir J. C. & S.

Instructions regarding War Diaries and Intelligence Summaries are contained in F. S. Regs., Part II. and the Staff Manual respectively. Title pages will be prepared in manuscript.

WAR DIARY
or
INTELLIGENCE SUMMARY.
(Erase heading not required.)

August (3)

Army Form C. 2118.

Place	Date	Hour	Summary of Events and Information	Remarks and references to Appendices
BARLIN.	Aug 12	1916.	Ordinary Routine continued. Unit medically inspected for Scabies 1400.	
	Aug 13	1916.	Ambulance inspected by Colonel Meek D.D.M.S. IV Corps, 1030. Colonel Meek appeared satisfied. Sunday Routine.	
	Aug 14	1916.	Ordinary routine continued. B Bearer Section stood off duty from 1200 cleaning billets & packing gear preparatory to moving off.	
	Aug 15	1916	B Bearer Section paraded 0830, under Captain Hutcheson R.A.M.C, in full marching order without packs. Gas helmets inspected. Captain Hutcheson with party moved off at 0900 for Aix Noulette. C Bearer Section with Captain Lewis arrived from Aix Noulette 2000	
	Aug 16	1916.	Routine – Necessary sanitary work & fatigues. Gas helmet drill. Iron rations inspected at 1700 Parade. two Iron rations found to be missing; one Private who had lost his through negligence fined the cost of an iron ration. Corps Routine Order 961 re casualties to horses from nails on roads read out on Parade.	
	Aug 17	1916	Captain McKnight R.A.M.C (S.R) taken on strength of this unit but remaining at IV Corps School of Instruction Pernes.	W Bradbury.

T.134. Wt. W708–776. 500000. 4/15. Sir J. C. & S.

Instructions regarding War Diaries and Intelligence Summaries are contained in F. S. Regs., Part II. and the Staff Manual respectively. Title pages will be prepared in manuscript.

WAR DIARY
or
~~INTELLIGENCE SUMMARY.~~
(Erase heading not required.)

Aug. (4)

Army Form C. 2118.

Place	Date	Hour	Summary of Events and Information	Remarks and references to Appendices
BARLIN	Aug 18	1916.	One Private reported superficially wounded at Aix Noulette; this is the first casualty in this Unit since arrival in France.	
	Aug 19	1916	Captain Forrester R.A.M.C who had previously been taken on Strength of this Unit, joined up from IV Corps School of Instruction at Pernes. Extract from Daily Orders "In future Officer next for Duty as well as Orderly Officer will remain in Camp". Routine continues the same.	
	Aug 20	1916.	Sunday Routine. C of E. parade service 10.00 R.C. Parade Service 08.30 Make & mend for all available hands from 12.00. Divisional Order re Ammunition & explosives read on Parade.	
	Aug 21	1916.	Captain Forrester R.A.M.C posted to C Bearers.	
	Aug 22	1916.	Captain Hutcheson & B Bearers were relieved at Aix Noulette by Lieut Walker and A Bearers.	
	Aug 23	1916	Captain Hutcheson R.A.M.C. evacuated to 18 C.C.S. suffering from Para typhoid Obs.	
	Aug 24	1916.	Routine continues the same. Gas helmet drill for all available hands.	W Bradbury
	Aug 25	1916.	Lieut Walker R.A.M.C. transferred to B Tent Section.	

T.134. Wt. W708-776. 500000. 4/15. Sir J. C. & S.

Instructions regarding War Diaries and Intelligence Summaries are contained in F. S. Regs., Part II. and the Staff Manual respectively. Title pages will be prepared in manuscript.

WAR DIARY
or
~~INTELLIGENCE SUMMARY.~~
(*Erase heading not required.*)

Aug. (5)

Army Form C. 2118.

Place	Date	Hour	Summary of Events and Information	Remarks and references to Appendices
BARLIN.	Aug 26	1916	Ordinary Routine with Gas helmet drill for all available hands.	
			The following are a list of promotions in this Unit approved by the A.D.M.S	
			S. 3027 Sergt. Warriner G. to Staff Sergt. (Paid)	
			S. 3839 Cpl. Tilton R. to Acting Sergt. Clerk (Paid)	
			S 3219. Lance Cpl. Swain E E. " Acting Corporal. (Paid).	
			S 3577. Lance Cpl. Clewes W to Acting Corporal (Paid)	
	Aug 27	1916.	Sunday routine C of E Parade Service 1000. R.C Parade Service 0830.	
	Aug 28	1916.	Surgeon Bradbury, Surgeon Grow & Captain Forrester R.A.M.C proceed at 1000 in Ambulance Car with A.D.M.S of the Division to inspect Advanced Dressing Station at Petit Servay preparatory to its being taken over by this Unit. arrived back at Unit 1400.	
			Corps Order re Currency & Notes read on Parade.	
	Aug 29	1916.	Lieut Walker R.A.M.C with A Bearers arrived at this Unit from Aix Noulette 1000	
			Lieut Wilson (Quartermaster) proceeded with C Section's gear to Petit Servay A.D.S. at 1800. N.C.O was left in charge of stores. Lieut Wilson & party	W Bradbury

T.134. Wt. W708-776. 500000. 4/15. Sir J. C. & S.

Instructions regarding War Diaries and Intelligence Summaries are contained in F. S. Regs., Part II. and the Staff Manual respectively. Title pages will be prepared in manuscript.

WAR DIARY
or
~~INTELLIGENCE~~ SUMMARY.
(*Erase heading not required.*)

Aug. (6)

Army Form C. 2118.

Place	Date	Hour	Summary of Events and Information	Remarks and references to Appendices
BARLIN.	Aug 29. 1916		(Continued) returning to Unit 2400.	
	Aug 30 1916.		Surgeon Gow, Captain Forrester R.A.M.C and party of 32 (C section) with two Ambulance Cars left here 0800 for Port Grenay, relief completed Port Grenay 1200.	
	Aug 31 1916.		Lieut Welker R.A.M.C took over charge of Medical Ward in place of Surgeon Gow. Ambulance inspected by Colonel Meek D.D.M.S of 1 Corps. expressed himself satisfied. Surgeon Bradbury visited A.D.S. taken over by this Unit at Port Grenay officers and men very comfortable there and making improvements.	WBradbury

Volume No 4

"Confidential"

Headquarters
3rd Field Ambulance
63rd (R N) Division
~~September 26 16.~~
Oct. 1. 16.

War Diary
of
3rd F. A.
from
September 1. 1916
to
September 30. 1916.

William Bradbury
Surgeon R.N.
O.C. 3rd F.A.

63rd Div

Sept 1916

Instructions regarding War Diaries and Intelligence Summaries are contained in F. S. Regs., Part II. and the Staff Manual respectively. Title pages will be prepared in manuscript.

WAR DIARY
or
~~INTELLIGENCE~~ SUMMARY. September (1)

(*Erase heading not required.*)

Army Form C. 2118.

Place	Date	Hour	Summary of Events and Information	Remarks and references to Appendices
Barlin BARLIN	Sept 1. 1916.		Ordinary routine continued + improvements to Camp continued Unit medically inspected by Orderly Officer (Captain Lewis (R A M C) no disease found. Iron ration + gas helmets inspected all found correct.	
	Sept 2 1916		Captain Lewis R.A.M.C. detailed by A.D.M.S of this Division, to report at Aire for duty with the X Ray Mobile Laboratory there, Captain Lewis proceeded there by Ambulance Car.	
	Sept 3. 1916.		Sunday routine; Make and mend for all available hands from noon. C of E services held in the Maire, Barlin:- Holy Communion 07.30 Parade Service 09.30 Evening service 1800. R.C services held in BARLIN Church:- Mass 06.30 Parade Service 08.30 Voluntary service 18.30.	
	Sept 4 1916		Surgeon Sewell R.N.V.R detailed Officer in charge of Motor transport. Improvements continued. Road leading to Medical Inspection Room covered with slag and made passable, secondary road from Ambulance to Med. Inspection Room, Officer's Mess, Stores + Orderly Room, made by bridging Gully	W Bradbury

T.131. Wt. W703–776. 500000. 4/15. Sir J. C. & S.

Instructions regarding War Diaries and Intelligence Summaries are contained in F. S. Regs., Part II. and the Staff Manual respectively. Title pages will be prepared in manuscript.

WAR DIARY
or
~~INTELLIGENCE~~ SUMMARY.

(*Erase heading not required.*)

Army Form C. 2118.

Sept. (2)

Place	Date	Hour	Summary of Events and Information	Remarks and references to Appendices
BARLIN	Sept 4	(1916)	(Continued) which runs between these places	
	Sept 5	1916	Improvements continued B section stood off duty from 12 noon, cleaning billets + packing gear preparatory to moving off following day to Pont Grenay to relieve section there.	
	Sept 6	1916	Surgeon Sewell with advance party of 12 other ranks paraded at 07 45 and moved off 0800 for Pont Grenay in Ambulance cars Lieut Walker R.A.M.C with remainder of party paraded 08 15 and moved off 08 30 in motor Lorry for same place. All gas helmets + Iron rations inspected before leaving. Surgeon Gow + Captain Forrester RAMC with C section arrived at this Unit from PONT GRENAY 1400.	
	Sept 7	1916	Captain Davys R.A.M.C placed in charge of Divisional Rest Station Ward. Captain Forrester i/c of Medical + Surgical Wards.	
	Sept 8 + 9.		Ordinary Routine continued	
	Sept 10.		Captain Macfarlane R.A.M.C joined this Unit from late 316th R.F.A. Corporal A. Dunkley of this Unit has been awarded the Distinguished Service	W Bradbury

T.134. Wt. W708–776. 500000. 4/15. Sir J. C. & S.

Instructions regarding War Diaries and Intelligence Summaries are contained in F. S. Regs., Part II. and the Staff Manual respectively. Title pages will be prepared in manuscript.

WAR DIARY
or
~~INTELLIGENCE SUMMARY~~.
(Erase heading not required.)

September (3)

Army Form C. 2118.

Place	Date	Hour	Summary of Events and Information	Remarks and references to Appendices
BARLIN	Sept 10		(Continued) Medal for Bravery in Gallipoli. Sunday routine & services remain the same as previous Sunday.	
	Sept 11. 1916		Ordinary routine Continued.	
	Sept 12.		Sergt. Major Ashton J.F.A reported for duty with Horse transport of this Unit, and taken on strength. A. section stood off duty from 12 noon cleaning billets and packing gear preparatory to relieving B section at Fort Gueray following day.	
	Sept 13.		Captain Davys with advance party of 12 men paraded at 0800 and moved off in two ambulance cars 0830 Captain Macfarlane with remainder of party paraded 0830 and moved off in Motor Lorry 0900 party relieving totalled 49 other ranks. Iron rations and gas helmets inspected before party moved off. B section Section being relieved arrived at Unit 1400.	
	Sept 14.		Ordinary routine continued.	W Bradbury.

T.134. Wt. W708–776. 500000. 4/15. Sir J. C. & S.

Instructions regarding War Diaries and Intelligence Summaries are contained in F. S. Regs., Part II. and the Staff Manual respectively. Title pages will be prepared in manuscript.

WAR DIARY
or
~~INTELLIGENCE SUMMARY.~~
(Erase heading not required.)

September (4)

Army Form C. 2118.

Place	Date	Hour	Summary of Events and Information	Remarks and references to Appendices
BARLIN	Sept 15.		Ordinary Routine continues. Corporal Swain S 3219 recommended and approved for ten days home leave. Corporal Swain has been away from England since February 1915.	
	Sept 16.		Captain Mac Farlane directed to report to A.D.M.S New Zealand Division at Merricourt for Duty authority IV Corps Medical. Captain Mac Farlane taken off strength. Captain Mac Farlane's duties at Advanced Dressing	
	Sept 16.		Station Port Grenay taken over by Surgeon Good.	
	Sept 17.		Secret orders received from A.D.M.S of this Division that Advanced Dressing Station at Port Grenay will be relieved by 48th F.A. this afternoon, Main dressing Station at Barlin will be relieved by 50th F.A. following day, on relief being completed F.A. to proceed to Bruay + occupy site vacated by 50th F.A. Relief of A.D.S at Port Grenay completed + section who were on duty there, arrived Main Dressing Station Station Barlin midnight.	
			One Officer and Advance Party from 50th F.A. arrived Main Dressing Station 1400 and were billeted.	W Bradbury

Instructions regarding War Diaries and Intelligence Summaries are contained in F. S. Regs., Part II. and the Staff Manual respectively. Title pages will be prepared in manuscript.

WAR DIARY
or
~~INTELLIGENCE SUMMARY.~~
(*Erase heading not required.*)

September (5)

Army Form C. 2118.

Place	Date	Hour	Summary of Events and Information	Remarks and references to Appendices
BRUAY	Sept 18.		Surgeon Sewell R.N.V.R moved off with Ambulance Cars and Advance Party. 09.00 Captain Davys and Horse transport with stores moved off 09.45 Surgeon Gow, Captain Forrester and Lieut. Walker moved off with main party 10.00, patients who could march, 40 in all, proceeded with this party; one patient left in wards and transferred to 50th F.A. Heavy downpour of rain. Surgeon Bradbury with 8 O.R. awaited arrival of O.C 50th F.A., who arrived 11 am and then proceeded to BRUAY. Arrived BRUAY and relief completed noon. Heavy rainfall continues + unfortunately no cover for horses. Latrines conspicuous by their absence	
	Sept 19.		Careful attention paid to Camp sanitation; Heavy rain continues. Camp drained and new latrines made. Men comfortably billeted but scattered. B + C section's gear repacked in waggons. A. section's gear required for use in Ambulance and can not be packed.	W Bradbury
	Sept 20.		Corporal Swain S/3219 proceeded on leave. Sanitation + improvements of Camp continue	

Instructions regarding War Diaries and Intelligence Summaries are contained in F. S. Regs., Part II. and the Staff Manual respectively. Title pages will be prepared in manuscript.

WAR DIARY
or
~~INTELLIGENCE SUMMARY~~.
(Erase heading not required.)

September (6)

Army Form C. 2118.

Place	Date	Hour	Summary of Events and Information	Remarks and references to Appendices
~~September~~ BRUAY.	Sept 21		Ordinary Routine continued. 9th D.S.C inspected by Surgeon Sewell & Captain Davys.	
	Sept. 22.		General improvements carried on in Camp. Lieut. Guthrie taken on strength from King Edward's Horse.	
	Sept. 23		Improvements on roads & wards carried on. Work on stables commenced. Lieut. Guthrie R.A.M.C posted to A section.	
	Sept. 24.		Ordinary Routine continues. One N.C.O and four privates detached to act as guard over stores etc left behind at Devion by 2nd F.A.	
	Sept. 25.		Routine continues. C section paraded in full marching order 9 am, and proceeded on Route march Captain Forrester in charge.	
	Sept. 26.		B Section & Transport paraded 9 am for Baths. B Section under Surgeon Sewell & Lieut. Walker route marching in full kit from 2 to 4 pm.	
	Sept 27.		Lieut. Guthrie & A Section proceeded on route march 9 am. and arrived in Camp 12 noon.	
	Sept 28.		Captain Davys & C Section paraded in full marching order 9 am &	W Bradbury.

Instructions regarding War Diaries and Intelligence Summaries are contained in F. S. Regs., Part II. and the Staff Manual respectively. Title pages will be prepared in manuscript.

WAR DIARY
or
~~INTELLIGENCE SUMMARY~~
(Erase heading not required.)

Sept. (7.)

Army Form C. 2118.

Place	Date	Hour	Summary of Events and Information	Remarks and references to Appendices
BRUAY	Sept (28)		Continued) proceeded on route march and arrived in Camp 12·30 pm.	
	Sept 29		Surgeon Sewell + Lieut Guthrie placed in Charge of Medical + Surgical Wards. Lieut. Walker in Charge of O.R.S ward.	
			Divisional manoeuvres held today. 3rd F.A. in Reserve.	
			Pte Bainbridge S/2045 placed under arrest for disobedience of orders & refusing to obey an order.	
	Sept 30.		Pte Bainbridge S/2045, Driver attached to 3rd F.A. sent under guard to A.P.M to undergo punishment. 28 days F.P. no 1.	W Madbury

T.131. Wt. W708-776. 500000. 4/15. Sir J. C. & S.

To.

A. G.'s Office
BASE.

"Confidential"

3rd Field Ambce
63rd (R.N.) Division
Nov. 1st 16.

War Diary

of.

3rd Field Ambce
63rd (R.N.) Division

from.

1st October to 31st October /16

William Bradbury.
Surgeon RN
i/c 3rd Field Ambce

Instructions regarding War Diaries and Intelligence Summaries are contained in F. S. Regs., Part II. and the Staff Manual respectively. Title pages will be prepared in manuscript.

WAR DIARY
or
~~INTELLIGENCE SUMMARY.~~
(Erase heading not required.)

October (1)

Army Form C. 2118.

Place	Date	Hour	Summary of Events and Information	Remarks and references to Appendices
BRUAY.	Oct. 1.		Private Bainbridge A. 3rd F.A. Transport. given 28 days Field punishment no 1. for disobeying orders. Surgeon Gow & 4. OR. returned from Gas School, where they were under course of Instructions. One N.C.O and 4. OR. returned from Divion, where they were acting as guard over stores left behind by 2nd F.A.; stores turned over to Town Major. Divion. Private Brown W 3rd F.A. Transport appointed Acting L/Cpl unpaid.	
	Oct. 2.		In accordance with orders, reported to A.D.M.S., and was informed that Unit will probably move off following day. Secret orders received 1600 all Transport to move off following day for Canottement; to be clear of Bruay by 08.30. other personnel to stand fast until further orders. Ambulance cleared of patients, with the exception of 10 who arrived from 'Howe' about 11 pm.	
	Oct. 3.		Captain Davys & Lieut Guthrie moved off at 08.15 with Horse transport. Staff Sergeant Warriner in Charge of Stores. Captain Forrester with Motor Convoy moved off 8.30. Further orders to be received by Transport at Canottement.	WBradbury.

T.134. Wt. W708-776. 500000. 4/15. Sir J. C. & S.

Instructions regarding War Diaries and Intelligence Summaries are contained in F. S. Regs., Part II. and the Staff Manual respectively. Title pages will be prepared in manuscript.

WAR DIARY
or
~~INTELLIGENCE SUMMARY.~~
(Erase heading not required.)

October (2)

Army Form C. 2118.

Place	Date	Hour	Summary of Events and Information	Remarks and references to Appendices
BRUAY.	Oct	3.	Secret orders received 1300 from A. D. M. S:- remainder of personnel to arrive at Ligny St Flochel by noon following day. For purpose of entraining, personnel to be divided into two parties.	
'On the March'	Oct	4.	Unit paraded at 0615 in full marching orders + moved off 0630 in two parties:- 1st Party consisted of Surgeon Bradbury, Surgeon Gow, Lieut Wilson, Interpreter and 74 O.R. 2nd Party consisted of Surgeon Sewell, Captain Baker, Lieut Walker and 86 O.R. Parties arrived at Ligny St Flochel 11.30, here I was informed by R.T.O that trains would be delayed 9 hours. Considerable rainfall, men housed temporarily in Barns etc close to station, and after much trouble managed to secure a hot meal for personnel. Private Boston S. discharged to 12 Stationary Hospital St. Pol with Influenza. 1st Party entrained 0930 and left 1030, 2nd Party entrained 2300 and left 0300 following day.	W Bradbury.
'En Route'	Oct	5.	1st Party arrived Acheux 0730, where they were met by guide. Formed up and marched to Varennes to hutments, where Motor transport	

T.134. Wt. W708–776. 500000. 4/15. Sir J. C. & S.

Instructions regarding War Diaries and Intelligence Summaries are contained in F. S. Regs., Part II. and the Staff Manual respectively. Title pages will be prepared in manuscript.

WAR DIARY
or
~~INTELLIGENCE SUMMARY~~.
(Erase heading not required.)

October (3)

Army Form C. 2118.

Place	Date	Hour	Summary of Events and Information	Remarks and references to Appendices
"On the March"	Oct 5		(Continued) of this Unit had arrived previous day. Orders received from A. D. M. S to move with 2nd F.A. to Clairfaye, where Unit will encamp for the night. Motor Ambulance despatched to Acheux station to meet 2nd party of this Unit, and guide it to Clairfaye; Car also sent to direct Horse transport to destination. Formed up at 1300 & marched to Clairfaye, where 2nd Party had just arrived. Encamped with 2nd F.A. Horse transport arrived Clairfaye 1830, Unit now complete, with exception of Pte Ferriday & Pte Ainscough, who contrary to orders got out of train at Belle Eglise; train moved off without them; these two privates joined up later in evening having marched remainder of distance fortunately only about 3 miles.	
	Oct. 6.		Privates Ferriday & Ainscough given 7 days F.P. no 1. for offence mentioned yesterday. Unit moved to 0.36. C 9.3. Map 57.D. site chosen by Surgeon Gow & myself previous day. Move completed 1800. About 150 men in Bivouacs, remainder in Tents.	W Bradbury

Instructions regarding War Diaries and Intelligence Summaries are contained in F. S. Regs., Part II. and the Staff Manual respectively. Title pages will be prepared in manuscript.

WAR DIARY
or
~~INTELLIGENCE SUMMARY~~.
(Erase heading not required.)

October (4)

Army Form C. 2118.

Place	Date	Hour	Summary of Events and Information	Remarks and references to Appendices
0 36 9.9.3 In Camp. Rt of VARENNES – HARPONVILLE Road	Oct	7th	Instructions received from A.D.M.S. to detail Med. Officer to report for duty at TANKODROME ALTON. Capt BAKER W G. R.A.M.C. proceeded there at 1400 but returned at 1730; a Med. Officer having arrived there in the meantime.	W Bradbury
			Erection of shelters for cookhouses & stores continued.	
	Oct	8th	Bad weather continues necessitating improvements in horse lines. ADMS wires instructions that 1 Officer and 8 Other Ranks proceed to AILT Rest Camp. Lieut WALKER. D. (RAMC) 1 N.CO & 7 other ranks left at 0900, the officer assuming charge of this and parties from 1st & 2nd Field Ambces	
	Oct	9th	Necessary fatigues and sanitation. "A & C" Sections parade at 0900 for route marches.	
	Oct	10th	Instructed by ADMS to detail 1 Medical Officer 2 N.CO's and 3 other Ranks to report at the Advanced Dressing Station of the 142nd Field Ambce at COLINCAMPS. Surgeon GOW (RN) and specially chosen party left at 0830 to arrive by 1000. They	W Bradbury

T.134. Wt. W708–776. 500000. 4/15. Sir J. C. & S.

Instructions regarding War Diaries and Intelligence Summaries are contained in F. S. Regs., Part II. and the Staff Manual respectively. Title pages will be prepared in manuscript.

WAR DIARY
or
~~INTELLIGENCE~~ SUMMARY.
(*Erase heading not required.*)

October (5)

Army Form C. 2118.

Place	Date	Hour	Summary of Events and Information	Remarks and references to Appendices
Oct 10th (Continued) 0 36 c 9.3			are to acquire as much knowledge as possible of routes of evacuation. Regt Aid Posts and Bearer Posts as well as Med. Matters pertaining to this particular sector	W Bradbury
			"A" & "C" Sections paraded for route march at 0900.	
	Oct	11th	"B & C" Sections carried on with Stretcher & Squad Drill. Later 70 Other Ranks proceeded to Baths at ACHEUX.	
	Oct	12th	Improvements in camp generally – sanitary arrangements improved.	
	Oct	13th	Surgeon POW AE. & party at A.D.S. COLINSCAMP relieved by Capt BAKER RAMC. & similar number of men. Maps of this sector issued to M.O's of unit and information, especially relating to Anti-gas precautions imparted to Med. Officers of Unit.	
	Oct	14th	"B & C" Sections under command of Surgeon SEWELL W.A. employed on Field work engaging Aid Posts, Advanced Dressing Station, Main Dressing Station and evacuation by Stretcher Squads & Horsed Ambs. Also practise in mounting parapet & collection of wounded.	W Bradbury

T.131. Wt. W708–776. 500000. 4/15. Sir J. C. & S.

Instructions regarding War Diaries and Intelligence Summaries are contained in F. S. Regs., Part II. and the Staff Manual respectively. Title pages will be prepared in manuscript.

WAR DIARY
or
~~INTELLIGENCE SUMMARY.~~
(Erase heading not required.)

October (6)

Army Form C. 2118.

Place	Date	Hour	Summary of Events and Information	Remarks and references to Appendices
			Capt BAKER (R.AMC) & party return from COLINSCAMP. to ~~Hdqrs~~ of unit	
O 36 c 9.3	Oct	15th	1 NCO & 8 other Ranks return from Army Rest Camp AULT reporting	
			that Lieut WALKER D. (RAMC) had been admitted to Hospital Sick.	W Bradbury
			Instructed by A.D.M.S. to detail parties as below:-	
			(a) Surgeon SEWELL W.S. (R.N.) 2 N.C.O's & 20 Stretcher Bearers to proceed to A.D.S. MESNIL to take over from 134 Field Amb^ce on the 16th inst this A.D.S. and the Bearer Posts connected with it.	
			(b) Surgeon GOW A.F. (R.N.) 1 N.C.O and 20 Stretcher Bearers to take over on the 16th inst the Posts at MAILLY and AUCHINVILLERS from the 134th Field Amb^ce & Bearer Posts in connection therewith.	
			Visited the Headquarters of the 134th Field Amb^ce and ascertained details of working these posts.	
			These two parties proceeded by Amb^ce Cars to the Headquarters of the 134th Field Amb^ce to remain for the night pending further orders from the A.D.M.S.	
			(c) Capt FORRESTER J. (RAMC) 2 N.C.O's & 20 Stretcher Bearers detailed	W Bradbury

T.134. Wt. W708–776. 500000. 4/15. Sir J. C. & S.

Instructions regarding War Diaries and Intelligence Summaries are contained in F. S. Regs., Part II. and the Staff Manual respectively. Title pages will be prepared in manuscript.

WAR DIARY
or
~~INTELLIGENCE SUMMARY~~.
(Erase heading not required.)

October (7)

Army Form C. 2118.

Place	Date	Hour	Summary of Events and Information	Remarks and references to Appendices
O 34 c 9.3.	Oct 15th (Continued).		to report at Headquarters of 132nd Field Ambce at A.D.S. LANCASHIRE DUMP. for duty at the A.D.S "THE COOKERS" and Bearer Posts in connection therewith.	W Bradbury
			(c) Sergeant WINGATE and 4 Other Ranks to report at Headquarters of 132nd Field Ambce for duty at Divisional Collecting Station on Left of road ENGLEBELMER – MARTINSART.	
			Visited the Headquarters of 132nd Fd Ambce & ascertained necessary particulars & requirements in connection with these posts.	
			The following equipment accompanied each Med. Officer: Days Rations, Stretchers, 1 Med. Companion & Water Bottle, 1 Surgical Haversack and Water Bottle.	
	Oct 16th		The above parties proceeded to their respective posts and relief was completed by 12 noon today.	
			Despatched TWO large Ambce Cars to the A.D.S MESNIL to remain there for duty. Cases sick & wounded to be evacuated	W Bradbury

Instructions regarding War Diaries and Intelligence Summaries are contained in F. S. Regs., Part II. and the Staff Manual respectively. Title pages will be prepared in manuscript.

WAR DIARY
or
~~INTELLIGENCE SUMMARY.~~
(Erase heading not required.)

Army Form C. 2118.

October (8)

Place	Date	Hour	Summary of Events and Information	Remarks and references to Appendices
O. 36 c 9.3	Oct 16th (Continued)		to the 1st Fd Ambce at FORCEVILLE. Urgent cases requiring immediate operation sent to Special Operating centres at AUTHIE & WARLOY. Rough accounts of cases treated kept at each A.D.S but slow admitted by 1st Field Ambce	W Bradbury
	Oct 17th		A Party from 2nd Field Ambce consisting of 1 Bearer Officer 3 Bearer N.C.O's and 6 Ptes attached to each A.D.S for instructional purposes. Collecting Stn vacated the 4 ratings going on to "COOKERS" Captain JACKSON RAM.C & Capt WATKINS RAM.C posted to 3rd Field Ambce for duty, the former being detailed for duty with C Tent Sub-section and the latter with B Tent Sub-section.	
	Oct 18th		Surgeon GOW AE (RN) and party at MAILLY MAILLET hand over the Collecting Post and Bearer Posts to the 1/2 Highland Field Ambce 57th (Highland) Division. Relief completed by 1500. Location. A.D.M.S from LEALVILLERS to HEDAUVILLE. 1st Field Ambce from FORCEVILLE to VARENNES	W Bradbury.

T.134. Wt. W708–776. 500000. 4/15. Sir J. C. & S.

Instructions regarding War Diaries and Intelligence Summaries are contained in F. S. Regs., Part II. and the Staff Manual respectively. Title pages will be prepared in manuscript.

WAR DIARY
or
~~INTELLIGENCE~~ SUMMARY.
(*Erase heading not required.*)

Army Form C. 2118.

October (9)

Place	Date	Hour	Summary of Events and Information	Remarks and references to Appendices
O 36c9.3.	Oct 19th		Seats made for G.S. wagons for transport of walking wounded in case of active operations.	W Bradbury
	Oct 20th		Advanced Party of 4 Ptes proceed to site on Right of ENGLEBELMER – MARTINSART ROAD to guard site selected as Divisional Collecting Station for walking wounded. Capt JACKSON proceeded to ADS "COOKERS" Parties consisting of 1 Bearer Officer 2 N.C.O's + 6 Other Ranks from 1st Field Ambce attached to each of A.D.S's for instructional purposes. Also 1 Bearer Officer 2 N.C.O's + 6 Other Ranks from the 2nd Field Ambce attached to A.D.S at "COOKERS" for the same purpose. Capt BAKER & CAPT. WATKINS proceed to A.D.S at MESNIL	
	Oct 21st		Detailed Sergt Major, 1 N.C.O and 11 Other Ranks to proceed to site selected for D.W. Collecting Stn and pitch camp also to prepare roads. Stretchers & Blankets surplus to Establishment held in reserve in the event of Active Operations. Supplies held in reserve:– 1000 Rations at Headquarters of unit 500 at A.D.S's MESNIL & "COOKERS"	W Bradbury

T.131. Wt. W708–776. 500000. 4/15. Sir J. C. & S.

Instructions regarding War Diaries and Intelligence Summaries are contained in F. S. Regs., Part II. and the Staff Manual respectively. Title pages will be prepared in manuscript.

WAR DIARY
or
~~INTELLIGENCE SUMMARY~~.
(Erase heading not required.)

Army Form C. 2118.

October (10)

Place	Date	Hour	Summary of Events and Information	Remarks and references to Appendices
O. 36 c 9. 3.			500 Rations at each Bearer Post KNIGHTSBRIDGE + HAMEL.	W Bradbury
			Med Stores held in reserve:-	
			3000 at H.qrs of unit, 2000 at MESNIL + "COOKERS" A.D.S's	
			1000 at each Bearer Post KNIGHTSBRIDGE + HAMEL	
	Oct 22nd		Great improvements needed at "CABSTAND" and D.W. Collecting Stn so	
			reinforced party at D. C. Stn by 6 Bearer Ptes from each A.D.S.	
	Oct 23rd		The Road to ADS MESNIL in bad condition from shell fire + traffic	
			Reported to ADMS the condition of two Cars through bad road.	
	Oct 24th		Changed Headqrs of Unit from O 36 c 9.3 Map Ref Sheet 57d France	
			to D.W. Collecting Stn Q. 31 b 7.7. (Map Ref 57d). leaving 1 N.CO +	
			3 men as guard over stores left behind in marquee. Transport not	
			required for move + spare horses left in old camp in charge of	
			Sergt DORRELL.	
			Parties from 1st + 2nd Field Ambces withdrawn.	
	Oct 25th		Weather greatly impairs the improvements in + around camp.	
			Camp site about 100 yds square. 3 marquees pitched parallel	W Bradbury

Instructions regarding War Diaries and Intelligence Summaries are contained in F. S. Regs., Part II. and the Staff Manual respectively. Title pages will be prepared in manuscript.

WAR DIARY
or
~~INTELLIGENCE SUMMARY.~~
(Erase heading not required.)

Army Form C. 2118.

October (11)

Place	Date	Hour	Summary of Events and Information	Remarks and references to Appendices
Q. 31 6 7.7 on Rt of ENGLEBELMER - HARTINSART road.			to road & about 40 yards from Road constitute (1) Reception Room (2) Dressing Room (3) Refreshment room. In addition there are shelters & seats for accommodation of cases in the event of an action.	W Bradbury
			Cross country routes indicative of route of evacuation for walking wounded marked by wooden direction boards from each A.D.S. to Div: Collecting Station.	
	Oct 26th		Bearer Sub-Sections provided each with SIX small wooden direction boards to mark out intended routes of evacuation during the action to Bearer Posts.	
			Intended day of attack. Postponed to 28th Inst.	
	Oct 27th		"CABSTAND" improvements continued. General improvements in the camp.	
			In the event of active operations 2 Bearer Divisions of 37th Division will be in reserve at "THE COOKERS" and one Bearer Sub-Division at MESNIL.	W Bradbury

T.134. Wt. W708-776. 500000. 4/15. Sir J. C. & S.

Instructions regarding War Diaries and Intelligence Summaries are contained in F. S. Regs., Part II. and the Staff Manual respectively. Title pages will be prepared in manuscript.

WAR DIARY
or
~~INTELLIGENCE SUMMARY~~.
(*Erase heading not required.*)

Army Form C. 2118.

October (12)

Place	Date	Hour	Summary of Events and Information	Remarks and references to Appendices
Q.31.b.7.7			3 Motor Ambces of this unit to be stationed at A.D.S. MESNIL and 3 Motor Ambces of 2nd F.A at "THE COOKERS" to be in position on day preceding the attack. Remainder of Cars will be stationed at the "CABRANK" on the morning of day of attack	W Bradbury
			2 Horsed Ambce wagons + 2 G.S. wagons from Nos 1 2 + 3 Fd Ambces, the Sanitary lorry + 4 Motor busses to be at Div. Collecting Stn on the evening of day preceding the attack.	
	Oct 28th		Day of attack postponed to 30th through bad weather Continued improvements of sheds for wounded.	
	Oct 29th		Day of attack further postponed 48 hours. No improvement in the climatic conditions. Definite roads made in Camp. Entrance to Station covered with broken stone, paths made to reception room, Dressing Room and sheds.	
	Oct 30th		Weather shows no improvement. Section of Tent Subdivision of 37th Division arrive about 1130 but called away again at 1400.	W Bradbury

T.131. Wt. W708-776. 500000. 4/15. Sir J. C. & S.

Instructions regarding War Diaries and Intelligence Summaries are contained in F. S. Regs., Part II. and the Staff Manual respectively. Title pages will be prepared in manuscript.

WAR DIARY

or

~~INTELLIGENCE SUMMARY~~.

(Erase heading not required.)

October (13)

Army Form C. 2118.

Place	Date	Hour	Summary of Events and Information	Remarks and references to Appendices
O.31.b.7.7	Oct	31st	Weather improving. Necessary fatigues & sanitation	

"Confidential"

3rd
FIELD AMBULANCE,
ROYAL NAVAL DIV.
No.
Date 1.12.16

War Diary
of
3rd Field Ambce
63rd (R.N.) Division
from
November 1st 1916
to
November 30th 1916.

To
The A.G's Office
3rd Echelon.

William Bradbury
Staff Surgeon
i/c 3rd Field Ambce
63rd R.N. Div.

107

Nov 916

63rd Div

140/1862

3rd RND Field Ambulance

Instructions regarding War Diaries and Intelligence Summaries are contained in F. S. Regs., Part II. and the Staff Manual respectively. Title pages will be prepared in manuscript.

WAR DIARY
or
~~INTELLIGENCE SUMMARY.~~
(Erase heading not required.)

(1)

Army Form C. 2118.

Place	Date	Hour	Summary of Events and Information	Remarks and references to Appendices
In the Field	Nov 1st/16		Capt Davys J.A. (RAMC) 4 N.C.Os + 23 other Ranks relieved at MESNIL leaving camp at 9am. On being relieved Captain Watkin + Capt Baker (RAMC) with party returned to the Divisional Collecting Station.	W Madbury
			Lieut Guthrie G. W. (RAMC) proceeded to "COOKERS" to relieve Surgeon Gow A.G. (RN) and Capt S Jackson RAMC. Gas helmets and iron rations being inspected prior to departure.	
	Nov 2nd/16		General fatigues + Sanitation of camp.	
	Nov 3rd/16		Reinforcements of 4 "other Ranks" join from Base Depôt.	
			Lieut D. Walker (RAMC) previously admitted to Hospital sick now struck off strength on authority from A.D.M.S.	
	Nov 4th/16	9 30am	Captain P. J. Watkins (RAMC) relieved Surgeon W A Sewell RNVR at A.D.S. MESNIL	
			Pte Ellis J S/4121 killed + 4 O.R. suffering from "Shell Shock" whilst on duty in region of Bearer Post KNIGHTSBRIDGE.	
	Nov 5th/16		Improvements in Camp. - footpaths paved and park for Motor Vehicles made. Entrance to camp widened & paved	W Madbury

T.131. Wt. W708-776. 500000. 4/15. Sir J. C. & S.

Instructions regarding War Diaries and Intelligence Summaries are contained in F. S. Regs., Part II. and the Staff Manual respectively. Title pages will be prepared in manuscript.

WAR DIARY
or
~~INTELLIGENCE SUMMARY.~~
(Erase heading not required.)

(2)

Army Form C. 2118.

Place	Date	Hour	Summary of Events and Information	Remarks and references to Appendices
In the Field	Nov 6th/16		Half of "C" Sub Division at "COOKERS" ADS and HAMEL Bearer Post return to D.W. Collecting Station for a brief rest.	W Madbury
	Nov 7th/16		Capt J.H. Davys (R.A.M.C) detailed to join up with ADMS 3rd Division and in accordance with ADMS 63rd RN Division instructions struck off strength	
	Nov 8th/16		Necessary fatigues and sanitation.	
	Nov 9th/16		Reinforced by 2 "Other Ranks" from Base Depôt. No change in bad weather. Deeper drains made throughout camp	
	Nov 10th/16		Bath parade 2pm. 50 "Other Ranks" proceeded to baths at Hédauville	
	Nov 11th/16		Shelter for wounded completed with floor paved, galvanised iron roof and felt sides supported by wire netting. "Queen" stoves placed in position and ventilation ensured.	
		9am	"B" Section paraded for inspection and moved off at 9.30 am for MESNIL	
			Capt S. Jackson (RAMC) Staff Sergt Booth + 7 "Other Ranks" moved off	W Madbury

T.134. Wt. W708–776. 500000. 4/15. Sir J. C. & S.

Instructions regarding War Diaries and Intelligence Summaries are contained in F. S. Regs., Part II. and the Staff Manual respectively. Title pages will be prepared in manuscript.

WAR DIARY
or
~~INTELLIGENCE SUMMARY.~~
(Erase heading not required.)

(3)

Army Form C. 2118.

Place	Date	Hour	Summary of Events and Information	Remarks and references to Appendices
In the Field			at 1 pm for "COOKERS".	
			Lieut G.W. Guthrie (RAMC) returned from "COOKERS" A.D.S. to Divisional Collecting Station	W Bradbury
	Nov 12th		Sections "B + C" at MESNIL + "COOKERS" completed up to strength with plentiful supply of stretchers + blankets. 3 Amb^ce Cars placed at the disposal of each A.D.S.	
			Lieut G.W. Guthrie (RAMC) with "A" Bearers proceeded to Headquarters of Anson Battalion ENGLEBELMER in readiness to proceed later to front line trenches. In position by 10 pm.	
			Capt W.A. Baker RAMC i/c "B" Bearers in position in front line by 10 pm in KNIGHTSBRIDGE region	
			Capt J.D. Forrester (RAMC) i/c "C" Bearers in position by 10 pm in region of HAMEL.	
	Nov 13th/16			
		5.45 am	Action Commenced.	
			At Mesnil A.D.S. Surgeon Sewell RNVR. + Capt E.J. Watkins (RAMC)	W Bradbury

Instructions regarding War Diaries and Intelligence Summaries are contained in F. S. Regs., Part II. and the Staff Manual respectively. Title pages will be prepared in manuscript.

WAR DIARY
or
~~INTELLIGENCE~~ SUMMARY.
(Erase heading not required.)

Army Form C. 2118.

(4)

Place	Date	Hour	Summary of Events and Information	Remarks and references to Appendices
In the Field.	Nov 13th		(Continued) with "B" Tent Sub section. Latter assisted by 1/3 Scottish Highland Fd Amb^ce. Later Surgeon Padwick RN + 3 other Ranks	W Bradbury
		8pm	went to assistance at Mesnil.	
			At "Cookers" A.D.S. Surgeon A.E. Gow (RN) Capt. S Jackson (RAMC) and "C" Tent Sub section. Later Capt Mathers RAMC assisted at the A.D.S. with Surgeon Adams RN + Surgeon Kay-Mouat. (RND)	
		7am	At Div. Coll. Stn. Horse Transport (6 G.S. wagons 6 Horse Amb^ces) were in position.	
			At this Station "A" Tent Sub section were on duty assisted by Surgeon Knowles RN, Surgeon Blackwell RN, Surgeon Padwick RN. Capt Mathers RAMC and 40 "Other Ranks".	
			Lieut G.W. Guthrie RAMC killed in action. 4/3921 Pte Bowden W.O killed in action and 2 other Ranks wounded.	
			In afternoon Capt Mathers proceeded to assistance of A.D.S "Cookers"	
	Nov 14th/16	9.40am	Bearer Sub-Division of 37th Div recalled to join up with Brigade of 37th near South end of Station Road	W Bradbury.

T.134. Wt. W708-776. 500000. 4/15. Sir J. C. & S.

Instructions regarding War Diaries and Intelligence Summaries are contained in F. S. Regs., Part II. and the Staff Manual respectively. Title pages will be prepared in manuscript.

WAR DIARY
or
~~INTELLIGENCE SUMMARY.~~
(Erase heading not required.)

(5)

Army Form C. 2118.

Place	Date	Hour	Summary of Events and Information	Remarks and references to Appendices
In the Field	Nov.	14th (Continued)		W Madbury
			3 Motor busses sent to "COOKERS" with instructions to send all sitting cases to 1st Field Ambce VARENNES. Reported to ADMS that COOKERS had 500 cases and congested, that M.A.C were evacuating but cases were not being dressed quickly enough and that more medical assistance was required, that 40 cars were working COOKERS. The ADMS called for report on situation at CAB RANK. Report sent as follows: "To 20 M.A.C. clearing "COOKERS", 22 cars reporting at CAB RANK and clearing MESNIL, 10 cars now at CAB RANK." Instructed NCO at Cab Rank to send all cars there to proceed to MESNIL	
		2.15 pm	Congestion at COOKERS due to lack of medical personnel. Surgeon A.E. Gow (RN) suggested more medical assistance, if possible 3 medical officers and 10 nursing orderlies.	
			Captain J.D. Forrester (RAMC) killed. S/4092 Pte T. Johnston killed S/3487 Pte J. Scales killed and 3 other Ranks wounded	W Madbury

T.134. Wt. W708-776. 500000. 4/15. Sir J. C. & S.

Instructions regarding War Diaries and Intelligence Summaries are contained in F. S. Regs., Part II. and the Staff Manual respectively. Title pages will be prepared in manuscript.

WAR DIARY
or
~~INTELLIGENCE SUMMARY.~~
(Erase heading not required.)

Army Form C. 2118.

(6)

Place	Date	Hour	Summary of Events and Information	Remarks and references to Appendices
In the Field	Nov 15th/16		1/3 Highland Fd Amb^ce recalled. 2 Offs + Tent Division of 49th Field Amb^ce 37th Div sent to relieve 63rd RN Div at MESNIL at 10pm. 6 Other Ranks wounded.	W Bradbury
	Nov 16th/16		"COOKERS" personnel relieved by 48th Field Amb^ce 37th Div. at 5pm and returned to Div. Coll: Stn.	
			MESNIL personnel relieved at 8 am and returned to Div Coll Stn.	
			A Tent Sub-Section of 49th Field Amb^ce 37th Division arrived at Divisional Coll Stn. to take over from this unit. All stores except sufficient to complete to WOF establishment turned over and relief completed at 12 midnight.	
	Nov 17th/16		"A" Section and portion of "B" Bearers remained in the line with 190th Inf Bde to clear the Battlefield. This party returned to camp during forenoon.	
	Nov 18th/16		Capt Baker with 1 N.CO + Surgeon Gow RN with 1st Party of "A + B" Sections left by motor bus for BEAUVAL.	W Bradbury

T.134. Wt. W708–776. 500000. 4/15. Sir J. C. & S.

Instructions regarding War Diaries and Intelligence Summaries are contained in F. S. Regs., Part II. and the Staff Manual respectively. Title pages will be prepared in manuscript.

WAR DIARY
or
~~INTELLIGENCE SUMMARY.~~
(Erase heading not required.)

Army Form C. 2118.

(7)

Place	Date	Hour	Summary of Events and Information	Remarks and references to Appendices
In the Field	Nov 18th/16		12 noon telegram received from ADMS that unit to proceed to AUTHIEULE. Despatch Rider sent off to pick up Capt Baker, Surgeon Gow & Lieut Wilson and instruct them of change of destination. Remaining party with O.C. and Surgeon Sewell left at 12.30 pm by road to march to AUTHIEULE arriving there at 8 pm. Unable to find billets. Surgeon Gow arrived about 9.30 pm with instructions to proceed to BEAUVAL. In the meantime Lieut Wilson RM and transport had received instructions through Surgeon Gow and by 12 pm the unit had completed move to BEAUVAL and billetted.	W Bradbury
	Nov 19th/16		Reveillé 6 am at Jute Factory BEAUVAL. Paraded unit at 9 am. and left at 10.30 am for HEUZECOURT. Destination reached by 3 pm and billetted.	
	Nov 20th/16		2 other Ranks proceeded on leave to England. Interpreter joined up from 2nd F.A. Unit remained here for whole of day. Winter clothing issued. Vehicles of Horse Transport re-packed	W Bradbury.

T.131. Wt. W708-776. 500000. 4/15. Sir J. C. & S.

Instructions regarding War Diaries and Intelligence Summaries are contained in F. S. Regs., Part II. and the Staff Manual respectively. Title pages will be prepared in manuscript.

WAR DIARY
or
~~INTELLIGENCE~~ SUMMARY.
(Erase heading not required.)

Army Form C. 2118.

(8)

Place	Date	Hour	Summary of Events and Information	Remarks and references to Appendices
In the Field	Nov 20th/16		The following ratings were recommended for awards for conduct in the field during Active Operations:-	W Bradbury
			S/ 3251 Staff Sergt Booth. Daniel	
			S/ 3346 Sergt Murray Richard.	
			S/ 3431 L.Cpl. Green Joseph Cowey.	
			S/ 4119 Pte. Carny Harold Hutton.	
			S/ 3897 L.Cpl Lawton. Richard.	
			S/ 3477 Pte. Davies. James	
			S/ 4072 Pte Hall James Whassier	
	Nov 21st/16		Reveille 6.30 am. Unit paraded at 8.30 am and moved off at 9 am for Agenville. Arrived Agenville at 11. am	
	Nov 22nd/16		Reveille 6.30 am Unit paraded 10.30 am and moved off to NOYELLE-en-CHAUSÉE.	
			S/ 3791 Corp Glover E. S/4038 Pte Mann C.W S/4064 Pte Barker A.G. left at 5.45 pm for Cadet School England to report to War Office re Candidature for Commissions.	W Bradbury

T.2134. Wt. W708–776. 500000. 4/15. Sir J. C. & S.

Instructions regarding War Diaries and Intelligence Summaries are contained in F. S. Regs., Part II. and the Staff Manual respectively. Title pages will be prepared in manuscript.

WAR DIARY
or
~~INTELLIGENCE SUMMARY.~~
(Erase heading not required.)

Army Form C. 2118.

(9)

Place	Date	Hour	Summary of Events and Information	Remarks and references to Appendices
In the Field	Nov 23rd/16		Reveillé 6·30 am Unit paraded at 8·30 am and moved off at 9.30 am for LAMOTTE-BULEUX arriving at destination by 12.30 pm.	W Bradbury
	Nov 24th/16		Reveillé 6 30 am. Unit paraded 9.15 am for inspection and dismissed. Paraded later at 12.15 pm to move off to NOLETTES. Arrived at destination at 3.30 pm. Signal from ADMS received for Officer to survey neighbourhood for accommodation of sick, a place suitable for a D.W. Rest Station with adjoining land suitable for the pitching of marquees. Capt Baker & orderly proceeded forthwith for this duty. Horse Ambce detailed to follow in rear of troops of 190th Inf Bde whilst on march.	
	Nov 25th/16		Necessary sanitation carried out in new camp. Sick Bay completed with accommodation for 20 patients.	
	Nov 26th/16		Unit refitted and equipped. Training Area Routine framed. Vehicles cleaned	W Bradbury

T.134. Wt. W708–776. 500000. 4/15. Sir J. C. & S.

Instructions regarding War Diaries and Intelligence Summaries are contained in F. S. Regs., Part II. and the Staff Manual respectively. Title pages will be prepared in manuscript.

WAR DIARY
or
~~INTELLIGENCE SUMMARY~~.
(Erase heading not required.)

Army Form C. 2118.

(10)

Place	Date	Hour	Summary of Events and Information	Remarks and references to Appendices
In the field	Nov 26th/16		Continued Routine. Reveillé 6.30 am Tea 4.15 pm Breakfast 7.30 am Cookhouse 7 pm Sick Bay 8.30 am 1st Post 8.15 pm Parade for all Lanes 9. am. Last Post 8.45 pm Roll call & Sick Bay 4 pm. Lights out 9 pm.	W Bradbury
	Nov 27th/16		Route march in accordance with Brigade orders. Moved off at 8.15 am. Surgeon Sewell RNVR in charge of medical section and Lieut Wilson RM in charge of Transport. A Tent Section was retained in camp on duty at Sick Bay. Capt William Frederick Gibson RAMC and Capt William Hamilton RAMC joined up from 1st Field Amb^ce^	
	Nov 28th/16		General improvements carried out. Issue of fur coats to personnel. 7.30 am to 8 am Physical Drill. Breakfast put back to 8 am. Recreative games to be played in the afternoons in accordance with Divisional Training Scheme.	W Bradbury.
			Visit from ADMS re accommodation of cases sick in barn near Chateau	

T.134. Wt. W708–776. 500000. 4/15. Sir J. C. & S.

Army Form C. 2118.

Instructions regarding War Diaries and Intelligence Summaries are contained in F. S. Regs., Part II. and the Staff Manual respectively. Title pages will be prepared in manuscript.

WAR DIARY
or
~~INTELLIGENCE~~ SUMMARY.
(Erase heading not required.)

(11)

Place	Date	Hour	Summary of Events and Information	Remarks and references to Appendices
In the Field	Nov 29th/16		Usual Routine pursued. Order for prevention of fires in billets reissued.	
	Nov 30th/16		Barn near Chateau NOLETTES. Cleansed and personnel re billetted. Barn prepared for whitewashing	W Madbury

T.131. Wt. W708–776. 500000. 4/15. Sir J. C. & S.

"Confidential" Headquarters

140/1903

War Diary
of
3rd Field Amb^ce
63rd (R.N.) Division
from
December 1st 16
to
December 31st 16

To The A.G's Office
3rd Echelon.

W Bradbury Staff Surgeon
i/c 3rd Field Amb^ce
63rd (R.N) Division

Instructions regarding War Diaries and Intelligence Summaries are contained in F. S. Regs., Part II. and the Staff Manual respectively. Title pages will be prepared in manuscript.

WAR DIARY
or
~~INTELLIGENCE~~ SUMMARY.
(*Erase heading not required.*)

Army Form C. 2118.

Place	Date	Hour	Summary of Events and Information	Remarks and references to Appendices
In the Field	Dec 1st/16.		Continued improvements at Sick Bay & Barn for the accommodation of patients.	W Bradbury
			Capt Gibson RAMC in charge of patients housed in ground floor of Sick Bay. Surgeon Gow RN. in charge of those in the attic. As before the Duty Surgeon will see all cases admitted during the 24 hours he is on duty & visit the sick bay at 8.45 am & 4 pm. & make round of wards between 8.45 pm and 8.45 am.	W Bradbury
	Dec 2nd 16.		Programme of training for coming week submitted to ADMS	
			Squad & wagon Drill in the morning; the afternoon being devoted to sports. One section "B" detailed for duty at Sick Bay.	W Bradbury
	Dec 3rd 16.		9am. Parade and inspection of all ranks by O.C. followed by inspection of Billets	
			Squad Drill and instruction in 2, 3, & 4 handed seats being given in the morning followed by Sports and organised games in the afternoon.	W Bradbury
			Continued improvements in sanitation and Sick Bay	

T2134. Wt. W708—776. 500000. 4/15. Sir J. C. & S.

Instructions regarding War Diaries and Intelligence Summaries are contained in F. S. Regs., Part II. and the Staff Manual respectively. Title pages will be prepared in manuscript.

WAR DIARY
or
~~INTELLIGENCE SUMMARY.~~
(Erase heading not required.)

Army Form C. 2118.

Place	Date	Hour	Summary of Events and Information	Remarks and references to Appendices
In the Field	Dec 3rd Continued.		Lieut G. A. Clement RAMC joined unit.	
	Dec 4th 16		9 am Inspection by the Orderly Officer. Brigade Day. Excused by Brigadier from "Field Day" owing to general fatigues and work necessary for accommodation and improvements in Sick Bay and Camp.	W Bradbury
	Dec 5th/16.		9 am Inspection by Orderly Officer. Squad Drill in the morning. Surgeon Gow RN + 4 other Ranks proceeded on Leave to England leaving camp at 4 am for NOYELLES-sur-MER. 9.30 am Inspection by O/C of Billets and Sick Bay. Great improvement in dress and appearance of men. The afternoon devoted to organised games and sports.	W Bradbury
	Dec 6th/16		7.30 am Physical Drill 9 am Parade and inspection by Orderly Officer. Capt Hamilton RAMC in charge of Upper Ward at Sick Bay for week ending Dec 11th 16. Capt Gibson RAMC to be in charge of Lower Ward at Sick Bay for week ending Dec 7th 16	W Bradbury

T2134. Wt. W708—776. 500000. 4/15. Sir J. C. & S.

Instructions regarding War Diaries and Intelligence Summaries are contained in F. S. Regs., Part II. and the Staff Manual respectively. Title pages will be prepared in manuscript.

WAR DIARY
or
~~INTELLIGENCE SUMMARY.~~
(Erase heading not required.)

Army Form C. 2118.

Place	Date	Hour	Summary of Events and Information	Remarks and references to Appendices
In the Field	Dec 6th/16		(continued) Lieut Wilson RM detailed to be in charge of sports.	W Bradbury
			The following is a list of sectional Officers	
			A Section { A. Tent. Staff Surgeon Bradbury RN	
			Capt Gibson RAMC	
			Lieut Wilson RM.	
			A. Bearers Lieut Clement RAMC	
			B. Section { B. Tent. Surgeon Sewell RNVR. (on leave)	
			Capt Watkins RAMC (Sick)	
			B. Bearers Capt Baker RAMC	
			C. Section { C Tent. Surgeon Gow RN.	
			Capt Hamilton RAMC	
			C. Bearers	
	Dec. 7th/16		7.30 am Physical Drill	
			9 am Parade. Inspection of Unit by Orderly Officer.	
			Stretcher Drill & Wagon Drill during the morning.	W Bradbury
			Capt Emmison R.F. (RAMC) and Capt ANDERSON A.S.K (RAMC)	

T2134. Wt. W708—776. 500000. 4/15. Sir J. C. & S.

Instructions regarding War Diaries and Intelligence Summaries are contained in F. S. Regs., Part II. and the Staff Manual respectively. Title pages will be prepared in manuscript.

WAR DIARY
or
~~INTELLIGENCE~~ SUMMARY.
(Erase heading not required.)

Army Form C. 2118.

Place	Date	Hour	Summary of Events and Information	Remarks and references to Appendices
	(Continued)			
In the Field	Dec 7th/16		and 28 Other Ranks taken on the strength of the unit from Base Depôt	W Bradbury,
			Capt Baker in charge of sanitation for districts Nolettes and Noyelles-sur-Mer.	
			Fire picquet of 1 N.C.O and 4 Other Ranks detailed to watch for infringements of "fire orders" & outbreaks of fire.	
			The afternoon devoted to sports.	
	Dec 8th/16		7.30 am Physical Drill	
			9 am Inspection of parade by Orderly Officer.	
			Necessary fatigues and sanitation. Squad Drill, Stretcher Drill and instruction in 2, 3 & 4 handed seats given during the morning.	W Bradbury
			The afternoon devoted to Sports.	
	Dec 9th/16		7.30 am Physical Drill.	
			9 am Inspection of parade. Programme of training for coming week submitted to A D M S.	W Bradbury

T2134. Wt. W708–776. 500000. 4/15. Sir J. C. & S.

Instructions regarding War Diaries and Intelligence Summaries are contained in F. S. Regs., Part II. and the Staff Manual respectively. Title pages will be prepared in manuscript.

WAR DIARY
or
~~INTELLIGENCE~~ SUMMARY.
(Erase heading not required.)

Army Form C. 2118.

Place	Date	Hour	Summary of Events and Information	Remarks and references to Appendices
In the Field	Dec 9th/16		Usual Bde programme. Lieut G. H. Clement (RAMC) left at 1.30pm for duties at 14th Worcesters (permanent) Surgeon Sewell RNVR & 3 other Ranks return from English leave. From Noon make and mend for all hands less Duty Section A	W Bradbury
	Dec 10th/16		7.30 am Physical Training. 9 am. Parade & inspection by O/C. Parade Service 11.15 am From noon make & mend or Sports or games.	W Bradbury
	Dec 11th/16		7.30 am Physical Training. Brigade Training. "A" Section less cooks, clerks & store party paraded in full marching order at 9 am. Capt Hamilton RAMC in charge. Transport accompanying them :- 2 G.S. wagons, 1 Limbered wagon & 1 water cart with Lieut Wilson RA in charge. A ration of bully beef & biscuits to be carried. 1 Horse Ambce was detailed to follow in rear of the 4th Bedford Regiment.	W Bradbury

T2134. Wt. W708—776. 500000. 4/15. Sir J. C. & S.

Instructions regarding War Diaries and Intelligence Summaries are contained in F. S. Regs., Part II. and the Staff Manual respectively. Title pages will be prepared in manuscript.

WAR DIARY

or

~~INTELLIGENCE~~ SUMMARY.

(Erase heading not required.)

Army Form C. 2118.

Place	Date	Hour	Summary of Events and Information	Remarks and references to Appendices
	(Continued)			
In the Field	Dec 11th/16		During the afternoon Boxing, Skipping and Tug-of-war.	W Bradbury
	Dec 12th/16		Usual Routine of Brigade Training	
			Capt Emmerson R.F. (R.A.M.C) left at 11 am for duty at	
			4th Bedford Regt in relief of Capt Jackson R.A.M.C.	W Bradbury
			Surgeon Sewell in charge of Upper Ward at Sick Bay.	
	Dec 13th/16		Staff Surgeon Bradbury R.N. proceeded on leave to England	Will A Sewell
			Surgeon Sewell R.N.V.R. assumed command of 3rd Field Amb ce	
			Capt Anderson R.A.M.C. proceeded to 7th Royal Fusiliers	
			in accordance with ADMS instructions 25/31 of 9th inst. to	
			relieve Lieut Robertson R.A.M.C on leave.	
		7.30 am.	Physical Drill.	
		9.–12.30pm	Continued Brigade training.	
	Dec 14th/16		Continued Brigade training.	Will A Sewell
			The undermentioned NCOs & men were awarded the "Military Medal for services rendered on the 'Ancre'"	
			S/3251 Staff Sergeant Booth D.	

T2134. Wt. W708–776. 500000. 4/15. Sir J. C. & S.

Instructions regarding War Diaries and Intelligence Summaries are contained in F. S. Regs., Part II. and the Staff Manual respectively. Title pages will be prepared in manuscript.

WAR DIARY

or

~~INTELLIGENCE SUMMARY.~~

(Erase heading not required.)

Army Form C. 2118.

Place	Date	Hour	Summary of Events and Information	Remarks and references to Appendices
In the Field	Dec. 14th/16		Awards continued :- S/ 3346. Sergt. Murray R. S/ 3431. Lance Corporal Green J. C S/ 3477. Pte Davies J. Continued improvements of accommodation for patients, improvements in latrines.	W. A. Sewell
	Dec. 15th/16		7.30 am to 4.30 pm Continued Brigade Training Stretcher + wagon drill. Surgeon Gow RN returned from leave.	W. A. Sewell
	Dec 16th/16		7.30 am to 4.30 pm Continued Brigade Training Squad Drill. Eleven promotions made by ADMS to complete establishment (1 Staff Sergt., 4 Sergts, 1 Lance Sergt, 4 Corporals + 1 Lance Corporal) Visit of Surgeon General and inspection of billets. Stated that cases of Scabies required more attention, that latrines should be covered and sheltered from wind by screens, that ablution stands be provided for patients, that tins after passing through the incinerator should be utilised for the making of paths.	W. A. Sewell

T2134. Wt. W708–776. 500000. 4/15. Sir J. C. & S.

WAR DIARY
or
INTELLIGENCE SUMMARY.
(Erase heading not required.)

Army Form C. 2118.

Instructions regarding War Diaries and Intelligence Summaries are contained in F. S. Regs., Part II. and the Staff Manual respectively. Title pages will be prepared in manuscript.

Place	Date	Hour	Summary of Events and Information	Remarks and references to Appendices
			Lieut Wilson RM and 7 O.R. proceeded on leave to England.	
In the Field	Dec	17th/16	Brigade Training. "C" Section paraded at 8.30 am under charge of Capt Hamilton R.A.M.C. for route march. Transport accompanying Section – 2 G.S. wagons, 1 Limbered wagon, 1 watercart. a horse ambulance to follow in rear of 10th Royal Dublin Fusiliers to pick up such cases as "fall out" on march.	Willi A. Sewell
	Dec	18th/16	"A + C" Tent Sections take over for ward duties for the week. Stretcher Drill during morning. One NISSEN Hut received. All available "hands" used for erection of hut behind Sick Bay. Visit from Brigadier General Finch. Continued improvements in camp sanitation & improvements in billets.	Willi A. Sewell
	Dec	19th/16.	Continued Brigade routine for training. Necessary fatigues for improvements for accommodation of sick	Willi A. Sewell
	Dec	20th/16	Brigade Training. Squad Drill & instruction in hand seats. Sports during the afternoon.	Willi A. Sewell
	Dec	21st/16	In accordance with instructions in Div. Routine Order 1228 of 20th inst.	

T2134. Wt. W708–776. 500000. 4/15. Sir J. C. & S.

Instructions regarding War Diaries and Intelligence Summaries are contained in F. S. Regs., Part II. and the Staff Manual respectively. Title pages will be prepared in manuscript.

WAR DIARY
or
INTELLIGENCE SUMMARY.
(*Erase heading not required.*)

Army Form C. 2118.

Place	Date	Hour	Summary of Events and Information	Remarks and references to Appendices
Sixth Field	Dec 21st/16		(Continued) All Sheepskin coats worn on all parades during the inclement weather. Arrival of 14 "Other Ranks" reinforcements. Reported to N.CO's in accordance with ADMS instructions. and with authority of 150/18, ADMS of 20th inst detailed 5 O.R. to proceed to 1st Field Ambce and 4 O.R to proceed to 2nd Field Amb'ce retaining 5 O.R.	WillASewell
	Dec 22nd/16.		Continued Brigade Training. Improvements in billets carried out. Road precautions put on from Noon.	WillASewell
	Dec 23rd/16		Capt Hamilton detailed to visit daily Fifth Army Artillery School at Sailly-le-Sec as Medical Officer.	WillASewell
	Dec 24th/16		7. Other Ranks proceeded on leave. Visit of RAMC Staff Officer from II Corps who inspected Sick Bay and site. Parade Service 9.am. at Noyelles-sur-Mer.	WillASewell
	Dec 25th/16.		B Tent Sub-Section take over for ward Duties at Sick Bay.	

T2134. Wt. W708—776. 500000. 4/15. Sir J. C. & S.

Instructions regarding War Diaries and Intelligence Summaries are contained in F. S. Regs., Part II. and the Staff Manual respectively. Title pages will be prepared in manuscript.

WAR DIARY
or
~~INTELLIGENCE~~ SUMMARY.
(*Erase heading not required.*)

Army Form C. 2118.

Place	Date	Hour	Summary of Events and Information	Remarks and references to Appendices
In the Field	Dec 25th/16		(Continued). Services 9 am. & 11 am Noyelles.	
		3.20pm	Staff Surgeon Bradbury RN returned from Leave and assumed command of unit.	W.Ll.A. Sewell
	Dec 26th/16		Continued Brigade routine of training. 3 "Other Ranks" proceeded to Rue for course of instruction in Signalling. Second NISSEN Hut received from Louvion. 92nd Field Coy RE. T. Capt Gibson RAMC proceeded on Leave to England.	W Bradbury
	Dec 27th/16		Usual Bde training. Stretcher & wagon Drill. Instruction given in Hand Seats. 1 NCO and 17 "OR" reinforcements arrived from Base Depot, Rouen. In accordance with ADMS instructions 9 "OR" detailed for 1st Field Ambce and 5 "OR" to 2nd Field Ambce. Retained. 1 NCO & 3. OR	W Bradbury
	Dec 28th/16		Preparations made to arrange accommodation for Scabies Personnel removed from large barn and place allotted and prepared as Scabies Ward.	
	Dec 29th/16		Lieut Wilson RM returned from English Leave. Capt Anderson RAMC	W Bradbury

T2134. Wt. W708–776. 500000. 4/15. Sir J. C. & S.

Instructions regarding War Diaries and Intelligence Summaries are contained in F. S. Regs., Part II. and the Staff Manual respectively. Title pages will be prepared in manuscript.

WAR DIARY
or
INTELLIGENCE SUMMARY.
(Erase heading not required.)

Army Form C. 2118.

Place	Date	Hour	Summary of Events and Information	Remarks and references to Appendices
In the Field	Dec 29th/16		(Continued) returned from 9th Royal Fusiliers. Visit from Divisional Commander Major General Shute who inspected the site and wards at Sick Bay. Remarked on unsuitability of present site for accommodation of sick. Difficulty experienced in obtaining a better place in this area. Work in making 'cots' for sick and provision for increased accommodation carried on. Party of Engineers from 92nd Field Coy RE detailed to provide and construct 'cots' in the wards.	W Bradbury
	Dec 30th/16		Continued the work for provision of washing & treatment of Scabies Cases. 7 O.R. proceeded on Leave to England. Sixteen Cots erected today.	W Bradbury
	Dec 31st/16		Continued improvements in billets. Usual Brigade training. T. Capt Anderson RAMC detailed to report as Med. Officer to Anson Battalion.	W Bradbury

T2134. Wt. W708—776. 500000. 4/15. Sir J. C. & S.

"Confidential"

Headquarters 3rd Fd Ambce
63rd (R.N.) Division
Feb. 1st 17.

War Diary
of.
3rd Field Ambce. 63rd (R.N.) Division.
from
Jan. 1st 1917.
to
Jan. 31st 1917.

[signature]
Lt. Col. R.A.M.C.
O/c 3rd Field Ambce
63rd (R.N.) Division

To
The A.G.'s Office
3rd Echelon.

Instructions regarding War Diaries and Intelligence Summaries are contained in F. S. Regs., Part II. and the Staff Manual respectively. Title pages will be prepared in manuscript.

WAR DIARY

or

~~INTELLIGENCE~~ SUMMARY.

(*Erase heading not required.*)

Army Form C. 2118.

Place	Date	Hour	Summary of Events and Information	Remarks and references to Appendices
In the Field	Jan 1st/17		9.0am Parade & Inspection. Continued improvements in billets and Scabies wards.	W Madbury
			L/4135 Corp. Hodgson detailed for a course at ROE in Cookery.	
			T. Capt. HAMILTON R.A.M.C. detailed to proceed to 10th Royal Dublin Fusiliers vice Lieut EVANS R.A.M.C on leave.	
			Received orders from 190th Brigade to move to NOUVION for the better accommodation of patients.	
			Deficiencies in animals 3 Chargers 1 Rider 4 Light Draught & 7 Heavy Draught.	
			Visited Chateau at NOUVION. Accommodation found for 45 sick and 25 Scabies cases. Find it impossible to move present sick. Reported the circumstances to Brigade and detailed a Medical Officer and Section - Tent Bearers to proceed tomorrow for NOUVION.	
	Jan 2nd/17		Surgeon Gow R.N. and 60 O.R. proceeded 9 am to Chateau	W Madbury

T2134. Wt. W708—776. 500000. 4/15. Sir J. C. & S.

Instructions regarding War Diaries and Intelligence Summaries are contained in F. S. Regs., Part II. and the Staff Manual respectively. Title pages will be prepared in manuscript.

WAR DIARY
or
~~INTELLIGENCE SUMMARY.~~
(*Erase heading not required.*)

Army Form C. 2118.

Place	Date	Hour	Summary of Events and Information	Remarks and references to Appendices
In the Field	Jan 2nd/17		NOUVION as working party. Engineers assisted in preparation of wards & beds	W Bradbury
	Jan 3rd/17		Surgeon GOW R.N. and 3 N.C.O's proceeded to Gas School at RUE for half days course.	W Bradbury
			Further evacuation of horses. Riders 3, Light Draught 3 Heavy Draught 4 sent to 53rd Mobile Veterinary Section	
			Inspection of animals by A.D.V.S. at 3pm.	
	Jan 4th/17		Engineers engaged in removing bunks from wards at NOLETTE. Material conveyed to NOUVION by G S wagons and Motor Lorry.	W Bradbury
			Continued arrangements at Chateau NOUVION	
	Jan 5th/17		Lieut WILSON R.M. & 2 N.C.O's left 9am for 2 days Gas Course at RUE. Surgeon GOW R.N. & 1 N.C.O from NOUVION also proceeded to RUE for 3 days gas course.	W Bradbury
	Jan 6th/17		Preparation made to move "A" Section to NOUVION	
			Requested permission of A.D.V.S. to take horses to NOUVION	W Bradbury

Instructions regarding War Diaries and Intelligence Summaries are contained in F. S. Regs., Part II. and the Staff Manual respectively. Title pages will be prepared in manuscript.

WAR DIARY
~~or~~
~~INTELLIGENCE SUMMARY.~~
(Erase heading not required.)

Army Form C. 2118.

Place	Date	Hour	Summary of Events and Information	Remarks and references to Appendices
			(Continued)	
In the Field	Jan 6th/17		Headquarters of unit moved to NOUVION. "B" Section under Surgeon SEWELL RNVR remained at NOLETTE until accommodation found for patients.	W Bradbury
	Jan 7th/17		Carried on improvements at Chateau. Detailed Horsed Ambce to follow in rear of 190th Bde on march to VRON for training Awards. 2/3080 Sergeant Major Evans H. awarded D.C.M. for Service in the Field Authority London Gazette Jan 1st 1917.	W Bradbury
	Jan 8th 17		"B" Section moved to NOUVION. No patients left at NOLETTE. Inspection of Ambce Cars by Brigadier General. Horse Transport unable to take part owing to deficiencies of animals. Carried on improvements at Chateau for increased accommodation of sick	W Bradbury
	Jan 9th 17		Fitted whole of unit out with Small box respirator. + Tested them under Supervision of Lieut Wilson RM. + Gas Sergeant.	W Bradbury

T2134. Wt. W708—776. 500000. 4/15. Sir J. C. & S.

Army Form C. 2118.

Instructions regarding War Diaries and Intelligence Summaries are contained in F. S. Regs., Part II. and the Staff Manual respectively. Title pages will be prepared in manuscript.

WAR DIARY
or
~~INTELLIGENCE SUMMARY.~~
(Erase heading not required.)

Place	Date	Hour	Summary of Events and Information	Remarks and references to Appendices
In the Field	Jan 9th/17		(Continued) NISSEN hut used for testing purposes. Second NISSEN hut received from Town Major	W Bradbury
			T. Capt JACKSON RAMC reported his arrival from leave	
			Arrival of advance party from 57th Division to arrange for incoming Field Ambce and to take over	
	Jan 10th/17		Improvements at Chateau & sanitation carried on.	W Bradbury
			Inspection by Corps Commander of Ambce Section of Transport	
			Horse Transport unable to take part owing to deficiencies of Horses. Shortage of horses 8 Heavy Draught 6 Light Draught 5 Riders.	
	Jan 11th 17		T. Capt JACKSON RAMC detailed to proceed to 7th Royal Fusiliers. Proceeded to relief of Capt ROBERTSON RAMC during the afternoon.	W Bradbury
			Arranged with Brigade that Battalions notify this unit of cases obviously requiring admittance to Field Ambce & to assist in collection and evacuation of cases.	

T2134. Wt. W708—776. 500000. 4/15. Sir J. C. & S.

Instructions regarding War Diaries and Intelligence Summaries are contained in F. S. Regs., Part II. and the Staff Manual respectively. Title pages will be prepared in manuscript.

WAR DIARY
or
INTELLIGENCE SUMMARY.
(Erase heading not required.)

Army Form C. 2118.

Place	Date	Hour	Summary of Events and Information	Remarks and references to Appendices
In the Field	Jan 12th/17		T. Capt GIBSON returned to this unit from leave. Capt ROBERTSON RAMC & Capt JACKSON RAMC rejoined unit from 7th Royal Fusiliers. Capt GIBSON RAMC permanently detailed as M.O. 7th Royal Fusiliers. Capt ROBERTSON RAMC temporarily detailed to assist 2nd Field Amb^ce at LE CROTOY. Preparations for move	W Bradbury
	Jan 13th/17		Paraded at 8.15 am. in full marching order. Left at 9 am for LAMOTTE BULEUX. Santary party left behind to clean up billets. The O/c remained until 11 am in case claims made regarding billets. Move completed by 11.30 am and reported to ADMS & Inf Bde. Headquarters of unit situated about 50 yards from Cross roads Lamotte Buleux on road to HAUTVILLERS	W Bradbury
	Jan 14th/17		The unit paraded at 8.15 am to move off at 9.17 am from starting point - railway crossing on LAMOTTE BULEUX - CANCHY Road. Route via CANCY L ARGENVILLERS - YVRENCH to HIERMONT	

T2134. Wt. W708-776. 500000. 4/15. Sir J. C. & S.

Instructions regarding War Diaries and Intelligence Summaries are contained in F. S. Regs., Part II. and the Staff Manual respectively. Title pages will be prepared in manuscript.

WAR DIARY
or
INTELLIGENCE SUMMARY.
(Erase heading not required.)

Army Form C. 2118.

Place	Date	Hour	Summary of Events and Information	Remarks and references to Appendices
In the Field	Jan 14th/17		(Continued) arrived at destination 3.30 pm. Headquarters of unit situated at café near Church. HIERMONT. T. Capt JACKSON RAMC posted to 3rd Field Ambce & T. Capt GIBSON R.A.M.C. posted to 7th Royal Fusiliers. Authority Divisional Routine Order No 1402 of 14th inst T. Capt ROBERTSON R.A.M.C. posted to 3rd Field Ambce from 7th Royal Fusiliers. Authority D.R.O. 1402 of 14th inst	WBradbury.
In the Field	Jan 15th/17		Reveille 6 am. Paraded unit at 8 am. Parties moved off at 8.15 am to GEZAINCOURT via AUXI-le-CHATEAU - WAVANS - HEMS to GEZAINCOURT. Completion of move 4 pm. Headquarters of unit situated in house at Cross Road. CANDAS to DOULLENS and GEZAINCOURT to BEAUVAL. Billeting parties met Staff Capt at GEZAINCOURT Church 10 am to arrange billets	WBradbury
In the Field	Jan 16th/17		Rest day. Carried on necessary fatigues and sanitation. T. Capt HAMITON RAM.C rejoins unit from 10th Royal Dublin Fusiliers, T Capt ANDERSON RAMC rejoins unit from Anson Batt.	WBradbury.

T2134. Wt. W708—776. 500000. 4/15. Sir J. C. & S.

Instructions regarding War Diaries and Intelligence Summaries are contained in F. S. Regs., Part II. and the Staff Manual respectively. Title pages will be prepared in manuscript.

WAR DIARY
or
~~INTELLIGENCE SUMMARY.~~
(Erase heading not required.)

Army Form C. 2118.

Place	Date	Hour	Summary of Events and Information	Remarks and references to Appendices
In the Field	Jan 16/1/17.		T. Capt WATKINS RAMC rejoins unit from Hospital. Lt Col R. E. Drake Brockman R.A.M.C assumes command of the 3rd Field Ambce vice Staff Surgeon W. Bradbury R.N. Staff Surgeon W. Bradbury. R.N., Surgeon RNVR W A Sewell and T. Surgeon RN A. E. Gow leave at 3.30 pm to return to Admiralty. Capt Macnaughton R.A.M.C., Capt Macleod R.A.M.C, and Lieut Kerby R.A.M.C., report for duty.	R Drake Brockman Lt Col
do.	17/1/17	9.30am	Paraded to move off at 10 am. Capt. Anderson RAMC in charge of Parade, Lieut Nelson R.M. i/c Transport. Route via: BEAUQUESNE to PUCHEVILLERS. The inclement weather and frost made it difficult for transport. The personnel arrived at destination 3 pm. Transport arrived 6 p.m. having had difficulties through bad roads and frost. Billetted near Church PUCHEVILLERS and in Hutments some 800 yards from Hdqrs of unit. Capt Hopkins RAMC reported for duty and taken on strength of unit.	R Drake Brockman Lt Col

T2134. Wt. W708—776. 500000. 4/15. Sir J. C. & S.

Instructions regarding War Diaries and Intelligence Summaries are contained in F. S. Regs., Part II. and the Staff Manual respectively. Title pages will be prepared in manuscript.

WAR DIARY
or
~~INTELLIGENCE SUMMARY.~~
(Erase heading not required.)

Army Form C. 2118.

Place	Date	Hour	Summary of Events and Information	Remarks and references to Appendices
In the Field	18/1/17	9am	Unit paraded for orders. Camp cleaned and necessary fatigues and sanitation dealt with. Day treated as rest day	
		10.30am	Kit inspection by sectional officers. Detailed lists of lost kit made. Capt Macleod RAMC detailed and proceeded to relieve Surgeon MacRitchie RN. Medical Officer Hood Battalion during absence on leave of this officer.	A.W. Drake Brockman Lt Col
do	19/1/17		Necessary fatigues and sanitation. All men's blankets(?) all gear cleaned and packed. Lieut Welsh RM & 2 N.C.O.s proceeded to CLAIRFAYE to take over and check stores etc left by outgoing Field Amb^e. Sergt Leake and 17 O.R. proceeded to No 4(?) C.C.S. VARENNES for fatigues at that place.	A.W. Drake Brockman Lt Col
do	20/1/17	9.30am	Unit paraded to move off at 10.20 am and under the command of Capt Anderson R.A.M.C. Capt Jackson R.A.M.C took temporary command of horse transport during the absence of Lieut Welsh RM. A/Corporal Hodgson detailed by A.D.M.S. & proceeded to NOUVION as assistant instructor at Divisional Cookery School.	A.W. Drake Brockman Lt Col

T2134. Wt. W708—776. 500000. 4/15. Sir J. C. & S.

Instructions regarding War Diaries and Intelligence Summaries are contained in F. S. Regs., Part II. and the Staff Manual respectively. Title pages will be prepared in manuscript.

WAR DIARY
or
INTELLIGENCE SUMMARY.
(Erase heading not required.)

Army Form C. 2118.

Place	Date	Hour	Summary of Events and Information	Remarks and references to Appendices
In the Field	20/7		Unit completed move to CLAIRFAYE at 3.30 pm. and relief of 34th Field Ambce 11th Division completed.	
		9.50pm	Capt Watkins R.A.M.C. and 8 O.R. proceeded on leave to England. Attached to this unit Capt Wallace R.A.M.C., Lieut Biggs R.A.M.C. and 19 O.R. of 56th Field Ambce 18th Division; also 34 other Ranks, 13 Riding Horses, 28 Heavy Draught horses from 1st Field Ambce 63rd (R.N.) Division for rations and duty. Difficulty experienced in Motor Transport Section. Only two Siddeley Deasy Cars and a Ford available for duty.	[signature] Lt Col
do.	21/7	6.30am	Unit parades daily. Detailed personnel for camp duties. Capt Hamilton R.A.M.C. detailed to visit the German Prison Camps at CLAIRFAYE, BELLE EGLISE & ACHEUX.	
			Distribution of Wards:-	
			Wards 1 – 5 — Capt Jackson R.A.M.C.	
			Wards 6 – 10 — Capt Anderson R.A.M.C.	
			Wards 11 – 15 — Capt Macnaughton R.A.M.C.	[signature] Lt Col

Instructions regarding War Diaries and Intelligence Summaries are contained in F. S. Regs., Part II. and the Staff Manual respectively. Title pages will be prepared in manuscript.

WAR DIARY
or
~~INTELLIGENCE SUMMARY.~~
(Erase heading not required.)

Army Form C. 2118.

Place	Date	Hour	Summary of Events and Information	Remarks and references to Appendices
CLAIRFAYE	21/1/17		Wards 16-20 Capt Hopkins R.A.M.C	
			Wards 21-24 Lieut Kirby R.A.M.C.	
			Wards D Section Capt Wallace R.A.M.C.	
			Wards E Section Lieut Biggs R.A.M.C.	
			Camp cleaned up and salvage of articles carried out	[illegible] Lt Col
do	22/1/17	8 am	10 German Prisoners of War reported to assist in fatigues of Camp. Great difficulty in obtaining water experienced. Supply at VARENNES frozen. Water obtained from FORCEVILLE	[illegible] Lt Col
do	23/1/17		Capt Hamilton R.A.M.C. detailed to act as Sanitary advisor to the Town Majors of FORCEVILLE, LEALVILLERS and ARQUÈVES in addition to his other duties	
			Capt Hopkins R.A.M.C detailed to proceed to 63rd Divisional Engineers. Capt Macnaughton R.A.M.C detailed to proceed to 63rd Divisional Train. These two officers struck off strength from today.	[illegible] Lt Col
do	24/1/17		Improvements in camp carried out. Commenced alterations of	

T2134. Wt W708-776. 500000. 4/15. Sir J. C. & S.

Instructions regarding War Diaries and Intelligence Summaries are contained in F. S. Regs., Part II. and the Staff Manual respectively. Title pages will be prepared in manuscript.

WAR DIARY
or
~~INTELLIGENCE~~ SUMMARY.
(Erase heading not required.)

Army Form C. 2118.

Place	Date	Hour	Summary of Events and Information	Remarks and references to Appendices
CLAIRFAYE	24/1/17		Cohhose:	
			Lieut Kitchall RAMC reported his arrival to relieve Lieut Biggs RAMC who rejoined his unit the 56th Field Amb^ce 18th Division	
			Redistribution of wards:	
			Capt Jackson RAMC took charge of Wards 1 – 8	
			" Anderson RAMC do do 9 – 17	
			Lieut Kirby RAMC do do 18 – 26	
			Capt Wallace RAMC do do B + C.	
			Lieut Kitchall RAMC do do D + E.	[signature] Lt Col
do.	25/1/17		Evacuating the L Sector to VARENNES from 9 am today	
			Continued the improvements in camp generally. Wards renumbered. Much difficulty still experienced in obtaining water. Severe frost still continued.	
			Difficulty also experienced in evacuation & collection of cases only 1 Siddeley Deasy Car available. Use made of the 1st/3rd Amb^ce Transport.	[signature] Lt Col

T2134. Wt. W708—776. 500000. 4/15. Sir J. C. & S.

Instructions regarding War Diaries and Intelligence Summaries are contained in F. S. Regs., Part II. and the Staff Manual respectively. Title pages will be prepared in manuscript.

WAR DIARY
or
~~INTELLIGENCE~~ SUMMARY.
(Erase heading not required.)

Army Form C. 2118.

Place	Date	Hour	Summary of Events and Information	Remarks and references to Appendices
CLAIRFAYE	25/1/17	9.30pm	S/3413 L/Cpl Cluster J and S/4045 Pte Eves C. E. proceeded to England as candidates for Commissions.	[illegible] Lt Col
do	26/1/17		Improvements carried out in camp. Still great difficulty with Motor Ambulance Cars. Ford Car placed at the disposal of O/c 21st Sanitary Section.	[illegible] Lt Col
do	27/1/17		Capt Hamilton RAMC detailed to relieve O/c 21st Sanitary Section with Ford Car at his disposal. Difficulty in arranging for Dental Surgeon to attend cases for Dental Treatment. Received instructions from ADMS that all Dental cases to be treated at 2nd Field Amb^ce on Wednesdays and Saturdays.	[illegible] Lt Col
do	28/1/17		Capt Jackson RAMC detailed to relieve Capt Hesketh RAMC Medical Officer Horse Battalion. Instructions received from ADMS to detail an officer to proceed to 61st Division. Proposed detailing Capt Hesketh RAMC for this duty. Capt Jackson RAMC proceeded to carry out relief.	[illegible] Lt Col

T2134. Wt. W708—776. 500000. 4/15. Sir J. C. & S.

Instructions regarding War Diaries and Intelligence Summaries are contained in F. S. Regs., Part II. and the Staff Manual respectively. Title pages will be prepared in manuscript.

WAR DIARY
or
~~INTELLIGENCE~~ SUMMARY.
(Erase heading not required.)

Army Form C. 2118.

Place	Date	Hour	Summary of Events and Information	Remarks and references to Appendices
CLAIRFAYE	29/1/17		Lieut Tutchell RAMC detailed to visit sick of Drake Battalion owing to Medical Officer of that Battalion being sick. Capt Metcalfe RAMC reported for unit and taken on the strength of unit from 2nd Field Amb^ce 63rd (RN) Division. Capt Robertson RAMC already attached to 2nd Field Amb^ce for temporary duty now struck off strength to 2nd Field Ambulance 63rd (R.N.) Div.	[illegible] Drake Brockman Lt Col
do	30/1/17		Continued improvements in camp. Frost continues only 2 Ford Cars and 1 Sunbeam Daimler Car fit to take the road. Visit of D.D.M.S. II Corps.	[illegible] Drake Brockman Lt Col
do	31/1/17		Continued daily routine. Lieut Hyatt RAMC reported for duty from 56th Field Amb^ce 18th Division to relieve Lieut Tutchell RAMC. Capt Nicholson RAMC reported for duty from Hood Battalion. Signal received from ADMS 63rd (RN) Division to draw 2 days forage from Refilling Point for thaw precautions.	[illegible] Drake Brockman Lt Col

T2134. Wt. W708—776. 500000. 4/15. Sir J. C. & S.

Instructions regarding War Diaries and Intelligence Summaries are contained in F. S. Regs., Part II. and the Staff Manual respectively. Title pages will be prepared in manuscript.

WAR DIARY

or

~~INTELLIGENCE SUMMARY.~~

(Erase heading not required.)

Army Form C. 2118.

Place	Date	Hour	Summary of Events and Information	Remarks and references to Appendices
Clairfaye	1/2/17		Orderly Officer - Lieut Kirby R.A.M.C. Carried on usual routine of fatigues and sanitation throughout Camp. Frost continues. Erection of cook house expedited.	
			Instructed by A.D.M.S. 63rd (R.N.) Division (F2/442) to attach Capt Maclean R.A.M.C. to Drake Battalion pending the return of Battalion Medical Officer - sick.	
			Received instructions from Hdqrs of Division to draw extra forage for thaw precautions.	
			Owing to irregular train service unable to despatch men discharged to duty via R.T.O. ACHEUX. Reported	[illegible]
	2/2/17		Orderly Officer - Capt Wallace R.A.M.C. attached from 56th Field Amb^ce 18th Division.	
			Captains ANDERSON, & HAMILTON & Lieut KERBY RAMC with 90 Bearers told off to report to O/c 2nd Field Ambulance by 12 noon on 3rd Inst.	
			Issued orders for prevention of Chilled Feet	[illegible]

"Confidential"

Vol 11

1407/1917

Headquarters
3rd Field Ambulance
63rd (R.N.) Division

War Diary

of

3rd Field Ambulance 63rd (R.N.) Division

from

February 1st 1917

to

February 28th 1917

To

A.G.'s Office.
3rd Echelon.

[signature]
Lt. Col RAMC
O/c 3rd Field Ambce
63rd (R.N.) Division

Feb 1917

Instructions regarding War Diaries and Intelligence Summaries are contained in F. S. Regs., Part II. and the Staff Manual respectively. Title pages will be prepared in manuscript.

WAR DIARY

or

~~INTELLIGENCE~~ SUMMARY.

(Erase heading not required.)

Army Form C. 2118.

Place	Date	Hour	Summary of Events and Information	Remarks and references to Appendices
Clairfaye	3/2/17		Orderly Officer - Lieut Hyatt RAMC (56th Field Amb^ce 18th Division)	
		8am.	Bearers paraded in Steel helmets, Box Respirator and Gas helmets. Overcoats carried bandolier fashion. Capt Anderson RAMC took charge of party and party moved off by gun to march to ENGLESART.	[initials illegible]
			O/c proceeded later to inspect ground and the Bearer Posts and lines of evacuation.	
			A.D.M.S. signal Fx/460 repeated D.G.M.S. wire to suspend evacuation of all cases except really urgent cases.	
	4/2/17		Orderly Officer - Capt Metcalfe RAMC.	
			Bearers take part in action - 1 O.R. wounded	[signature illegible] Lt Col
		11.30am	Service C. of E. in the Dining Hall.	
	5/2/17		Orderly Officer - Capt Wallace R.A.M.C.	
			Bearers return from front line. 1 N.C.O. sent to FORCEVILLE for 3 days Gas Course. Reported the difficulty to ADMS of clearing the patients discharged to duty of the 11th & 61st Div.	[initials illegible]

T2134. Wt. W703—776. 500000. 4/15. Sir J. C. & S.

Army Form C. 2118.

WAR DIARY
or
INTELLIGENCE SUMMARY.
(Erase heading not required.)

Instructions regarding War Diaries and Intelligence Summaries are contained in F. S. Regs., Part II. and the Staff Manual respectively. Title pages will be prepared in manuscript.

Place	Date	Hour	Summary of Events and Information	Remarks and references to Appendices
Clairfaye	5/2/17		Corps instructs us to overcome difficulty & [illegible] [illegible] somewhere. All Officers to become familiar with Thomas' Splints which shortly will replace Liston's Splints.	
	6/2/17		Orderly Officer - Lieut Hyatt RAMC. Capt Metcalfe RAMC leaves for the 61st Division and is struck off strength from today. Capt Jackson RAMC rejoins the unit from temporary duties with the [illegible] Battalion. Evacuation & Collection of cases carried out by Horsed Ambces and G.S. wagons owing to lack of Ambulance Cars through breakdowns.	[signature] Lt Col
	7/2/17		Orderly Officer - Capt Watkins RAMC. A.D.M.S. instructions received to detail one Medical Officer to proceed at once to 1st Field Ambulance by Car. On arrival there Capt Watkins RAMC detailed to act as Medical Officer to 4th Bedfords.	[initials]

T2134. Wt. W708-776. 500000. 4/15. Sir J. C. & S.

Army Form C. 2118.

WAR DIARY
or
~~INTELLIGENCE~~ SUMMARY.
(Erase heading not required.)

Instructions regarding War Diaries and Intelligence Summaries are contained in F. S. Regs., Part II. and the Staff Manual respectively. Title pages will be prepared in manuscript.

Place	Date	Hour	Summary of Events and Information	Remarks and references to Appendices
Clairfaye	7/2/17	10pm	A.D.M.S. instructions C.1. received to detail 25 Bearers to stand by ready to proceed to 1st Field Ambulance. Motor Lorry provided to convey them if needed.	[illegible signature]
	8/2/17	8am	Bearers not required and Lorry dismissed to proceed to D.A.D.O.S.	
			Orderly Officer - Capt Jackson RAMC.	
			Capt Byrne RAMC & Lieut Lewis RAMC from 56th Field Ambulance 18th Division join unit to assist at Rest Station.	[illegible signature]
			3 N.C.O's and 9 O.R. arrive from Base as reinforcements.	
	9/2/17		Orderly Officer - Lieut Kirby RAMC.	
		9.30am	As per A.D.M.S. Signal F.2/527 Capt Anderson RAMC and 2 Bearer N.C.O.s proceeded to No 6 Field Ambulance 2nd Division at OVILLERS HUTS (X.7.d. 5.2.) to learn routes of evacuation in the 2nd Division Sector.	[illegible signature]
	10/2/17		Orderly Officer - Capt Wallace RAMC.	
		10am	Capt Anderson RAMC and TWO N.C.O.s proceeded from	[illegible initials]

T2134. Wt. W708—776. 500000. 4/15. Sir J. C. & S.

Instructions regarding War Diaries and Intelligence Summaries are contained in F. S. Regs., Part II. and the Staff Manual respectively. Title pages will be prepared in manuscript.

WAR DIARY
or
~~INTELLIGENCE~~ SUMMARY.
(Erase heading not required.)

Army Form C. 2118.

Place	Date	Hour	Summary of Events and Information	Remarks and references to Appendices
Chartfaye	10/2/17		No 6 Field Ambce to [illegible] to 57 Field Ambulance at AVELUY POST. [illegible] routes of evacuation of that sector as per A.D.M.S. instructions F2/527.	[initials]
	11/2/17		Orderly Officer Capt. Wynne R.A.M.C. Issued orders that instruction, by means of classes, should be given to all unacquainted with the use of the new Box Respirator. Until further orders the Officer next for duty will assist the Orderly Officer in seeing the morning sick. The Officer next for duty will visit the Dining Hall and attend to any complaint made. D.M.S. order that all Frost Bite Feet be termed Trench Feet	[initials]
	12/2/17		Orderly Officer – Lieut Lewis 118 men of the Hood Battalion sent to Rest Station with minor ailments. Paraded unit at 2pm. for inspection of equipment	[initials]

T2134. Wt. W708–776. 500000. 4/15. Sir J. C. & S.

Instructions regarding War Diaries and Intelligence Summaries are contained in F. S. Regs., Part II. and the Staff Manual respectively. Title pages will be prepared in manuscript.

WAR DIARY
or
INTELLIGENCE SUMMARY.
(*Erase heading not required.*)

Army Form C. 2118.

Place	Date	Hour	Summary of Events and Information	Remarks and references to Appendices
In the Field	12/7		Sent up to ENGLESART 2nd Field Amb^ce 90 Stretcher Bearers. under Capt ANDERSON RAMC and Lieut Kirby RAMC to take part in coming action	[initials]
	13/7		Orderly Officer Capt Jackson RAMC.	
			Arrangements made for the Dentist of No 49 C.C.S. to attend Clairfaye on Tuesdays and Fridays at 9 am. for units in the Central area.	[initials]
			Wire received from 63. (RN) Div Supply Column No L.P. 397 warning the expectation of severe frost during the night & that all precautions relative to Amb^ce Cars be taken	
	14/7		Orderly Officer Capt Wallace RAMC	
			Severe frost continues. Difficulty in obtaining sufficient water from present supplies. Improvements carried out in camp. Patients certified by Medical Officer as fit for Light Duty utilised for work in Camp.	[initials]
			NISSEN Huts erected on site of old canvas huts.	

T2134. Wt. W708—776. 500000. 4/15. Sir J. C. & S.

Instructions regarding War Diaries and Intelligence Summaries are contained in F. S. Regs., Part II. and the Staff Manual respectively. Title pages will be prepared in manuscript.

WAR DIARY
or
INTELLIGENCE SUMMARY.
(*Erase heading not required.*)

Army Form C. 2118.

Place	Date	Hour	Summary of Events and Information	Remarks and references to Appendices
In the Field	15/7		Orderly Officer Capt Byrne RAMC. Carried on improvements in camp, necessary fatigues & sanitation.	[illegible]
	16/7		Orderly Officer Lieut Lewis RAMC. Casualties reported from active Operations 1 O.R. wounded and 1 OR Shell Shock.	[illegible]
	17/7		Orderly Officer Capt Jackson RAMC. Distinct change in the weather. Thaw precautions issued. Roads almost impassable through thaw.	[illegible]
	18/7		Orderly Officer Capt. Wallace RAMC. Carried on improvements in camp and necessary fatigues. 1 OR. "Shell Shock" reported from active Operations.	[illegible]
	19/7		Orderly Officer Capt Byrne RAMC. Carried on daily routine in camp and improvements generally. Nissen Huts in course of construction	[illegible]

T2134. Wt. W708–776. 500000. 4/15. Sir J. C. & S.

Instructions regarding War Diaries and Intelligence Summaries are contained in F. S. Regs., Part II. and the Staff Manual respectively. Title pages will be prepared in manuscript.

WAR DIARY
or
INTELLIGENCE SUMMARY.
(Erase heading not required.)

Army Form C. 2118.

Place	Date	Hour	Summary of Events and Information	Remarks and references to Appendices
In the Field	20/7		Orderly Officer Lieut Lewis RAMC Bearers return from front line & stand off for half day.	[illegible]
	21/7		Orderly Officer Capt Jackson RAMC. Sergt Major Evans H. evacuated to No 4 C.C.S. Varennes	[illegible]
	22/7		Orderly Officer Capt Anderson RAMC. Capt Jackson detailed to see the sick of 63rd D.A.C. at Varennes at 8 am daily in addition to his other duties. During this period he will be excused the duties of Orderly Officer	[illegible]
		2pm	Lecture on "The Evacuation of Wounded" by the O/c.	
	23/7		Orderly Officer Lieut Kerby RAMC. Orders issued in Daily Orders re Salvage of old clothing deposited in and around camp.	[illegible]
	24/7		Orderly Officer Lieut Lewis RAMC. Lieut Biggs. RAMC (56 Field Amb^ce 18th Division) reported for	[illegible]

Instructions regarding War Diaries and Intelligence Summaries are contained in F. S. Regs., Part II. and the Staff Manual respectively. Title pages will be prepared in manuscript.

WAR DIARY
or
~~INTELLIGENCE SUMMARY.~~
(Erase heading not required.)

Army Form C. 2118.

Place	Date	Hour	Summary of Events and Information	Remarks and references to Appendices
In the Field	24/7/17		(Continued). Lieut Hyatt R.A.M.C. 56 Field Ambulance 18th Division returns from Hospital sick. Unit paraded at 2 pm for inspection Iron Rations. Staff Sergeant Booth detailed to act as Sergeant Major vice Sergt Major Evans sick. Rewards. The undermentioned men have been awarded the Military Medal (Authority C.R.O 418.) S/3398 Pte Fellow G.T. and S/4025 Pte Makin J.	[initials]
	25/7/17		Orderly Officer Lieut Biggs R.A.M.C. Received wire F2/763 warning units of the danger of mines in captured territory. Services held in the Dining Hall	[initials]
	26/7/17		Orderly Officer Lieut. Hyatt R.A.M.C. Gas precautions removed. Systematic disinfection of wards carried out. Blankets disinfected at FORCEVILLE.	[initials]

T2134. Wt. W708—776. 500000. 4/15. Sir J. C. & S.

Army Form C. 2118.

Instructions regarding War Diaries and Intelligence Summaries are contained in F. S. Regs., Part II. and the Staff Manual respectively. Title pages will be prepared in manuscript.

WAR DIARY
or
INTELLIGENCE SUMMARY.
(Erase heading not required.)

Place	Date	Hour	Summary of Events and Information	Remarks and references to Appendices
In the Field	27/7		Orderly Officer Lieut Sorby R.A.M.C. Working Party return from 1st Field Ambulance. Hastened construction of cookhouse and continued cleansing of the wards.	[illegible] Lt Col
	28/7		Orderly Officer. Capt Anderson R.A.M.C. Carried on usual routine and cleansing of the wards. Awards. Capt A.S.H. ANDERSON R.A.M.C. awarded Bar to Military Cross. Authority D.R.O. 1697 of 27th inst.	[illegible]

T2134. Wt. W708—776. 500000. 4/15. Sir J. C. & S.

"Confidential"

Vol XI
140/2042

Hdqrs 3rd Field Amb^ce
63rd (R.N.) Division
April 1st 1917

War Diary

of

3rd Field Ambulance 63rd (R.N) Division

from

March 1st 1917

to

March 31st 1917

To

The A.G's Office.
3rd Echelon.

Mar 1917

[signature], Capt R.A.M.C.
for O/c 3rd Field Amb^ce
63rd (R.N.) Division

Instructions regarding War Diaries and Intelligence Summaries are contained in F. S. Regs., Part II. and the Staff Manual respectively. Title pages will be prepared in manuscript.

WAR DIARY
or
~~INTELLIGENCE~~ SUMMARY.
(Erase heading not required.)

Army Form C. 2118.

Place	Date	Hour	Summary of Events and Information	Remarks and references to Appendices
CLAIRFAYE	1/3/17		Orderly Officer Lieut Hyatt R.A.M.C.	
			Captain A.S.K. Anderson M.C. R.A.M.C. awarded Bar to Military Cross Authority D.R.O. 1697.	
			Owing to scattered area over which the unit of this Division are billeted cases of the 63 (R.N.) Division are to be conveyed in motor Amb^ce cars as follows:-	[signature]
			188th Bde - BOUZINCOURT, 189th Bde HEDAUVILLE, 190th Bde MARTINSART	
			The cars of 1st + 2nd F.A.s are to be used.	
			Acquainted the A.D.M.S. of the shortage of Horses.	
	2/3/17		Orderly Officer Lieut Biggs R.A.M.C.	
			Carried on with the improvements in camp. - cookhouses, latrines pathways.	[signature]
			Leave granted of 1 O.R. for 10 Days.	
	3/3/17		Orderly Officer Lieut Biggs R.A.M.C.	
		2 pm	The Unit paraded at 2pm. for the Inspection of P.H. Helmets and Box Respirators	[signature]

T2134. Wt. W708—776. 500000. 4/15. Sir J. C. & S.

Instructions regarding War Diaries and Intelligence Summaries are contained in F. S. Regs., Part II. and the Staff Manual respectively. Title pages will be prepared in manuscript.

WAR DIARY
or
INTELLIGENCE SUMMARY.
(*Erase heading not required.*)

Army Form C. 2118.

Place	Date	Hour	Summary of Events and Information	Remarks and references to Appendices
Clairfaye	3/3/17		(Continued). Officers appointed to Sections as below.	
			A. Section. Lt Col. R. E. Drake-Brockman RAMC	
			Capt A.S.K. Anderson M.C. RAMC	
			Capt D.R. Baillie RAMC	
			B. Section. Capt A.W. Baker RAMC	
			Capt S.J. Watkin RAMC	
			Lieut C.C. Kerby RAMC	
			C. Section. Capt S. Jackson RAMC.	
			Capt D. Hamilton RAMC	
			Capt K. Macleod RAMC.	
			appointed Gas N.C.O's to Sections for instructional purposes.	
	4/3/17		Orderly Officer Lieut Kerby RAMC	
			The Tent Division of the 51st Field Amb^ce 17th Division relieved the Tent Division of the 56th Field Ambulance 18th Division. Relief completed by noon.	
			The Ford Car detailed to be at the disposal of O/c 21st Sanitary Section	

Instructions regarding War Diaries and Intelligence Summaries are contained in F. S. Regs., Part II. and the Staff Manual respectively. Title pages will be prepared in manuscript.

WAR DIARY
or
INTELLIGENCE SUMMARY.
(Erase heading not required.)

Army Form C. 2118.

Place	Date	Hour	Summary of Events and Information	Remarks and references to Appendices
Clairfaye	5/2/17		Orderly Officer Capt Baillie RAMC.	
			Thaw precautions adopted. Great improvements in camp in sanitary conditions and pathways.	[illegible]
	6/2/17		Orderly Officer Capt. Jackson RAMC.	
			Capt Anderson M.C. RAMC temporarily detached for duty at the Office of the A.D.M.S.	
			Lieut Kerby RAMC temporarily detached to Hawke Battalion vice Surgeon Padwick RN sick.	[illegible]
			Supply Wagons to report daily to Refilling Points by 8.30 am.	
	7/2/17		Orderly Officer. Captain Walker RAMC.	
			The Wards thoroughly cleansed and bedding and clothing disinfected.	[illegible]
	8/2/17		Orderly Officer Lieut. Lewis RAMC.	
			Thaw precautions removed. Carried on general improvements in camp. New sanitary appliances erected, double rows. Duck Boards laid down. - Wards re-numbered	[illegible]

T2134. Wt. W708—776. 500000. 4/15. Sir J. C. & S.

Army Form C. 2118.

WAR DIARY
or
INTELLIGENCE SUMMARY.
(*Erase heading not required.*)

Instructions regarding War Diaries and Intelligence Summaries are contained in F. S. Regs., Part II. and the Staff Manual respectively. Title pages will be prepared in manuscript.

Place	Date	Hour	Summary of Events and Information	Remarks and references to Appendices
Clairfaye	9/3/17		Orderly Officer Capt Jackson RAMC.	
			Capt Blockley RAMC joins from the 51st Field Amb^ce	
			Improvements in the Sanitary Services in camp.	
	10/3/17		Orderly Officer Capt Baillie RAMC	[illegible]
			The Unit paraded at 2pm. for the inspection of P.H. helmets and Box respirators	
			ADMS instructions 2 Large Cars sent to report O/C to 26 M.A.C. ALBERT (Rue de BAPAUME) at 9 a.m. to be at the disposal of O/C M.A.C. These cars were not needed and returned by 4 pm.	[illegible]
	11/3/17		Orderly Officer Capt Walker RAMC.	
			Capt Blockley RAMC proceeded on leave.	
			On ADMS instructions 3 N.C.O.'s detailed to proceed to HEDAUVILLE to undergo a course of Gas Instruction – Course lasting 3 days. L/Cpl Green being specially recommended for Gas Instructor, the other 2 N.C.O's also passed.	[illegible]

T2134. Wt. W708—776. 500000. 4/15. Sir J. C. & S.

Instructions regarding War Diaries and Intelligence Summaries are contained in F. S. Regs., Part II. and the Staff Manual respectively. Title pages will be prepared in manuscript.

WAR DIARY
or
~~INTELLIGENCE SUMMARY.~~
(*Erase heading not required.*)

Army Form C. 2118.

Place	Date	Hour	Summary of Events and Information	Remarks and references to Appendices
Clairfaye	12/3/17		Orderly Officer Captain Levis RAMC	
			Capt Gibson joins from 1st Field Ambulance	
			Cookhouse finished and in use.	[illegible]
	13/3/17		Orderly Officer Capt Gibson RAMC.	
			Capt Walker & Capt Levis R.A.M.C. visit the Tent Div. of the 57th Field Ambulance Offs at 3pm. to join up with their unit preparatory to moving into new area.	
			O/c Laundry writes that he is unable to fumigate clothes & blankets from Corps Rest Station as Foden disinfector is required by Division	[illegible]
	14/3/17		Orderly Officer Capt. Baillie RAMC	
			Capt Anderson M.C. RAMC returns from temporary duty at the Office of ADMS.	
			Water drawn daily from ACHEUX Sucrerie 750 galls.	
			V Corps Q. wire request that water be drawn from the Standpipe on ACHEUX - BERTRANCOURT road as water supply at ACHEUX is to be curtailed.	[illegible]

T2134. Wt. W708—776. 500000. 4/15. Sir J. C. & S.

Instructions regarding War Diaries and Intelligence Summaries are contained in F. S. Regs., Part II. and the Staff Manual respectively. Title pages will be prepared in manuscript.

WAR DIARY
or
INTELLIGENCE SUMMARY.
(Erase heading not required.)

Army Form C. 2118.

Place	Date	Hour	Summary of Events and Information	Remarks and references to Appendices
Clairfaye	15/3/17		Orderly Officer Capt Anderson M.C. R.A.M.C. Unit paraded at 2 pm. preparatory to inspection by D.D.M.S. II Corps. Dress - Marching order less pack. Awards. The undermentioned men of this unit awarded the Military Medal for conduct during recent operations. S/4012 Pte J.W. Hall S/4153 Pte J Hampson S/3960 Do E Parkinson Authority D.R.O 1792 dated 13/3/17	
	16/3/17		Orderly Officer Capt Jackson R.A.M.C. Improvements carried on, in and around camp. Inspection by D.D.M.S II Corps at 3.45 pm Unit paraded at 3.15 pm in marching order less pack in "Column by the right". Officers mounted. A.D.M.S. 63rd (R.N.) Division accompanied D.D.M.S on inspection. After the inspection the unit formed "Hollow Square" and was addressed by D.D.M.S who expressed his appreciation	

T2134. Wt. W708—776. 500000. 4/15. Sir J. C. & S.

Instructions regarding War Diaries and Intelligence Summaries are contained in F. S. Regs., Part II. and the Staff Manual respectively. Title pages will be prepared in manuscript.

WAR DIARY
or
~~INTELLIGENCE SUMMARY.~~
(Erase heading not required.)

Army Form C. 2118.

Place	Date	Hour	Summary of Events and Information	Remarks and references to Appendices
Clairfaye	16/3/17		(Continued) of the manner in which all ranks had carried out their work both in the line and at the Corps Rest Station and also of the manner in which all ranks had turned out on parade.	
	17/3/17		Orderly Officer Captain Baillie R.A.M.C.	
			Inspection at 2 p.m. of unit of P.H. Helmets and Box Respirators	
			Squared up things in camp generally	
	18/3/17		Orderly Officer Capt. Gibson R.A.M.C.	
			Arrival of a section of 54 Field Amb^ce^ 18th Division to take over the patients of the 18th Division who were sent to AVELUY CHATEAU	
			All patients unfit for discharge to duty evacuated to Casualty Clearing Station VARENNES.	
			Preparation made to hand over Stores Surplus to Mob. Establishment to 54th Field Ambulance.	

Instructions regarding War Diaries and Intelligence Summaries are contained in F. S. Regs., Part II. and the Staff Manual respectively. Title pages will be prepared in manuscript.

WAR DIARY
or
INTELLIGENCE SUMMARY.
(Erase heading not required.)

Army Form C. 2118.

Place	Date	Hour	Summary of Events and Information	Remarks and references to Appendices
CLAIRFAYE	19/3/17		Orderly Officer Captain Jackson R.A.M.C.	
			Captain Anderson M.C. R.A.M.C. left on 18th for duty in the Office of A.D.M.S. 63rd (R.N.) Division.	
			A Section detailed to pack wagons, the remaining Sections detailed to strike Tents and clean up camp.	
			All men discharged to duty cleared and stores handed over to 54th Field Ambulance 18th Division by 5 p.m.	[illegible] Lt Col.
	20/3/17		Orderly Officer Capt Baillie RAMC	
			The unit to parade for moving off at 12 noon under the command of Capt Gibson RAMC and to fall in behind the 190th Inf. Bde. Headquarters and proceed behind them to BEAUVAL. Route via LEALVILLERS – ARQUEVES – RAINCHEVAL – BEAUQUESNE. Move completed 5.30 pm.	
BEAUVAL	21/3/17		Orderly Officer Capt Gibson RAMC.	
		9 am	Breakfast.	
		10.50 a	Parade. The march continued to BONNERS	

Instructions regarding War Diaries and Intelligence Summaries are contained in F. S. Regs., Part II. and the Staff Manual respectively. Title pages will be prepared in manuscript.

WAR DIARY
or
INTELLIGENCE SUMMARY.
(Erase heading not required.)

Army Form C. 2118.

Place	Date	Hour	Summary of Events and Information	Remarks and references to Appendices
BEAUVAL	21/3/17		(Continued) Route via DOULLENS – BOUQUEMAISON – MON LE BLOND to BONNIERS	
BONNIERS	22/3/17		Orderly Officer Lieut Kerby RAMC	D.M.Baker Capt & Qrmr for O.C.
		9am	Breakfast	
		11.10am	Parade. The march continued to BLANGERMONT. Starting time altered by 190th Inf Bde from 9.40 am to 11.45 am. Route via FREVENT – NUNCQ – HAUTE COTE – FLERS. As water reported scarce in the new area, the water for Horses carried in water carts. Capt Hamilton RAMC detailed to look after the sick on line of march. Cases evacuated to 2/1 Northumbrian CCS and 3 Canadian Hospital.	
BLANGERMONT	23/3/17		Orderly Officer Capt Hamilton RAMC. The unit halted for the day. Necessary fatigues & sanitation carried out. Kit and Horse Transport vehicles cleaned up for march	D.M.Baker Capt & Qrmr for O.C.

T2134. Wt. W708–776. 500000. 4/15. Sir J. C. & S.

Instructions regarding War Diaries and Intelligence Summaries are contained in F. S. Regs., Part II. and the Staff Manual respectively. Title pages will be prepared in manuscript.

WAR DIARY
or
~~INTELLIGENCE~~ SUMMARY.
(Erase heading not required.)

Army Form C. 2118.

Place	Date	Hour	Summary of Events and Information	Remarks and references to Appendices
BLANGERMONT	24/3/17		Orderly Officer Capt Jackson RAMC.	
		7am	Breakfast	
		8am	Parade. The march was continued to HESTRUS via LINZEUX OEUF - BEAUVOIS - PIERREMONT - WAVRANS - HESTRUS.	
			Rear party attended to sanitation & cleanliness of billets on leaving BLANGERMONT.	
			Move completed 1.30 pm.	
HESTRUS	25/3/17		Orderly Officer Capt Baillie RAMC.	
		7am	Breakfast	
		8.15am	Parade - The march continued to LIVOSSART Route via EPS - BOYAVAL - HEUCHIN - FONTAINE LES BOULANS - PALFART.	
			Captain Macleod returned to unit from detached duty as Medical Officer of Drake Battalion.	
			Captain Macleod temp detached to 1st H.A.C. Battalion until further notice.	

(signature) Capt RAMC for O.C.

Instructions regarding War Diaries and Intelligence Summaries are contained in F. S. Regs., Part II. and the Staff Manual respectively. Title pages will be prepared in manuscript.

WAR DIARY
or
INTELLIGENCE SUMMARY.
(Erase heading not required.)

Army Form C. 2118.

Place	Date	Hour	Summary of Events and Information	Remarks and references to Appendices
	25/3/17		Move completed by 1.40 pm.	D.H. Baker Capt RAMC for O.C.
LIVOSSART	26/3/17		Capt Hamilton RAMC Orderly Officer	
		8am	Breakfast	
		8.50am	Parade. The unit continued the march to LA. CORNET BOORDOIS	
			Route via PALFART - WESTREHEM - ST HILAIRE - LILLERS - LA	
			CORNET BOORDOIS. Distance about 13½ miles	
			Rear Party clean up Billets as before.	
			Railhead - BETHUNE	
			Move completed by 2 p.m.	
			Destination should have been LA. MIQUELLERIE but altered by	
			190th Inf Bde to LA. CORNET BOORDOIS.	
			H.Qrs of unit situated at LA FLANDRIE	D.H. Baker Capt RAMC for O.C.
LA FLANDRIE	27/3/17		Orderly Officer Capt Gibson RAMC.	
		7am	Reveillé	
		8am	Breakfast.	
		9am	Parade. All kit to be cleaned up. All vehicles to be cleaned up	

Instructions regarding War Diaries and Intelligence Summaries are contained in F. S. Regs., Part II. and the Staff Manual respectively. Title pages will be prepared in manuscript.

WAR DIARY
or
~~INTELLIGENCE SUMMARY.~~
(Erase heading not required.)

Army Form C. 2118.

Place	Date	Hour	Summary of Events and Information	Remarks and references to Appendices
LA FLANDRIE	27/3/17		Lieut Kerby RAMC, until further notice, temporarily attached as Medical Officer to Anti Aircraft Battery LA PIERRIÈRE.	
			All cases sick evacuated to No 57 CCS ST. VENANT.	
			Infectious Cases to No 7 General Hosp MALASSISE.	M Baker Capt RAMC for OC.
"	28/3/17		Capt Jackson RAMC Orderly Officer.	
		7.30am	Parade for Physical Training.	
		8am	Breakfast.	
		9am	Commanding Officer's Parade.	
		11am	Sectional Officers will give a lecture daily in First Aid to their sections.	
		2pm	The afternoon recreation – Football matches.	M Baker Capt RAMC for OC.
"	29/3/17		Orderly Officer Capt Baillie RAMC.	
		7.30am	Physical Training.	
		11am	Visit of D.D.M.S. of XIII Corps.	
		2pm	Parade for inspection of gas gear.	
			Capt Macleod RAMC posted to 1st H.A.C. & struck off strength.	M Baker Capt RAMC for OC.

Army Form C. 2118.

Instructions regarding War Diaries and Intelligence Summaries are contained in F. S. Regs., Part II. and the Staff Manual respectively. Title pages will be prepared in manuscript.

WAR DIARY
or
INTELLIGENCE SUMMARY.
(Erase heading not required.)

Place	Date	Hour	Summary of Events and Information	Remarks and references to Appendices
LA FLANDRIE	30/3/17		Orderly Officer Capt Baker RAMC.	
			All ranks inspected for Scabies by Sectional Officers.	
			Lt Col R.E. Drake-Brockman RAMC & Capt Anderson M.C. RAMC.	
			left at 2.30pm for leave to England.	
			Usual daily routine of training carried out.	RHBaker Capt RAMC for O.C.
"	31/3/17		Orderly Officer Captain Jackson RAMC.	
			Usual daily routine of training carried out.	
			T. Capt Watkin RAMC posted to 4 Bedfordshire Batt and	
			struck off the strength of this unit.	RHBaker Capt RAMC for O.C.

T2134. Wt. W708—776. 500000. 4/15. Sir J. C. & S.

"Confidential"

Vol 17

140/2086

War Diary

of

3rd Field Ambce 63rd (RN) Division

from

April 1st 1917

to

April 30th 1917.

To/

The A. G's Office
3rd Echelon.

M Baker Capt RAMC
for/c 3rd F Ambce
63rd (RN) Division

S

April '17

B.E.F.

SUMMARY OF MEDICAL WAR DIARIES FOR 3rd R.N. F.A., 63rd Div. 13th Corps.

1st Army.

3rd Army from 11/4/17.

WESTERN FRONT. April-May. '17.

R.E.

O.C. Lt. Col./Drake-Brockman.

SUMMARISED UNDER THE FOLLOWING HEADINGS.

Phase "B" Battle of Arras-April- May. 1917.

1st Period Attack on Vimy Ridge April.

2nd Period Capture of Siegfried Line May.

3rd R.N. F.A., 63rd Divn. 13th Corps. WESTERN FRONT.

O.C. Lt. Col. Drake-Brockman. April. '17.

1st Army.

3rd Army from 11/4/17.

Phase "B" Battle of Arras- April- May. '17.

1st Period Attack on Vimy Ridge April.

1917.	Headquarters.	at La Flandrie 0.36.c.4.7. (36A)
April. 8th.	Moves:	To Bruay J.16.c.8.2.
11th.	Transfer.	3rd Army.

3rd R.N. F.A., 63rd Divn. 13th Corps. WESTERN FRONT.
O.C. Lt. Col. Drake-Brockman. April. '17.
3rd Army.

Phase "B" Battle of Arras- April- May. 1917.
1st Period Attack on Vimy Ridge April.

1917.
April. 11th. Transfer. 3rd Army.

12th. Moves: To Bajus.

14th. " To St Catherine Arras.

15th. Moves Detachment: Assistance. 3 and 110 Brs. attached from No. 2 Field Ambulance.

16th. Medical Arrangements:-

R.A.Ps.	H.3.c.5.0.	Drake and Bn. H.Q.
	H.3.d.4.8.	Nelson.
	H.1.c.6.6.7.	Hawke.
	G.6.c.9.6.	Hood.
	H.1.d.4.8.	189 M.G.C.
	C.6.c.5.2.	S.M. Coy. Map 51 b.

17th. A.D.S. opened at Bailleul.
Adv. Coll.P." " "

19th. O.C. 3rd R.N. Field Ambulance in charge of collection and evacuation from forward area to M.D.S. St Catherine. R.A.Ps. re-inforced.

20th. Brs. of 1st and 3rd Field Ambulance sent to forward area and worked from R.A.Ps to Adv. Coll.Post Bailleul and R. and L. Br. Relay Post to Advanced Dressing Station.

22nd. Transport:-

6 M.A.C. Cars)
8 Cars 31st Divn.) attached to clear from M.D.S.
? Motor Lorries.)

3rd R.N. F.A., 63rd Divn. 13th Corps. WESTERN FRONT.
O.C. Lt. Col. Drake-Brockman. April. '17.
3rd Army.

Phase "B" cont.

1st Period cont.

1917.		
April.	22nd. cont.	Divisional cars used solely between A.D.S. and M.D.S.
	23rd.	Operations. "Z" day attack commenced 4.30 a.m.
		Casualties: Evacuation: 1st Walking wounded arrived 7.30 a.m. Congestion until 3 p.m. Evacuation from Main Dressing Station proceeded regularly and Main Dressing Station cleared at 5 p.m.
		Medical Arrangements: R.A.Ps opened at Gavrelle by Btln.
	24th.	2 T.D.Ss 3rd Field Ambulance 1 " 2nd " " 1 " 3rd " " on duty at M.D.S.
	26th.	Transport. Cars of 31st Divn. returned to Division.
		Medical Arrangements: Minimun of Brs. retained at Forward Posts. Remainder withdrawn for a rest at Main Dressing Station.
	27th.	Casualties. Few wounded received who had lain out 4 days.
	28th.	Medical Arrangements: Personnel moved to forward Post ready for attack on 29th.
	29th.	Operations. " Attack".

Instructions regarding War Diaries and Intelligence Summaries are contained in F. S. Regs., Part II. and the Staff Manual respectively. Title pages will be prepared in manuscript.

WAR DIARY
or
~~INTELLIGENCE SUMMARY.~~
(Erase heading not required.)

Army Form C. 2118.

Place	Date	Hour	Summary of Events and Information	Remarks and references to Appendices
LA FLANDRIE	1/4/17		Orderly Officer Capt Hamilton RAMC.	
O. 36 c. 4.7		7.30 to 8am	Physical Training.	
Map 36A		9.30am	Small Box Respirators + Gas Helmet Drill. Squad + Stretcher Drill.	
Edition 6		11am–12 noon	Lecture in 1st Aid	
France.		2–3pm } 3–4pm }	Football Match	
			In accordance with D.R.O. 1918 a Unit Temp. dump arranged with ONE O.R in charge. – Situation O. 36 c. 4.9. Map 36A.	MBaker Capt RAMC for OC.
do.	2/4/17		Orderly Officer Capt Baillie RAMC	
			Daily Routine Training continued.	
			Sections "A + B" paraded 9am. in marching order for Route March.	
			Deficiencies in Horses + Chargers 3 Heavy Draught Horses	MBaker Capt RAMC for OC.
do	3/4/17		Orderly Officer Captain Gibson RAMC.	
			Daily Routine Training continued.	
		2pm	Lecture on "Treatment of Gas Poisoning" given by Capt Hamilton RAMC	

Instructions regarding War Diaries and Intelligence Summaries are contained in F. S. Regs., Part II. and the Staff Manual respectively. Title pages will be prepared in manuscript.

WAR DIARY
or
~~INTELLIGENCE~~ SUMMARY.
(Erase heading not required.)

Army Form C. 2118.

Place	Date	Hour	Summary of Events and Information	Remarks and references to Appendices
LA FLANDRIE			to all Medical Officers of 190th Inf Bde.	
			All "G.S" waggons now loaded with Sectional Mobilization Equipment.	
		11am	Reinforcements arrived during past month parade with gear to have Small Box Respirators tested in the gas chamber.	M Baker Capt for O.C. Ramc
do	4/10/17		Orderly Officer Capt Jackson RAMC.	
			All kit & gear surplus to Mobilization Table to be dumped in Unit dump between 3pm & 5pm.	
			Sheepskin coats withdrawn & returned to Ordnance.	
			All cases not likely to be fit to march within 4 days to be evacuated.	
			Acting on ADMS instructions all units of 190th Inf Bde intimated to send to Field Ambulance all men not fit to march within 4 days.	M Baker Capt for O.C. Ramc
do.	5/10/17		Orderly Officer: Captain Hamilton R.A.M.C.	
			Daily Routine training continued.	

Instructions regarding War Diaries and Intelligence Summaries are contained in F. S. Regs., Part II. and the Staff Manual respectively. Title pages will be prepared in manuscript.

WAR DIARY
or
~~INTELLIGENCE SUMMARY.~~
(Erase heading not required.)

Army Form C. 2118.

Place	Date	Hour	Summary of Events and Information	Remarks and references to Appendices
LA FLANDRIE	5/4/17		(Continued) The unit paraded 9am for Route March in the formation laid down by D.M.S. as below A Tent Sub Division A Bearer Sub Division B Bearer Sub Division C Bearer Sub Division.	
	6/4/17		Orderly Officer Capt Baillie RAMC. The unit divided into Groups as laid down in DMS Instructions. Bearer Division and one Tent Sub Division to march and billet with the Brigade and Two Tent Sub Divisions to march and billet with the Divisional Train. Lieut Kerby RAMC relieved from attending Anti Aircraft Battery at LA. PERRIERE	W Baker Capt RAMC for O.C.
	7/4/17		Orderly Officer: Captain Gibson RAMC. Daily Routine training continued. Preparations made for moving.	W Baker Capt RAMC for O.C.

T2134. Wt. W708–776. 500000. 4/15. Sir J. C. & S.

Instructions regarding War Diaries and Intelligence Summaries are contained in F. S. Regs., Part II. and the Staff Manual respectively. Title pages will be prepared in manuscript.

WAR DIARY
or
~~INTELLIGENCE SUMMARY.~~
(Erase heading not required.)

Army Form C. 2118.

Place	Date	Hour	Summary of Events and Information	Remarks and references to Appendices
LA FLANDRIE	8/4/17		Orderly Officer Capt Jackson RAMC	
		7.30am	Breakfast	
			Parades Bearer Division ~~10~~.15 am Tent Divisions 9 am.	
			The unit will move from its present area to BRUAY in the following formation.	
			Bearer Division (a) A Tent Sub Division (c) { 2 Horse Ambces	
			(b) { A Bearer Sub Division — 2 G.S. Wagons	
			B do — 1 Limber	
			C do. — 1 Water Cart.	
			1 Motor Ambce & 1 Motor Cycle	
			Capt Gibson RAMC will be in charge of party and Capts Baillie RAMC & Hamilton RAMC will accompany party.	
			Tent Division (a) { B. Tent Sub Division	
			C Tent Sub Division.	
			(b) Remainder of Transport Horse with Lt Wilson RM in charge	
			(c) Remainder of Motor Ambces	D.M.Baker Capt RAMC for O.C.

T2134. Wt. W708—776. 500000. 4/15. Sir J. C. & S.

Instructions regarding War Diaries and Intelligence Summaries are contained in F. S. Regs., Part II. and the Staff Manual respectively. Title pages will be prepared in manuscript.

WAR DIARY
or
~~INTELLIGENCE~~ SUMMARY.
(Erase heading not required.)

Army Form C. 2118.

Place	Date	Hour	Summary of Events and Information	Remarks and references to Appendices
			(Continued)	
LA FLANDRIE	8/4/17		Captain Jackson RAMC took charge of Tent Divisions who joined up with No 4 Coy Div Train at BUSNES CHURCH at 10 a.m. & marched with them. The Corps Commander inspected unit whilst on the march.	
			Capt Baillie RAMC & party formed a Rear Party to see to the Cleanliness of camp.	
			Route via BUSNES - L'ECLEME - BUSNETTES - BAS RIEUX - HAUTRIEUX - LOZINGHEM - MARLES les MINES. - BRUAY.	
BRUAY. J. 16 c. 8.2			The unit arrived in BILLETS at 4 pm.	A.W. Baker Capt RAMC for OC
	9/4/17		Orderly Officer Lieut Kerby RAMC.	
		9.30 am	Breakfast.	
		10 am	Foot & Boot Inspection	
		2 pm	Small Box Respirator & Gas Helmet Drill.	
			The Vehicles of Transport Section were cleaned up.	
		1.15 pm	Received Warning Order from 190th Inf Bde to stand bye ready to move at 3 hours notice.	

Instructions regarding War Diaries and Intelligence Summaries are contained in F. S. Regs., Part II. and the Staff Manual respectively. Title pages will be prepared in manuscript.

WAR DIARY
or
~~INTELLIGENCE~~ SUMMARY.
(Erase heading not required.)

Army Form C. 2118.

Place	Date	Hour	Summary of Events and Information	Remarks and references to Appendices
BRUAY.	9/4/17		Lieut Col. R.C. Drake-Brockman RAMC returned from English Leave.	DR Baker Capt RAMC for OC
J 16 c. 8.2	10/4/17		Orderly Officer Capt Hamilton R.A.M.C.	
			The unit continued to stand by, to move at 3 hours notice	
			Routine as per Brigade Training carried out.	
			Issue 3rd Field Amb^ce Operation Order No 1. in view of Active Operations.	
			Capt Anderson M.C. R.A.M.C assisted by Capt Gibson RAMC & Lieut Kerby RAMC will be command of Bearer Division	
			Capt Baker RAMC will be in charge of "A" Tent Sub division	
			Capt Hamilton R.A.M.C do "B" do.	
			Capt Jackson R.A.M.C do "C" do.	
			The Bearer Division with "A" Tent Sub-Division will march and billet with 190th Inf Bde.	
			Lieut Wilson R.M. in command of Transport will march & billet with Divisional Train.	
			Sunbeam Cars C.3, C4, C5 will be detailed for duty with the Reserve Motor Amb^ce Convoy on receipt of instructions from A.D.M.S.	DR Baker Capt RAMC for OC

T2134. Wt. W708–776. 500000. 4/15. Sir J. C. & S.

Instructions regarding War Diaries and Intelligence Summaries are contained in F. S. Regs., Part II. and the Staff Manual respectively. Title pages will be prepared in manuscript.

WAR DIARY
or
~~INTELLIGENCE SUMMARY.~~

(Erase heading not required.)

Army Form C. 2118.

Place	Date	Hour	Summary of Events and Information	Remarks and references to Appendices
BRUAY	11/4/17		Orderly Officer Capt Baillie RAMC.	
		7.15am	Orders received from Bde to be ready to move off at 9am.	
		9am	Marching orders received from Bde	
		9.45am	Tent Sub-Division of unit paraded to move off & accompanied Div Train & march under orders of O/c Div. Train.	
			Route – Direct Road via HOUDAIN to LA COMPTE	
		10.45	Bearer Division with "A" Tent Sub-Division paraded & moved off marching with Bde	
			Route – Direct Road via HOUDAIN to BAJUS.	
			Arrived in billets	O M Baker Capt RAMC for OC
BAJUS	12/4/17		Orderly Officer. Capt Gibson RAMC.	
			Only necessary fatigues carried on	
		11am	Conference of Medical Officers of 190th Inf. Bde. at HdQrs of unit at BAJUS.	O M Baker Capt RAMC for OC
	13/4/17		Orderly Officer Lieut Kerby RAMC.	
			Unit under orders to move at 2 hours notice.	

Instructions regarding War Diaries and Intelligence Summaries are contained in F. S. Regs., Part II. and the Staff Manual respectively. Title pages will be prepared in manuscript.

WAR DIARY
or
~~INTELLIGENCE SUMMARY.~~
(Erase heading not required.)

Army Form C. 2118.

Place	Date	Hour	Summary of Events and Information	Remarks and references to Appendices
BAJUS	13/4/17		Dump formed to dump all blankets surplus to 1 per man.	
			Location of Dump BAJUS O.22.a 1.3 Map 36 B.	
	14/4/17		Orderly Officer Capt Baker RAMC.	DMBaker Capt RAMC for OC
		2.30am	Received Secret Orders Bde order to 74 and Bde 1984 of 13/4/17 re move to front line.	
		3 am	Issued written instructions to Capt Jackson RAMC at LA COMPTE and to Sergt Major Ashton re transport.	
		7am	Detailed two guides to direct 2 buses from 7th Royal Fusiliers and 3 buses from 1/HAC and 1 from 190th Bde to Stagg's point at BAJUS.	
			Locations: HAC -- 9.6.d.9.8. 51B. & 7 R.F. -- B 25 d 9.2 51B	
		7.8am	Transport under Sergt Major Ashton moved off from starting point at Road Junction (1 mile S.W of MAGNICOURT EN COMPTE.	
		7.20am	Lieut Wilson RAMC and transport moved off from same starting point.	
		9am	Motor Ambulance Convoy under charge of N/c moved off to ARRAS	

T2134. Wt. W708—776. 500000. 4/15. Sir J. C. & S.

Instructions regarding War Diaries and Intelligence Summaries are contained in F. S. Regs., Part II. and the Staff Manual respectively. Title pages will be prepared in manuscript.

WAR DIARY
or
~~INTELLIGENCE~~ SUMMARY.
(Erase heading not required.)

Army Form C. 2118.

Place	Date	Hour	Summary of Events and Information	Remarks and references to Appendices
BAJUS	14/4/17	11.15am	The personnel under command of Capt Gibson RAMC moved off in busses to ARRAS	
			Route. via TINQUES - MAIN ST POL ARRAS Road.	
			De-bussing point at G 21 b 5.7 ARRAS OCTROI.	
			The Transport lines situated at G. 9 d	
		4.35pm	The Unit had completed its move to ARRAS. Headquarters of unit situated at ST. CATHERINE G.15.a.2.4 (51 B).	
			T. Capt GIBSON RAMC evacuated sick to No 7 Canadian CCS AUBIGNY.	
			Received Signal from ADMS to use A.D.S at St Catherine as a Main Dressing Station.	
		9 pm	The 34th Division Field Ambulance relieved and the Collecting post at H.1.c 3.8. and Main Dressing Station G 15 a 2.4 taken over.	[signature] Capt RAMC for OC
ST. CATHERINE ARRAS.	15/4/17		Orderly Officer. Capt Jackson RAMC.	
			Surgeon Morgan RN temp attached for duty from 1st (RN) Fd Amb[ce]	

Instructions regarding War Diaries and Intelligence Summaries are contained in F. S. Regs., Part II. and the Staff Manual respectively. Title pages will be prepared in manuscript.

WAR DIARY
or
~~INTELLIGENCE SUMMARY.~~
(Erase heading not required.)

Army Form C. 2118.

Place	Date	Hour	Summary of Events and Information	Remarks and references to Appendices
St Catherine Arras	15/4/17		3 Officers + 110 OR Bearers temp. attached for duty from 2nd (RN) Fd Ambce 6. M.A.C. Ambce Cars and 2 2nd (RN) Field Ambce Cars. temp. attached for duty.	MBaker Capt RNVR for OC
	16/4/17		Orderly Officer Capt Hamilton R.A.M.C.	
			Liaison Guides (TWELVE) detailed for the Battalions of 190th Bde and Bde Headquarters + 189th Bde and Bde Hdqrs. R.A.P's of Drake + Bn Hdqrs H 3 c 5.0, Nelson H. 3 d 4.8, Hawke H.1.c.6.6, Hood G.6 c 9.6. 189 M.G.C. H 1 d 4.8 and 189 S.M. Coy C.6.c.5.2. Map 51 B	
St Catherine			Sick for CRS who sent to No 6. Field Ambce at ECOIVRES.	MBaker Capt RNVR for OC
ARRAS.	17/4/17		Orderly Officer. Lieut Kerby RAMC.	
			An Advanced Dressing Station opened at BAILLEUL.	
			Capt Iles RAMC took over command of BLANCHE MAISON Collecting Post.	
			Capt Anderson MC RAMC returned from English leave.	
			Advanced Collecting Post opened at BAILLEUL	MBaker Capt RNVR for OC

T2134. Wt. W708—776. 500000. 4/15. Sir J. C. & S.

WAR DIARY

Place	Date	Hour	Summary of Events and Information.	
ST. CATHERINE	18/4/17		Orderly Officer - Surgeon Starforth RN.	
			Captain Jackson RAMC in charge of Advanced Collecting	
			Post. Capt Anderson RAMC took over charge of Bearers.	
			Surgeon Starforth RN proceeded to Advanced Collect. Post.	DMBaker Capt RAMC
ST. CATHERINE.	19/4/17		Orderly Officer - Capt Hamilton RAMC.	
			Capt Emmison RAMC taken on strength of the unit.	
			O/c 3rd Field Ambulance in charge of all Arrangements for the	
			collecting & evacuation of wounded from the forward area to Main	
			Dressing Station St Catherine	
			Reinforced each R.A.P. by 6 & M.G. Coy by two Stretcher Bearers.	DMBaker Capt RAMC
ST. CATHERINE	20/4/17		Orderly Officer Capt Baillie RAMC.	
			Capt Emmison RAMC posted as Med. Officer to 1/H.A.C. vice Capt	
			Macleod RAMC wounded. Bearers of 1st and 3rd Field Ambces	
			sent to forward area working from R.A.P.s to Advanced Collecting	
			Post at BAILLEUL and Right & Left Bearer Relay Posts to A.D.S.	DMBaker Capt RAMC for O.C.

WAR DIARY

Place	Date	Hour	Summary of Events	Remarks
ST. CATHERINE	21/4/17		Orderly Officer Capt. Clarke RAMC. Lieut Kirby RAMC returned from C.C.S. to duty. Runners detailed to proceed to Battalions of 190th Bde and to Stations of 189th + 190th Bde	M Baker Capt RAMC for O.C.
	22/4/17		Orderly Officer Capt Hamilton RAMC. 6. M.A.C. Cars and 8 cars of 31st Division and Motor Lorries arrive to clear from M.D.S. Divisional Cars used solely for clearing from A.D.S. to M.D.S.	M Baker Capt RAMC for O.C.
	23/4/17		'Z' Day. Action commenced 4.30 am. Walking wounded cases arrived from 7.30am and congested until 3pm. Clearing from M.D.S proceeded regularly and Dressing Station clear by 5pm. R.A.P.'s formed by Bn at GAVRELLE and cases cleared quickly.	M Baker Capt RAMC for O.C.
	24/4/17		Clearing still carried on. 2 Tent Sub Divisions of No 3 Field Amb^ce and 1st Tent Sub Division from each of No 1 + No 2 Fd Amb^ce	

WAR DIARY

Place	Date	Hour	Summary of Events	Remarks
ST. CATHERINE	24th/7		On duty at M.D.S.	R.M.Baker Capt RAMC for O.C.
	25th/7		Capt Wrigley RAMC reported for duty and taken on strength of unit. The Bearer Division of 2nd Field Ambulance relieved from forward area to rest at the M.D.S.	R.M.Baker Capt RAMC for O.C.
	26th/7		Cars of the 31st Division released to join their Division. Minimum of Bearers retained at the Bearer Posts & Collecting Posts. - the remainder sent down to M.D.S. for a rest.	
	~~27/7~~ 27th/7		Capts Jackson, Iles, relieved by Captains Hamilton & Baillie. Only few cases arriving. Wounded who had been lying out 4 days brought in. Everything quiet.	R.M.Baker Capt RAMC for O.C.
	28th/7	4.a.m	Bearers leave by motor lorry to assemble at their posts for second attack. Bearer Division of 31st Division arrive to take on reliefs. Continual flow of wounded arriving - no congestion.	R.M.Baker Capt RAMC for O.C.
	29th/7		Enemy attacked again and Bearers retained in forward area. No fresh posts created. Evacuation carried out systematically	R.M.Baker Capt RAMC for O.C.

WAR DIARY

Place	Date	Hour	Summary of Events	
ST. CATHERINE	29/7/17		Tent Divisions of No. 95th Field Amb^ce arrive.	
			Books closed at 9 a.m. and M.D.S. taken over.	M Baker Capt RAMC for O.C.
	30/7/17		Relief by 95th Field Ambulance completed.	
			Lt Col. R.E. Drake Brockman RAMC proceeded to England on leave	
			All Bearers of No 3 Field Amb^ce return to M.D.S.	
			Preparations made to march off on 1st prox.	M Baker Capt RAMC for O.C.

3rd
FIELD AMBULANCE
ROYAL NAVAL DIV.
No. W.D. 5
Date. 1. 6. 17

3/13

"Confidential"

Headquarters
3rd Field Ambulance
63rd (R.N.) Division

War Diary
of
3rd (R.N.) Field Ambulance.
from
May 1st 1915
to
May 31st 1915.

140/2161

To
The A.G's Office.
3rd Echelon.

[signature]
Lt. Col. RAMC
O/c 3rd Field Amb.
63rd (R.N.) Division

B.E.F.

SUMMARY OF MEDICAL WAR DIARIES FOR 3rd R.N. F.A., 63rd Div. 13th Corps.
1st Army.
3rd Army from 11/4/17.

WESTERN FRONT. April-May. '17.

R.E.
O.C. Lt. Col./Drake-Brookman.

SUMMARISED UNDER THE FOLLOWING HEADINGS.

Phase "B" Battle of Arras-April- May. 1917.

1st Period Attack on Vimy Ridge April.

2nd Period Capture of Siegfried Line May.

3rd R.N. F.A.,63rd Div. 13th Corps. WESTERN FRONT.

O.C. Lt. Col. Drake-Brookman. May. '17.

3rd Army.

Phase "B" Battle of Arras April- May. '17.

2nd Period Capture of Siegfried Line May.

1917.

May. 1st. Moves: To Guestreville on relief by 95th Field Ambulance.

2/20th. Operations R.A.M.C. Unit in rest. Routine.

21st. Moves: To Anzin-St- Aubin.

25th. Decoration:-

Pte. H. Andrews R.M.)
" J. Hathway) awarded M.M.
(A.S.C. Attached))

27th. Medical Arrangements:-

A.D.S. H.1.d.4.2. (518) 2 and 28.

Coll. Posts (a) B.28.a.2.8. 2 and 27.

(b) Gun Pits. 1 " 27.

(c) B.29.c. central 0 and 21.

Ambulance cars attached from 1st Field Ambulance

3rd R.N. Field Ambulance took over evacuation from forward Area.

Transport: Evacuation: Disposition of Ambulance Cars.

1. L.S. 1 Ford. at Bailleul 2 large cars at A.D.S.

2. R.S. 1 Ford and 2 large cars at Point du Jour.

30th. Casualties R.A.M.C. 0 and 2 wounded.

3rd R.N. F.A., 63rd Div. 13th Corps. WESTERN FRONT.

O.C. Lt. Col. Drake-Brookman. May. '17.

3rd Army.

Phase "B" Battle of Arras April- May. '17.

2nd Period Capture of Siegfried Line May.

1917.

May. 1st. Moves: To Guestreville on relief by 95th Field Ambulance.

2/20th. Operations R.A.M.C. Unit in rest. Routine.

21st. Moves: To Anzin-St- Aubin.

25th. Decoration:-

Pte. H. Andrews R.M.)
" J. Hathway) awarded M.M.
(A.S.C. Attached))

27th. Medical Arrangements:-

A.D.S. H.1.d.4.2. (518) 2 and 28.

Coll.Posts(a)B.28.a.2.8. 2 and 27.

(b)Gun Pits. 1 " 27.

(c)B.29.c. central 0 and 21.

Ambulance cars attached from 1st Field Ambulance 3rd R.N. Field Ambulance took over evacuation from forward Area.

Transport: Evacuation: Disposition of Ambulance Cars.

1. L.B. 1 Ford at Bailleul 2 large cars at A.D.S.

2. R.S. 1 Ford and 2 large cars at Point du Jour.

30th. Casualties R.A.M.C. 0 and 2 wounded.

WAR DIARY

Place	Date	Hour	Summary of Events & Information	Remarks
St. CATHARINE	1/5/17		Unit had been completely relieved at the Main Dressing Station St. Catharines & in the forward areas.	[illegible] Lt Col
		9am.	The unit paraded at 9am in full marching order to proceed to GUESTREVILLE. Route - Main Arras Road, Linques [?] & Guestreville. Move completed at 3.45pm. Arrival of 38 Other Rank Reinforcements. ADMS wire F3/302 orders their transfer to 2nd Field Ambce. This cancelled by ADMS F3/307. Headqrs of unit situated at V.13.c.3.6.	
	2/5/17		Orderly Officer Capt Baillie RAMC. Unit at rest. Only necessary fatigues and sanitation of camp continued. Lieut Cerby [?] RAMC detailed to proceed as Medical Officer of 10th Royal Dublin Fusiliers vice Capt Evans RAMC sick. 28 "O.R" reinforcements taken on strength. Remainder distributed 2 to 1st Fd Ambce and 8 to 2nd Field Ambce.	[illegible]
	3/5/17		Orderly Officer Capt Wrigley RAMC. 3 "O.R" reinforcements arrived and taken on strength. Bell Tents & Marquees pitched to house sick. — 4 "O.R" sick under treatment.	[illegible]

WAR DIARY

Place	Date	Hour	Summary of Events & Information	Remarks
GUESTREVILLE	3/5/17		(Continued). Kit Inspection	
			T. Capt Howlett RAMC. taken on strength.	[illegible]
	4/5/17		Orderly Officer - Capt Jackson RAMC.	
			Capt Baker RAMC proceeded on leave to England.	[illegible]
			Continued necessary fatigues and sanitation.	
	5/5/17		Orderly Officer Capt Hamilton RAMC.	[illegible]
			Capt Gibson RAMC struck off strength (Evacuated sick to Hospital)	
	6/5/17		Orderly Officer - Capt Howlett RAMC.	[illegible]
			Congratulatory message received from Brig. General of 188th Inf Bde on work done "in the line" by "Officers, N.C.O's & men."	[illegible]
		9.30am	Unit parade in Drill order for Route - March.	
			Capt Baillie RAMC detailed to supervise Sanitary arrangements in camp.	
			Capt Hamilton R.AM.C detailed to attend sick while in this area.	
	7/5/17		Orderly Officer Capt Baillie R.AMC	[illegible]
			Assembly of court for trial by F.G.C.M at 11 am of 1/3346 Sergt R. Murray of this Unit. Lieut Reily struck off strength.	

WAR DIARY

Place	Date	Hour	Summary of Events & Information	Remarks
GOESTREVILLE	8/7/17		Orderly Officer. Capt. Wigley RAMC.	[illegible]
			Carried on Squad Drill. Necessary fatigues & Sanitation.	
	9/7/17		Orderly Officer Capt. Hamilton RAMC.	
			Warning Order received from ADMS to move to CAMBLIGNEUL on 10th inst.	
		10am	Lecture given by Capt Howlett RAMC to all latest reinforcements	[illegible]
		9.30am	Unit paraded for Route March. Dress - Marching Order.	
	10/7/17		Orderly Officer - Capt Howlett R.A.M.C.	
			Capt A.S.K. Anderson M.C. R.A.M.C. returned from English Leave.	
		9am	The Unit paraded in full marching order & moved off to CAMBLIGNEUL. Hqrs of unit situated at W. 14.d. 8.6	[illegible]
			Rear party detailed for cleaning up of camp after unit had move. Move completed by 11.30am.	
	11/7/17		Orderly Officer Capt. Baillie R.A.M.C.	[illegible]
			Capt Howlett RAMC detailed to attend the [illegible] of Div Lewis Gun School at MINGOVAL.	
			Four Lance Corporals made & 1 Corporal to complete establishment.	

WAR DIARY

Place	Date	Hour	Summary of Events & Information	Remarks
CAMBLIGNEUL	12/5/17		Orderly Officer Capt Jackson RAMC.	
			Capt Wrigley RAMC detailed to proceed to 1/H.A.C as Med. Officer vice Capt Emerson RAMC sick (Auth. ADMS 109/104)	
			Capt Hamilton RAMC detailed to proceed to 63rd Div. Train for temp. duty as Med. Officer (Auth. ADMS 109/107)	
		11am	Parade Service and presentation of Military Medals by G.O.C. 63rd (R.N) Division.	[signature]
	13/5/17	7.30am	Daily Routine of Physical Training.	
			Capt Emerson RAMC taken on the strength of the Field Amb^ce from the 1st H.A.C.	
			Capt Baillie RAMC detailed to proceed to 63rd Div. Amm. Column as Med. Officer and struck off the strength of the unit (Auth ADMS 109/107)	[signature]
	14/5/17		Orderly Officer Capt Jackson RAMC	
			Daily Training continued.	
			Court of Enquiry held at 10.30 am on loss of instruments from panniers	[initials]
	15/5/17		Orderly Officer Capt Howlett RAMC.	
			Continued necessary fatigues and Daily Training	[initials]

WAR DIARY.

Place	Date	Hour	Summary of Events & Information.	Remarks
CAMBLIGNEUL	15 5/17		(Continued) Capt Simmons RAMC taken on the strength of the unit.	[signature]
	16 5/17		Orderly Officer Capt Emerson RAMC. Continued Daily Routine of Training. Lt Col R.E. Drake-Brockman RAMC and Capt Baker RAMC return from English Leave. Carried on Inoculation 18 per day of men of unit with T.A.B. Lecture given on 1st Aid and gas to the latest Reinforcements.	[signature]
	17 5/17		Orderly Officer Capt Simmons RAMC. Daily Training Inoculation & games principal routine for the day. Bell Tents utilised as Dressing Tent for the few sick attending daily. Cases requiring more attention sent direct to 2nd (RN) Field Amb^ce where better accommodation was available.	[signature]

Instructions regarding War Diaries and Intelligence Summaries are contained in F. S. Regs., Part II. and the Staff Manual respectively. Title pages will be prepared in manuscript.

WAR DIARY
or
INTELLIGENCE SUMMARY.
(Erase heading not required.)

Army Form C. 2118.

Place	Date	Hour	Summary of Events and Information	Remarks and references to Appendices
CAMBLIGNEUL	18/5/17		Orderly Officer Capt. Jackson RAMC.	
			Duty Section engaged on the necessary fatigues – cleaning up camp & erection of new latrines etc. Remainder of men proceeded with Daily Training and games and sports in the afternoon.	[illegible signature]
	19/5/17		Orderly Officer Capt Howlett RAMC.	
			Daily Training pursued.	
			ADMS instructions carried out by detailing large ambulance car to report for duty at the XIII Corps Rest Station (1/6 Field Ambulance at ECOIVRES.	[illegible signature]
	20/5/17		Orderly Officer Capt. Anderson RAMC.	
			Preparations made to move to new area.	
			Capt Howlett RAMC 1. N.C.O. and 4 Other Ranks selected to proceed as an advance party to ANZIN ST. AUBIN preparatory to the relief of the 94th Field Ambce.	[illegible signature]
	21/5/17		Orderly Officer. Capt Baker RAMC	
		4 am.	Reveillé	
		5.50 am.	The unit paraded ready to march off to new area.	[illegible initials]

A7092 Wt. W128 9/M1293 750,000. 1/17. D. D & L. Ltd. Forms/C2118/14.

Army Form C. 2118.

WAR DIARY
or
INTELLIGENCE SUMMARY.
(*Erase heading not required.*)

Instructions regarding War Diaries and Intelligence Summaries are contained in F. S. Regs., Part II. and the Staff Manual respectively. Title pages will be prepared in manuscript.

Place	Date	Hour	Summary of Events and Information	Remarks and references to Appendices
ANZIN S.T. AUBIN	21/5/17		(Continued) The whole personnel of 3rd (R.N.) Field Amb^ce has arrived by Gun and completed relief as per A.D.M.S instructions.	
			Headquarters of unit situated at G.1.d.42 (Map 51B)	
			Rear Party 1 N.C.O and 6 O.R. remain behind at CAMBLIGNEUL to clear up camp and billets and certified sanitary by Town Major	
			Capt Howlett RAMC detailed to proceed to A.D.S. to assist 2nd (R.N.) Field Ambulance at H.1.c. (Map 51 B.)	[signature]
	22/5/17		Orderly Officer Capt Jackson RAMC	
			Two Hospital Marquees accommodate the few sick admitted. Cases not likely to be fit for duty within [illegible] days and not warranting evacuation were sent to XIII Corps Rest Stn at ECOIVRES	
			Billets cleaned and area round camp put into sanitary condition.	[signature]
	23/5/17		Orderly Officer. Capt Anderson R.A.M.C.	
			All ranks put on cleaning up.	
			All ranks exercised in the use of the Small Box Respirator & P.H. Helmet	[signature]

A7092 Wt. W125 9/M1293 750,000. 1/17. D. D & L. Ltd. Forms/C2118/14.

Instructions regarding War Diaries and Intelligence Summaries are contained in F. S. Regs., Part II. and the Staff Manual respectively. Title pages will be prepared in manuscript.

WAR DIARY
or
INTELLIGENCE SUMMARY.
(Erase heading not required.)

Army Form C. 2118.

Place	Date	Hour	Summary of Events and Information	Remarks and references to Appendices
ANZIN ST AUBIN	24/5/17		Orderly Officer. Captain Baker RAMC	
			Continued Training and cleaning up of Billets. Very few sick & no wounded admitted.	[illegible]
	25/5/17		Orderly Officer Capt Jackson RAMC.	
			No 19010 A/Sergeant Major B. J. BULL R.A.M.C. taken on strength of the unit from No 1st Field Ambulance.	
			Training Routine carried on	
			Military Medals awarded to S/4077 Pte A. Andrew RM and 176108 Pte J. Hathway ASC.M.T. attached 3rd Field Amb^ce Authority D.R.O 2264.	
			Capt Howlett R.A.M.C. returns from temp duty with 2nd (RN) Field Ambulance.	[illegible]
	26/5/17		Orderly Officer Capt Anderson M.C. RAMC.	
			Continued Daily Training and necessary fatigues	[illegible]
			Signal received from ADMS re 'Gas alert on'	
	27/5/17		Orderly Officer Capt Baker RAMC	
			Preparations made then detailed to parade at 1.20 pm ready to	[illegible]

A7092 Wt. W128 9/M1293 750,000. 1/17. D. D & L. Ltd. Forms/C2118/14.

Army Form C. 2118.

WAR DIARY
or
INTELLIGENCE SUMMARY.
(Erase heading not required.)

Instructions regarding War Diaries and Intelligence Summaries are contained in F. S. Regs., Part II. and the Staff Manual respectively. Title pages will be prepared in manuscript.

Place	Date	Hour	Summary of Events and Information	Remarks and references to Appendices
ANZIN. ST AUBIN.	27/5/17		(Continued) proceed to forward area to relieve 2nd (RN) Field Ambulance in accordance with ADMS instructions "Order No 35." and take over the evacuation of the forward area.	
			The following posts were taken over.	
			Advanced Dressing Station A.1 d.2.2 (Map 51 B) 2 Officers. 28 O.R.	
			Composed of Tent Section and 10 O.R. Bearers	
			Collecting Posts. (a) B 28 a.2.8 (Map 51 B) 2 Officers 27 O.R.	
			(b) Gun Pitts 1 Officer 27 O.R.	
			(c) B 29 C Central 21 O.R.	
			The 1st (RN) Field Ambce placed at the disposal of O/C 3rd (RN) Field Ambce 2 Medical Officers, 1 Ford Car and 2 Large Ambce Cars.	
			Disposition of Ambce Cars.	
			(1) Left Side: 1 Ford Car at BAILLEUL 2 Large Cars at the Advanced Dressing Station	
			(2) Right Side 1 Ford Car & 2 Large Cars at POINT du JOUR.	
			The relief was completed by 6 pm and reported to ADMS	[signature]

A7092 Wt. W128 9/M1293 750,000. 1/17. D. D & L. Ltd. Forms/C2118/14.

Instructions regarding War Diaries and Intelligence Summaries are contained in F. S. Regs., Part II. and the Staff Manual respectively. Title pages will be prepared in manuscript.

WAR DIARY
or
INTELLIGENCE SUMMARY.
(Erase heading not required.)

Army Form C. 2118.

Place	Date	Hour	Summary of Events and Information	Remarks and references to Appendices
ANZIN ST AUBIN.	28/5/17		Orderly Officer Capt Baker RAMC. The remainder of men left in camp employed on Camp fatigues and nursing duties. Capt Hamilton RAMC returned from temporary duty with 63rd (RN) Divisional Train.	[illegible]
	29/5/17		Orderly Officer Capt Baker RAMC. Arrangements made in forward area working smoothly and few casualties. "Gas Alert Off" declared by ADMS 63rd (RN) Div.	[illegible]
	30/5/17		Orderly. Officer Capt Baker RAMC. 2 "O.R." slightly wounded amongst personnel at "Gun Pits" on Right sector. Disposition of Medical Officers in the forward area. Advanced Dressing Station — Capt Jackson RAMC & Capt Craig RAMC Gavrelle Sector — Capt Anderson RAMC & Capt Howlett RAMC Bailleul Sector — Capt Laverick RAMC & Capt Hamilton.	[illegible]
	31/5/17		Orderly Officer Capt Baker RAMC. T. Surgeon Baxter RN detailed by ADMS to report at Advanced Dressing	[illegible]

A7092 Wt. W128 9/M1293 750,000. 1/17. D. D & L. Ltd. Forms/C2118/14.

Instructions regarding War Diaries and Intelligence Summaries are contained in F. S. Regs., Part II. and the Staff Manual respectively. Title pages will be prepared in manuscript.

WAR DIARY
or
INTELLIGENCE SUMMARY.
(Erase heading not required.)

Army Form C. 2118.

Place	Date	Hour	Summary of Events and Information	Remarks and references to Appendices
ANZIN ST AUBIN	31/7		(Continued) Station and was attached for temp. duty at that post relieving Capt Laverick RAMC who returned to his unit the 1st (N.Z.) Field Ambulance. Carried on in Camp the necessary camp fatigues and attended few cases necessitating removal to XIII Corps Rest Station at ECOIVRES.	[illegible signature]

A7092 Wt. W128 9/M1293 750,000. 1/17. D. D & L. Ltd. Forms/C2118/14.

FIELD AMBULANCE,
ROYAL NAVAL DIV.
No. W.S.
Date 1.7.17

June 1917

Confidential

Headquarters
3rd (R.N.) Field Ambce
63rd Division

War Diary
of
3rd (R.N) Field Ambce.
from
June 1st 1917
to
June 30th 1917

To

The A.G.'s Office
3rd Echelon.

[signature]
Lt. Col. R.A.M.C.
O/c 3rd (R.N.) Field Ambce
63rd (R.N.) Division

Instructions regarding War Diaries and Intelligence Summaries are contained in F. S. Regs., Part II. and the Staff Manual respectively. Title pages will be prepared in manuscript.

WAR DIARY
or
~~INTELLIGENCE~~ SUMMARY.
(Erase heading not required.)

Army Form C. 2118.

Place	Date	Hour	Summary of Events and Information	Remarks and references to Appendices
ANZIN ST AUBIN	June 1st		T. Capt C. J. Timms returned from English leave	A.W. Baker Capt. Adjt.[?]
	" 2nd		T. Lieut H. O'Neil reported for duty with the unit	AWB
	" 3rd		T. Lieut H. O'Neil detailed for temporary duty with 14th Worcester Regt in place of Capt Matthew on leave	
			Bearer Division returned to H.Q. Ambulance from forward area Relief reported complete 7.15 pm	AWB
	" 4th		Colonel Bree D.D.M.S. 13th Corps visited the ambulance and inspected the transport	AWB
	" 5th		T. Capt Jackson detailed for temporary duty with the 7th R.F. Batt in place of T. Capt Davidson on leave	AWB
	" 6th		All blankets handed into Q.M. Store for return to base. General Lawrie inspected the Horse Transport. Four reinforcements joined (5th)	AWB AWB
	" 7th		Two reinforcements joined from Divisional Train.	
			During the week considerable improvements were made in the billets of the ambulance, the bunks have been entirely repaired, the yards of the billets have been drained and levelled and the re-painting of the horse transport vehicles practically completed. All men were tested & drilled in gas respirators	AWB
	" 8th		Nothing of note.	
	" 9th		"	
	" 10th		Advance Party under Capt Hamilton proceeded to Sombligneul	AWB
			Capt Timms returned from detached duty with the 2nd F.A.	AWB
	11th		The ambulance in charge of Capt Anderson marched out with transport at 6. am for	AWB

A7092 Wt. W128 9/M1293 750,000. 1/17. D. D. & L. Ltd. Forms/C2118/14.

Instructions regarding War Diaries and Intelligence Summaries are contained in F. S. Regs., Part II. and the Staff [illegible] respectively. Title pages will be prepared in manuscript.

WAR DIARY

or

~~INTELLIGENCE SUMMARY.~~

(Erase heading not required.)

Army Form C. 2118.

Place	Date	Hour	Summary of Events and Information	Remarks and references to Appendices
Bambliegnies	11.6.17		Bambliegnies. ~~Move~~ completed 9 a.m. H.Q. W.14 d.38. Map. 51.C.	
			1 Motor Cyclist detailed for temporary duty with D.D.M.S. XIII Corps.	
			Capt Emmerson struck off strength	
			Capt Howlett & Capt Hamilton & 4 O.R. proceeded on leave to UK.	DWB.
	12.6.17		Capt Watkins & Capt Timms awarded M.C., both whilst attached to Battalions of 190th Brigade	
			S/3251 Staff Sgt Booth awarded D.C.M. (Authority DRO. 2381)	
			Daily Routine Training commenced – Physical Exercises 7.30-8.00., Squad & Stretcher Drill 9.30-11.30 a.m., Cricket, Baseball 2-4 p.m.	DWB
	13.6.17		Training continued.	DWB
	14.6.17		Ambulance moved to Marœuil and took over Nissen Hut Encampment previously occupied by 527th Field Coy R.E. Transport marched off 5 a.m. Remainder of ambulance under Capt Anderson at 6 a.m. Move completed 9 a.m.	
			At the Divisional Horse Show the unit entered (a) Transport Turnout (Ambulance Wagon & Watercart (b) Limbered Wagon G.S.. In each event the first prize was awarded to the unit.	
	15.6.17		All sections continued to clean up camps and billets. Five Nissen Huts were put aside for the accomodation of sick cases, the greater part of the Bearer & Tent Sections being billeted in tents. Horse Transport, Motor Transport and a number of special duty men being housed in the remaining two Nissen Huts.	DWB
			T Capt Atkinson R.A.N., R.A.M.C. taken on the strength of unit.	DWB
	16.6.17		All sections continued to clean up camp, fill in trenches, level ground & mark off limits of encampment.	DWB

[illegible signature] Lt Col RAMC

Army Form C. 2118.

Instructions regarding War Diaries and Intelligence Summaries are contained in F. S. Regs., Part II. and the Staff Manual respectively. Title pages will be prepared in manuscript.

WAR DIARY
or
~~INTELLIGENCE SUMMARY.~~
(Erase heading not required.)

Place	Date	Hour	Summary of Events and Information	Remarks and references to Appendices
Marœuil	17.6.17		T. Capt R.A.H. Atkinson RAMC detailed to report to A.D.M.S. 5th Div for duty	AWB
			T. Capt Jackson rejoined unit from temporary duty with 7th R.F.	
	18.6.17		T. Capt Timms RAMC proceeded to 63rd Div R.E. & was struck off strength from 16th inst	
			Capt Dowse RAMC taken on strength from 16th inst & temporarily attached to A.D.M.S.	
			T. Capt Jackson proceeded on leave to U.K.	
			T Lieut O'Neil RAMC rejoined from 14th Worcester Regt.	AWB.
	19.6.17		The unit has been occupied daily in improving the site of the camp & the wards. A new pack store has been made. Arrangements have also been made with the Town Major for the erection of new latrines for personnel and patients. T Lieut O'Neil posted to 4th Bedfords & struck off strength (20.6.17)	AWB
	20.6.17		XIIIth Corps Horse Show. One Ambulance and Water Cart entered. These had been very carefully overhauled during the last few days but failed to obtain prizes.	AWB
	21.6.17		Gas Drill & Scabies Inspection. The men do the drill with respirators very efficiently. They are very free from Skin Diseases.	AWB
	22.6.17		Promotions. M/2 098568 A/Sgt Smith G. to Sergeant Subtant. M/2 175659 A/2Cpl Bennett E.J. " Corpl	AWB
	24.6.17		T. Capts Howlett & Hamilton returned from leave. T Capt. Hamilton RAMC to R.N.D.A.C. in place of T Capt Baillie to ambulance to proceed on leave.	AWB
	25.6.17		T Capt Baillie proceeded on leave.	AWB
	26.6.17		Work of improving camp is being continued. The kitchens have been rebuilt and rearranged. A meat safe has been built. A barbers room is in the process of erection. The wards are being relined with matchboarding where that is deficient.	AWB
	27.6.17			AWB
	28.6.17		Inspection 10.30 a.m. by Col. Bree A.M.S. D.D.M.S. XIII Corps. Lieut Wilson RM reported from leave. T Capt Howlett detached to XIII Corps School of Sanitation for course of instruction.	
	30.6.17		Lieut-Col. Scott Harden, Town Major, visited the camp and inspected the improvements made since taking over. He expressed his surprise at the amount of work that had been accomplished & his complete satisfaction with the camp.	AWB

[illegible signature] RAMC

A7092 Wt. W125 9/M1293 750,000. 1/17. D. D & L. Ltd. Forms/C2118/14.

63RD DIVISION

150TH(RN) FIELD AMBULANCE

~~JLY 1917-DEC 1918~~

1916 MAY - 1919 MAY

"Confidential"

Vol 19

Headquarters
150th (R.N.) Field Ambce
August 1st 17.

War Diary

of

150th (R.N.) Field Ambulance

from

July 1st 1917

to

July 31st 1917

To

The A.G.'s Office
3rd Echelon

[signature]
Lt Col R.A.M.C.
O/c 150th (R.N.) Field Ambce

Instructions regarding War Diaries and Intelligence Summaries are contained in F. S. Regs., Part II. and the Staff Manual respectively. Title pages will be prepared in manuscript.

WAR DIARY
or
~~INTELLIGENCE SUMMARY.~~
(Erase heading not required.)

Army Form C. 2118.

Place	Date	Hour	Summary of Events and Information	Remarks and references to Appendices
Maroeuil	July 1st		T Capt S Jackson R.A.M.C. rejoined from English leave	JHwlr
	" 2nd		Preparation of billets & land occupied, for a permanent Field Ambce site	JHwlr
	" 3rd		T.Capt J.E.M. Wigley R.A.M.C. rejoined from English leave	
			T.Capt W. Hamilton R.A.M.C struck off strength of unit from 24/6/17 on posting to 63rd (R.N) Div. Amm Column. T.Capt D.M. Baillie taken on strength from above date. Authority A.D.M.S. 109/33 of 1/7/17	JHwlr
ANZIN-St. AUBIN	- 4th		Unit paraded 7am & moved from present area to ANZIN-ST-AUBIN as Field Ambce in reserve. Arrived 8.30 am. H.Q situated in the Mairie G.8 a 2.8 (Map 51B.)	JHwlr
	- 5th		Cleaning & improvement of billets carried on with. Copies of estimates for material etc in connection with site at MAROEUIL handed over to 95th Field Ambce. Present site prepared for permanent Field Ambce billet	JHwlr
	- 6th		T.Capt L.W. Howlett RAMC rejoined from XIII Corps School of Sanitation	JHwlr
	- 7		Unit paraded in full marching order at 11am for inspection by D.M.S. 1st Army	
			T.Capt D.M. Baillie RAMC rejoined from English leave. 2 O.R. proceeded on leave	JHwlr
	- 8th		T.Capt J.E.M Wigley RAMC proceeded to XIII Corps School of Sanitation for Course of Instruction	
			1 O.R. proceeded to XIII Corps School of Sanitation for temporary duty as cook	
	- 9th		T.Capt S. Jackson RAMC & T.Capt D.M Baillie RAMC detailed to attend a Medical Board, assembling at 1st (R.N) Field Ambce, to examine such men as may be brought before it for 253rd Divl Employment Company	JHwlr
	- 10th		4 O.R. proceeded on leave	JHwlr
	11th		Anti Gas Goggles withdrawn & returned to Q.M. stores	
			132 Officers & O.R. paraded at 9.30am to proceed to Rendezvous near Madagascar for Special parade on occasion of the visit of H.M. the King	JHwlr
	12th		Gas Alert ON (A.D.M.S F 3/852)	JHwlr
	13th		T.Capt D.M Baillie RAMC posted to A. section of this unit	
			" L.W. Howlett - - - B - - -	
			" J.E. M Wigley - - - C	JHwlr

A7092 Wt. W128 9/M1293 750,000. 1/17. D. D & L. Ltd. Forms/C2118/14.

Army Form C. 2118.

WAR DIARY
or
~~INTELLIGENCE SUMMARY.~~
(Erase heading not required.)

Instructions regarding War Diaries and Intelligence Summaries are contained in F. S. Regs., Part II. and the Staff Manual respectively. Title pages will be prepared in manuscript.

Place	Date	Hour	Summary of Events and Information	Remarks and references to Appendices
ANZIN-ST-AUBIN	July 14th/17		Sports Meeting held by the Unit from 1·30 pm to 7·30 pm on ground adjoining billets. RMLI Band present. Brig. Gen. Hutcheson C.M.G. D.S.O. presented the prizes. Cost defrayed by Unit Canteen fund.	JHulo
	" 15th		T. Capt J. E. M. Wigley R.A.M.C. rejoined from XIII Corps School of Sanitation	JHulo
	" 16th		Kit Inspection 2 pm	JHulo
	" 17th		The following promotions were sanctioned by A.D.M.S 63rd (R.N.) Division S/3577 Cpl Clewes W to be Sergeant G.D. S/4062 a/L/cpl Brien CP to be Corporal G.D. S/4153 Pte Hampson J. - - L/cpl (paid)	JHulo
			T. Capt L. W. Howlett RAMC detailed for temporary duty with 63rd (R.N) Div. Train vice Capt. Macnaughton RAMC evacuated sick	JHulo
	" 18th		This unit relieved 1st (R.N) Field Amb.ce in the forward area. Relief complete by 6 pm. Dispositions - T. Capt. D. M. Baillie + 26 O.R. at Bearer Collecting Post in Railway Cutting (B.27 a.5.4) T. Capt. A.S.K. Anderson MC + 12 O.R. - A.D.S on Bailleul Road (A.1 a) T. Capt. J. E. M. Wigley + 32 O.R. - Bearer Collecting Post in Sunken on Gavrelle Rd (H.5 c.)	JHulo
			Application made to A.D.M.S for 1 N.C.O + 5 Bearer Squads to augment numbers of this unit depleted by evacuation of personnel sick during past few weeks	
	" 19th		Z day for raid on enemy trenches by Howe Bn.	
	" 20th		1 officer + 36 O.R. passed through Collecting Post at Gun Pits (between 4 am + 7.30 am) as casualties from raid. Patients in C.C.S. 12 hours after collecting on field.	JHulo
			The 63rd (R.N) Divisional Area administered by 62nd Sanitary Section. Two trucks for use on light railway between Railway Cutting (B27 a.5.4) + M.D.S (St Catherines), placed at disposal of Medical Unit by Corps Tramways Officer	JHulo
	" 21st		The 3rd (R.N) Field Amb.ce becomes the 150th (R.N) Field Amb.ce (Auth.y A.C.I. 1046 dated 3/7/17) Routine Order 1319 of 17.7.17 re painting + marking of Field Amb.ce transport rec.d 20 Med/111 Amb.)	JHulo
	" 22nd		Suggestions of Div.l Gas Officer that the collecting post at B27 a.5.4 be fitted with anti gas appliances. 16 Aydon anti gas fans drawn from gas school for distribution.	JHulo

A7092. Wt. W123 9/M1293 750,000. 1/17. D. D. & L. Ltd. Forms/C2118/14.

Instructions regarding War Diaries and Intelligence Summaries are contained in F. S. Regs., Part II. and the Staff Manual respectively. Title pages will be prepared in manuscript.

WAR DIARY
or
~~INTELLIGENCE~~ SUMMARY.
(Erase heading not required.)

Army Form C. 2118.

Place	Date	Hour	Summary of Events and Information	Remarks and references to Appendices
ANZIN-ST.-AUBIN	1917 July 23		T. Capt S Jackson RAMC left the unit for duty with No. 39 Stationary Hospital & is struck off the strength from this date. (auth. ADMS 109/142)	
			T. Capt. J. S. Stewart RAMC reported for duty & was taken on strength (auth. ADMS 109/142)	JHuls
	24th		Visit of C.E. Corps to Horse lines at 10am	
			Inspection of transport by O.C. 63rd (R.N.) Divl Train at 2pm.	
			T. Capt. L. W. Howlett RAMC assumes command of C section vice T. Capt S Jackson RAMC	JHuls
			T. Capt. J. S. Stewart RAMC posted to B section	
			Capt. J. C. Dowse RAMC posted to 148th (R.N.) Field Ambce & is struck off the strength of this unit from 23rd incl. (auth. ADMS 149/148)	
	25th		T. Capt. L. W. Howlett left unit for temporary duty with the 5th Army (auth. ADMS 109/149)	
			T. Capt. J. S. Stewart RAMC relieved T Capt. [illegible] RAMC at Collecting Post at Gun Pits ([illegible])	JHuls
			Work continued on improvements at A.D.S. & Railway Cutting Collecting Post (B27a5.0) H5 c)	
			Indents for necessary material submitted to CRE	
	26		Work of improvement of billets, construction of wire beds meatsafes etc proceeded with	JHuls
	27		Auth. 180/70 ADMS received for indent on CRE for material required for construction of Horse Standings.	JHuls
	28		Work at A.D.S. comprising officers & mens latrines completed. Cookhouse improved. Ground levelled & trenches & shell holes filled in.	[illegible]
	29		Captain Baker RAMC evacuated last night to No 42 C.C.S. Operated on acute haemorrhagic pancreatitis found – condition critical. Work on embankment in Railway Cutting opposite C.P. (B.27.a.5.6) nearing completion plinth on which new hut to stand completed	[illegible]
	30		Work at A.D.S. & C.P. continued. Dinner hut for personnel completed.	[illegible]
	31		19 O.R's of "C" Tent Sub Division withdrawn from forward area as they leave early tomorrow for No 23. C.C.S.	

Instructions regarding War Diaries and Intelligence Summaries are contained in F. S. Regs., Part II. and the Staff Manual respectively. Title pages will be prepared in manuscript.

WAR DIARY
or
INTELLIGENCE SUMMARY.
(Erase heading not required.)

Army Form C. 2118.

Place	Date	Hour	Summary of Events and Information	Remarks and references to Appendices
ANZIN ST AUBIN	July 31		D.M.S. 1st Army & A.D.M.S. XIII Corps visited Advanced Dressing Station and Collection Post (B. 27. a. 5. 4). Capt Wright RAMC relieved Capt Stewart RAMC at Gavrelle Gueldre Collecting Post. Latter in three cars with 13 O.R. of "C" Tent Sub Division & Capt [illegible] RAMC of 149th F.A. left 10.55 a.m. for No 23 C.C.S. at Lozinghem for temporary duty.	[illegible] Brooke

150TH (R.N.)
FIELD AMBULANCE.
No. W.D. 8
Date 1. 9. 17

"CONFIDENTIAL"

Headquarters 150(R.N.) Field Ambulance.

1st. September 1917.

Vol 16

140/2304

WAR DIARY

of

150 (R.N.) FIELD AMBULANCE.

from

1st. AUGUST 1917.

to

31st. AUGUST 1917.

To

The A.G's Office,
3rd. Echelon.

C B Knox
Lieut-Colonel R.A.M.C.
O.C. 150 (R.N.) Field Ambulance.

7
Aug. '17

Instructions regarding War Diaries and Intelligence Summaries are contained in F. S. Regs., Part II. and the Staff Manual respectively. Title pages will be prepared in manuscript.

WAR DIARY
or
~~INTELLIGENCE~~ SUMMARY.
(Erase heading not required.)

Army Form C. 2118.

Place	Date	Hour	Summary of Events and Information	Remarks and references to Appendices
ANZIN ST. AUBIN	Aug. 1.		The 150th (R.N.) Field Ambulance was relieved by the 148th (R.N.) Field Ambulance, in the forward area. Plans for suggested improvements at the various posts, handed over to relieving unit.	
			The Quarter Master - Lt Wilson R.M. and transport sergeants attended ECURIE for a demonstration of the use of Tump Lines + Yukon Pack.	A.M.C.
	2nd "		T/Capt WIGLEY RAMC detailed for medical duties to the 2nd R.M.L.I (ADMS. 109/152) during the absence, on leave, of Surgeon McBEAN ROSS R.N.	A.M.C.
	3rd "		Work on Horse Standings for winter started.	
	4th "		Application to Town Major to erect beds in MAPLE CHATEAU (L 25 a) so that accommodation might be increased.	A.M.C.
	5th "		One Officer (Capt. BAILLIE RAMC) and 18 OR detailed to	

A7092 Wt. W125 9/M1293 750,000. 1/17. D. D & L. Ltd. Forms/C2118/14.

Instructions regarding War Diaries and Intelligence Summaries are contained in F. S. Regs., Part II. and the Staff Manual respectively. Title pages will be prepared in manuscript.

WAR DIARY
or
~~INTELLIGENCE SUMMARY.~~
(Erase heading not required.)

Army Form C. 2118.

Place	Date	Hour	Summary of Events and Information	Remarks and references to Appendices
ANZIN ST AUBIN	5th (cont)		Attend Commemorative Church Parade Service. This was held at RANCHICOURT CHATEAU under the auspices of the 1st Army.	A. Cha.
	6th		T/CAPT. D.M. BAILLIE RAMC detached for temporary duty with 7th Royal Fusiliers, during the absence, while on a sanitary course, of T/CAPT. DAVIDSON RAMC.	A. Cha
	~~[illegible]~~		Clothing parade + kit inspection held.	
	7th		T/CAPT. A.S.K. ANDERSON MC RAMC took over duties as 2nd in command vice T/CAPT. A.W. BAKER RAMC. – Reg. Orders 24 7/8/17	A. Cha
	8th		General Routine.	A. Cha
	9th		Inspection of Gas Helmets + Small Box Respirators, followed by gas drill and some hints as to the detection of this new "Mustard Gas"	A. Cha

A7092 Wt. W128 9/M1293 750,000. 1/17. D. D & L. Ltd. Forms/C2118/14.

Instructions regarding War Diaries and Intelligence Summaries are contained in F. S. Regs., Part II. and the Staff Manual respectively. Title pages will be prepared in manuscript.

WAR DIARY
or
~~INTELLIGENCE SUMMARY.~~
(*Erase heading not required.*)

Army Form C. 2118.

Place	Date	Hour	Summary of Events and Information	Remarks and references to Appendices
ANZIN ST. AUBIN	10th		Work on Horse standings continued with.	G.C.C.
	11th			
	12th		Erection of wire beds in MAPLE CHATEAU started.	G.C.C.
	13 -			
	14th		All riding horses surplus to eight sent to D.H.Q. - VICTORY CAMP S3 6 5.s. Map 51B Four sent; of which one was returned.	
			150th (R.N.) Field Ambulance relieved the 148th (R.N.) Field Ambulance in the forward area.	
			7 CAPT. JOHNSON RAMC & Lt. DAW R.A.M.C. of 149th (R.N.) Field Ambulance detailed to be at the disposal of OC 150th (R.N.) Field Ambulance.	
			Detail. Map 51B — Left Sector	
			H12.38 A.D.S. - CAPT. BAILLIE - 7 O.R. Bearer Posts GOSE ALLEY - 9 O.R.	
			Collecting Post - (Railway Cutting) B27 6 6.2 } Lt. DAW - 26 OR	

Instructions regarding War Diaries and Intelligence Summaries are contained in F. S. Regs., Part II. and the Staff Manual respectively. Title pages will be prepared in manuscript.

WAR DIARY
or
~~INTELLIGENCE SUMMARY.~~
(Erase heading not required.)

Army Form C. 2118.

Place	Date	Hour	Summary of Events and Information	Remarks and references to Appendices
ANZIN ST AUBIN	14/4		Detail (cont) Right Sector	
			Collecting Post – Green Pits H4 C 5.4 } T/CAPT. WIGLEY R.A.M.C. T/CAPT. JOHNSON RAMC. 26 O.R.	
			Bearer Post in MARINE TRENCH } 1. N.C.O & 8 O.R.	
			A holding party of 4 O.R at B 28 a 0.8.	
				L.H.G.

A7092 Wt. W125 9/M1293 750,000. 1/17. D. D & L. Ltd. Forms/C2118/14.

Instructions regarding War Diaries and Intelligence Summaries are contained in F. S. Regs., Part II. and the Staff Manual respectively. Title pages will be prepared in manuscript.

WAR DIARY
or
~~INTELLIGENCE SUMMARY.~~
(Erase heading not required.)

Army Form C. 2118.

Place	Date	Hour	Summary of Events and Information	Remarks and references to Appendices
ANZIN St AUBIN.	15th August.		Twenty O.R. arrived as reinforcements from the Base.	A.H.G.
	16th "		Lt. Col. E.B. KNOX R.A.M.C. assumed command of 150th (R.N) Field Ambulance vice Lt-Col. R.E. DRAKE-BROCKMAN R.A.M.C who left to take command of 95th Field Ambulance – (authority – 109/161 A.DMS 16.8.17)	A.H.G.
	17th "		Advanced Dressing station – H1.C3.8 Map 51^B and Collecting Post (B27C6.2) visited. Work of improving A.D.S. being continued – viz – levelling of ground, improving the entrance to dugouts.	A.H.G.
	18th "		T/Capt Clarke RAMC 149th (R.N.) Field Ambulance relieved Lt Daw RAMC as officer in charge of Collecting Post in Railway Cutting B27.C6.2 (Map 51^B).	A.H.G.
	19th "		————	

A7092 Wt. W125 9/M1293 750,000. 1/17. D. D & L. Ltd. Forms/C2118/14.

Instructions regarding War Diaries and Intelligence Summaries are contained in F. S. Regs., Part II. and the Staff Manual respectively. Title pages will be prepared in manuscript.

WAR DIARY
or
~~INTELLIGENCE SUMMARY.~~
(*Erase heading not required.*)

Army Form C. 2118.

Place	Date	Hour	Summary of Events and Information	Remarks and references to Appendices
ANZIN ST. AUBIN.	20th August		Work on Horse standings continued.	GHG
	21st		—	
	22nd		T/Capt. Wigley RAMC relieved T/Capt. Baillie RAMC at A.D.S. H1.c 3.4 Map 51B.	
			T/Capt. Baker RAMC struck off the strength of the unit 63rd D.R.O. 2826 22.8.17.	GHG
	23rd		A.Ds.M.S. of 63rd Division & 5th Division visited ANZIN ST. AUBIN to arrange billets.	
			Box Respirators & P.H. Helmets – inspected.	GHG
	24			
	25.		Six O.R. as reinforcements arrived from Base	GHG

A5834 Wt. W4973/M687 750,000 8/16 D. D. & L. Ltd. Forms/C.2118/13.

Instructions regarding War Diaries and Intelligence Summaries are contained in F. S. Regs., Part II. and the Staff Manual respectively. Title pages will be prepared in manuscript.

WAR DIARY
or
~~INTELLIGENCE SUMMARY~~.
(*Erase heading not required.*)

Army Form C. 2118.

Place	Date	Hour	Summary of Events and Information	Remarks and references to Appendices
ANZIN St. AUBIN.	August 26th		T/Capt. MATTHEW R.A.M.C. reported from 1st Artist Rifles and was taken on the strength of 150th (R.N.) Field Ambulance.	A.C.A.G.
	27th		Commanding Officer accompanied by D.D.M.S. of 13th Corps visited Advanced Dressing Station H.1.c.3.8 and Collecting Post in Railway Cutting B.27.c.6.2 (Map 51B).	A.C.A.G.
	28th		150th (R.N.) Field Ambulance relieved in forward area by 148th (R.N.) Field Ambulance. T/Capt. WIGLEY R.A.M.C. Transferred to 95th Field Ambulance & struck off the strength of unit. (~~[illegible]~~) (D.D.M.S. XIII Corps 53/106) T/Capt. YOUNG R.A.M.C. transferred from 95th Field Ambulance & taken on the strength. (D.D.M.S. XIII Corps 53/106).	A.C.A.G.

Instructions regarding War Diaries and Intelligence Summaries are contained in F. S. Regs., Part II. and the Staff Manual respectively. Title pages will be prepared in manuscript.

WAR DIARY
or
INTELLIGENCE SUMMARY.
(*Erase heading not required.*)

Army Form C. 2118.

Place	Date	Hour	Summary of Events and Information	Remarks and references to Appendices
ANZIN ST. AUBIN	August 29th		A Medical Board – (the Commanding Officer as President and two Officers of the unit as members) examined and reclassified men of 39th Labour Company.	G.F.H.G
"	30th		Same Board continue & examine & reclassify men of 253rd Employment Company.	G.S.K.A
"	31st		More men of 253rd Employment Company examined and reclassified. Three NISSEN Huts erected in grounds of unit.	G.C.H.G

1st Sept 17

C B Knox
Lt Col
OC 150 Fd Amb
63rd (RN) Division

A5834 Wt. W4973/M687 750,000 8/16 D. D. & L. Ltd. Forms/C.2118/13.

Sept-1917

140/2438

No. 150 7 a.

11

"Confidential"

Headquarters,
150th.(R.N.)Field Ambulance,
1st.October 1917.

WAR DIARY
of
150th.(R.N.) Field Ambulance,

from
1st September 1917.
to
30th.September 1917.

To,
The A.G's Office,
3rd.Echelon.

C Knox
Lieut-Col.R.A.M.C.,
Commanding 150th.(R.N.)Field Ambce.

150TH (R.N.)
FIELD AMBULANCE.
No.
1 OCT 1917

Instructions regarding War Diaries and Intelligence Summaries are contained in F. S. Regs., Part II. and the Staff Manual respectively. Title pages will be prepared in manuscript.

WAR DIARY
or
INTELLIGENCE SUMMARY.
(Erase heading not required.)

Army Form C.2118.

Vol 17

Place	Date	Hour	Summary of Events and Information	Remarks and references to Appendices
ANZIN St.Aubin. Map 51 B. G.7.c.7.8.	Sept.12th. 1917.		150th.(R.N.)Field Ambulance relieved 148th.(R.N.) Field Ambulance in the forward area.	G.A.K.A.
-do-	Sep.24th. 1917.		150th.(R.N.)Field Ambulance relieved by 1/5th London Field Ambulance. 47th.Division.	G.S.A.A.
BEUGIN. Map 36 B. P.1.d.0.2.	Sep.24th. 1917.		150th.(R.N.)Field Ambulance moved into Billets at BEUGIN.	G.A.K.A.
do	-do-		T/Capt.R.M.Soames R.A.M.C.,taken on strength of Unit.	
-do-	25th.Sep. 1917.		T/Capt.L.W.Howlett R.A.M.C.,rejoined Unit from 2nd. Canadian Casualty Clearing Station.	G.A.K.A.
-do-	27th.Sep, 1917.		T/Capt.L.W.Howlett R.A.M.C.,proceeded to England and struck off strength of Unit.	G.A.K.A.

Instructions regarding War Diaries and Intelligence Summaries are contained in F. S. Regs., Part II. and the Staff Manual respectively. Title pages will be prepared in manuscript.

WAR DIARY

or

INTELLIGENCE SUMMARY.

(Erase heading not required.)

Army Form C. 2118.

Place	Date	Hour	Summary of Events and Information	Remarks and references to Appendices
BEUGIN. Map.36 B. P.1.d.O.2.	29th.Sept. 1917.		T/Capt.Soames R.M.,R.A.M.C.,struck off strength to A.D.M.S.,12th.Division.	[illegible] [illegible]

T2134. Wt. W708—776. 500000. 4/15. Sir J. C. & S.

"CONFIDENTIAL"

Headquarters.
150th(RN) Field Ambulance.
November 1st.1917.

War Diary
of
150th(RN) Field Ambulance.
from
October 1st.
to
October 31st.1917.

To
The A.G's Office.
3rd.Echelon.

E B Knox
Lieut-Col. R.A.M.C.
Commanding 150th(RN) Field Ambulance

Instructions regarding War Diaries and Intelligence Summaries are contained in F. S. Regs., Part II. and the Staff Manual respectively. Title pages will be prepared in manuscript.

WAR DIARY

or

~~INTELLIGENCE SUMMARY.~~

(Erase heading not required.)

Army Form C. 2118.

Place	Date	Hour	Summary of Events and Information	Remarks and references to Appendices
BEUGIN Map 36 B P1 d 0.2.	October 1		1st Lieut. BROWN U.S.A. M.O.R.C. attached for duty from 149th (R.N.) Field Ambulance.	G.A.Q.
do	3rd		150th (R.N.) Field Ambulance entrained at LIGNY St. FLOCHEL T23 d 6.0 Map 36 B and detrained at BAVINCHOVE O16 c 5.8 (Map BELGIUM and France Sheet 27) – and marched to ZERMEZEELE I27 d 4.6.	G.A.Q.
ZERMEZEELE I27 d 4.6 Map Belgium and France Sheet 27	7th		Unit marched to HOUTKERQUE area. Headquarters situated at D 18 b 6.3 (Map – Belgium & France Sheet 27)	G.A.Q.
HOUTKERQUE Map BELGIUM d 18.b 6.3 FRANCE Sheet 27	11th		1st Lt. BROWN U.S.A. M.O.R.C. detached for duty to 64 C.C.S.	G.A.Q.
do.	15th		Lt-Col. E.B. KNOX R.A.M.C. assumed command XVIII Corps Main Dressing Station.	G.A.Q.

T2134. Wt. W708—776. 500000. 4/15. Sir J. C. & S.

Army Form C. 2118.

Instructions regarding War Diaries and Intelligence Summaries are contained in F. S. Regs., Part II. and the Staff Manual respectively. Title pages will be prepared in manuscript.

WAR DIARY
or
~~INTELLIGENCE SUMMARY.~~
(Erase heading not required.)

Place	Date	Hour	Summary of Events and Information	Remarks and references to Appendices
HOUTKERQUE d.18.b.6.3 Map. Belgium & France Sheet 27.	October 17th		T/Capt. J.S. STEWART R.A.M.C struck off strength of unit on evacuation to ENGLAND.	G.H.G
do.	21st		T/Lieut. H.F. POWELL RAMC " S.E CATHCART " " 7 R SMYTH " } Taken strength of unit from Base.	G.H.G.
DUHALLOW C25.d.3.0 sheet 28 Belgium & France	24th		Headquarters moved to XVIII Corps Main Dressing Station	CBK
	29th		T/Lieut Smyth RAMC transferred to 1st RMLI & struck off strength	CBK
	30th		T/Lieut Powell RAMC transferred to Anson Batt: & struck off strength	
	"		6 Men of the unit Killed in action at C12.b.7.3 (Sheet 28)	CBK

"CONFIDENTIAL"

Headquarters, 150th. (RN) Field Ambce.

1st. December 1917.

WAR DIARY OF

150th. (R.N.) FIELD AMBULANCE

FROM

1st. November 1917

TO

30th. November 1917.

E B Knox

To A.G.'s Office,
3rd. Echelon.

Lieut-Col., R.A.M.C.,
Commanding 150th. (R.N.) Field Ambce.

No. 150. F.A.

140/2578

S

Instructions regarding War Diaries and Intelligence Summaries are contained in F. S. Regs., Part II. and the Staff Manual respectively. Title pages will be prepared in manuscript.

WAR DIARY
or
INTELLIGENCE SUMMARY.
(Erase heading not required.)

Army Form C. 2118.

Vol 19

Place	Date	Hour	Summary of Events and Information	Remarks and references to Appendices
Duhallow	Nov.			
C.25.d.3.0.	4th.		One other rank killed in action.	G.H.Q.
Sheet 28. Belgium &			T/Lieut.H.R.Sinclair R.A.M.C.,taken on strength.	
France.	5th.		One other rank killed in action.	G.H.Q.
	6th.		T/Lieut. P.J.Flood R.A.M.C., and 1st.Lieut.H.W.Goos M.O.R.C.,U.S.A. taken on strength.	G.H.Q.
	8th.		T/Lieut.H.R.Sinclair R.A.M.C.,struck off strength.	G.H.Q.
	18th.		Five Military Medals and One Bar awarded to One Sergeant and Five Other Ranks of Unit.	G.H.Q.

T2134. Wt. W708—776. 500000. 4/15. Sir J. C. & S.

140/2018

No. 150. F. A.

63 Div

"CONFIDENTIAL"

14

Headquarters,150th.(R.N.)Field Amb.
1st.January 1918.

150TH (R.N.)
FIELD AMBULANCE.
No. W.D. 1
Date 1 JAN 1918

WAR DIARY OF

150th.(R.N.)FIELD AMBULANCE

FROM

1st.DECEMBER 1917.

TO

31st.DECEMBER 1917.

C B Knox

To, A.G.'s Office,
3rd.Echelon.

Lieut-Col.R.A.M.C.,
Commanding 150th.(R.N.)Field Ambulance.

Instructions regarding War Diaries and Intelligence Summaries are contained in F. S. Regs., Part II. and the Staff Manual respectively. Title pages will be prepared in manuscript.

WAR DIARY
or
INTELLIGENCE SUMMARY.
(Erase heading not required.)

Army Form C. 2118.

Vol 20

Place	Date	Hour	Summary of Events and Information	Remarks and references to Appendices
DUHALLOW C.25.d. 3.0.	Dec. 1.		110 Sick and Wounded (including Officers & O.R.) evacuated to CCS from 2nd. Corps Main Dressing Station.	AKA
Sheet 28	2.		104 do. do. do.	AKA
Belgium & France	6.		Unit moved from 2nd. Corps Main Dressing Station and was conveyed in busses to GODEWAERSVELDE, Q.23.a.3.5. Sheet 27 Belgium and France.	AKA
GODEWAERSVELDE, Q.23.a. 3.5. Sheet 27 Belgium & France	10.		Unit, accompanied by transport, entrained at local station. Train left 3.45 a.m., arrived 12.30 p.m. at MIRAUMONT, where they detrained. From there Unit marched to ROCQUINY, O.27.d.4.8. Sheet 57c, where they billeted.	AKA
ROCQUINY O.27.d. 4.8.	11.		T/Capt. D.M.Baillie, R.A.M.C. proceeded to report to O.C. 39 General Hospital for duty and was struck off strength.	AKA
Sheet 57c	13.		Unit marched to and billeted at ETRICOURT, V.13.a.3.9. Sheet 57c.	AKA
ETRICOURT V.13.a. 3.9. Sheet 57c	14.		Unit marched to NURLU, V.28.d., Sheet 57c, and billeted there. 1/Lieut. A.J.Gordon, M.O.R.C., U.S.A., 1/Lieut. R.O.Rogers, M.O.R.C., U.S.A. and 1/Lieut. A.G. Heard, M.O.R.C., U.S.A. arrived from Base for duty and were taken on strength.	AKA
NURLU, V.28.d. Sheet 57c	16.		Unit marched to and billeted at LECHELLE, P.25.c., Sheet 57c. T/Lieut. S.E.Cathcart, R.A.M.C., struck off strength. 50 Bearers reported for duty to O.C. 149th. (R.N.) Field Ambce.	AKA
LECHELLE P.25.c. Map 57c.	30.		Unit proceeded to METZ, Q.19.b.9.2. and relieved 149th. (R.N.) Field Ambulance in the forward area. Headquarters of Unit in METZ.	CBK

A5834 Wt. W4973/M687 750,000 8/16 D. D. & L. Ltd. Forms/C.2118/13.

Jan. 1918

140/2696

No. 150 7. A.

Army Form C. 2118.

Instructions regarding War Diaries and Intelligence Summaries are contained in F. S. Regs., Part II. and the Staff Manual respectively. Title pages will be prepared in manuscript.

WAR DIARY
or
~~INTELLIGENCE SUMMARY~~
(Erase heading not required.)

150th (RN) Field Ambulance

Volume XX Vol 21

Place	Date 1918	Hour	Summary of Events and Information	Remarks and references to Appendices
METZ, Q.19.b.9.1. Sheet 57c	Jan. 2		Lieut. P.J. Flood, R.A.M.C. detached to Composite Battn. 3rd and 5th. Corps Cyclists attached 190th. Inf. Bde. 1/Lieut. A.J. Gordon, M.O.R.C., U.S.A., detached to C.R.E. 63rd. (R.N.) Division.	AJ
	3		Operation Order 68 of A.D.M.S./63rd.(RN) Div. 19th. Division to place 3 bearer squads at Bearer Relay Posts, (R.8.b.2.8., Sheet 57c) for evacuation from R.A.Ps, which 19th. Division have taken over.	AJ
	4		37 Re-inforcements (other ranks) arrived from base. Lieut. P J. Flood, R.A.M.C. re-joins Unit.	AJ
	6		1/Lieut. H.W. Coos, M.O.R.C., U.S.A. struck off strength.	AJ
	7		1/Lieut. A.J. Gordon, M.O.R.C., U.S.A. re-joins Unit. Lieut. P.J. Flood, R.A.M.C. detached to Anson Battn. Lieut. W. Taylor, R.A.M.C. taken on strength, from 1st. Div.	AJ
	8		Horse Transport section moved from LECHELLE (P.25.c. Sheet 57c) to Headquarters, METZ.	AJ
	9		Lieut. P J. Flood, R.A.M.C. re-joins Unit. 1/Lieut. A.J. Gordon, M.O.R.C., U.S.A. detached to Anson Battn	AJ
	15th.		Lieut. P J. Flood, R.A.M.C. struck off strength (To 1st.Div)	AJ
	16		1/Lieut. A.J. Gordon, M.O.R.C., U.S.A. struck off strength, (To Anson Battn.)	AJ
	21		1/Lieut. R.O. Rogers, M.O.R.C., U.S.A. to 1/4 K.S.L.I., struck off strength. Captain C. Scales, R.A.M.C. taken on strength from 1/4 K.S.L.I	AJ

Instructions regarding War Diaries and Intelligence Summaries are contained in F. S. Regs., Part II. and the Staff Manual respectively. Title pages will be prepared in manuscript.

Army Form C. 2118.

WAR DIARY
or
~~INTELLIGENCE SUMMARY~~.
(Erase heading not required.)

Place	Date	Hour	Summary of Events and Information	Remarks and references to Appendices
	1918 Jan.			
METZ, Q.19.b.9.1. Sheet 57c	23		Personnel in forward area relieved by 5th. Field Ambulance, 2nd. Division and returned to headquarters.	
	24		Unit relieved by 5th. Field Ambulance, 2nd. Division and proceeded by light railway to billets at ROCQUIGNY (O.27.d.0.4 All transport proceeded by road. Captain A.S.K.Anderson, DSO, MC, detached to A.D.M.S. 63rd.Div	
ROCQUIGNY O.27.d.0.4. Sheet 57c	25		T/Surgeon A.L. Pearce-Gould R.N. taken on strength and detached to V. Corps Main Dressing Station for duty.	
	30		Captain A.S.K.Anderson, DSO, MC, evacuated sick to 48 C.C.S.	

A Young Capt.
for Lieut-Colonel, R.A.M.C.
Commanding,
150th Field Ambulance,
63rd (R.N.) Division.

A5834 Wt. W4973/M687 750,000 8/16 D. D. & L. Ltd. Forms/C.2118/13.

Feb. 1915

No. 150 F. O.

Army Form C. 2118.

Instructions regarding War Diaries and Intelligence Summaries are contained in F. S. Regs., Part II. and the Staff Manual respectively. Title pages will be prepared in manuscript.

WAR DIARY
or
~~INTELLIGENCE SUMMARY~~.
(*Erase heading not required.*)

150th (RN) Field Ambulance

Volume 21.

VR 22

Place	Date 1918	Hour	Summary of Events and Information	Remarks and references to Appendices
ROCQUIGNY, O.27.d.0.4. Sheet 57c.	Feb.9		~~XXXXX~~ D.M.S. Third Army, Surgeon General Sir Murray Irwin, K.C.M.G. inspected camp.	a.h.a.
BARASTRE, O.15.b.5.4. Sheet 57c.	Feb.14		Unit moves from ROCQUIGNY to BARASTRE, Map Ref. O.15.b.5.4. Sheet 57c and takes over the 63rd. (RN) Div. Rest Station.	a.h.a.

C B Knee
Lieut-Col RAMC
Commanding 150th (RN) Field Ambce.

A5834 Wt. W4973/M687 750,000 8/16 D. D. & L. Ltd. Forms/C.2118/13.

150 F.A.

140/2849.

March
1918

Instructions regarding War Diaries and Intelligence Summaries are contained in F. S. Regs., Part II. and the Staff Manual respectively. Title pages will be prepared in manuscript.

150th (R.N.) FIELD AMBULANCE
No.
Date

WAR DIARY
or
~~INTELLIGENCE SUMMARY.~~
(Erase heading not required.)

150 Fd Amb
VR 23

Army Form C. 2118.

Place	Date	Hour	Summary of Events and Information	Remarks and references to Appendices
	MARCH.			
BARASTRE O15 65.4 Sheet 57.C.	1st		Lt. Col. E. B. KNOX R.A.M.C appointed Assistant Director of Medical Services 15th Division, and was struck off the strength of the unit. (authority 183/26 A.D.M.S 63rd Div. 27/2/18) T/Capt. YOUNG R.A.M.C assumed temporary command of the unit.	A.H.K.G
do.	3rd		Lt. A.G. HEARD U.S.A. M.O.R.C proceeded as medical officer to 7th Entrenching Batt. and struck off strength of the unit. (A.D.M.S 109/257 1/3/18)	A.H.K.G
do.	10th		T/Capt. A.S.K. ANDERSON D.S.O. M.C. R.A.M.C and T/Capt. H. YOUNG R.A.M.C appointed acting Majors pending approval and to date January 4th 1918. (authority D.R.O 3815 10/3/18).	A.H.K.G
do.	15th		Lt. A.J. GORDON M.O.R.C. struck off strength of unit - (A.D.M.S 109/267 13/3/18)	A.H.K.G
BARASTRE.	16th	—	Major. G.E. FERGUSON. R.A.M.C. reported his arrival for duty and took over command of the Unit vice Lt. Col. E. BLAKE-KNOX. R.A.M.C. appointed A.D.M.S 15th Division	Ferguson Major

T2134. Wt. W708—776. 500000. 4/15. Sir J. C. & S.

Instructions regarding War Diaries and Intelligence Summaries are contained in F. S. Regs., Part II. and the Staff Manual respectively. Title pages will be prepared in manuscript.

WAR DIARY
or
~~INTELLIGENCE SUMMARY.~~
(Erase heading not required.)

Army Form C. 2118.

Place	Date	Hour	Summary of Events and Information	Remarks and references to Appendices
BARASTRE	16 3/18	✓	Major G. E. Ferguson. R.A.M.C. appointed to rank of T/Lieut-Col. whilst in command of the Unit.	
do.	17 3/18	✓	Visited A.D.M.S. 63rd Division; also G.O.C. 63rd Division to report my arrival. Usual routine work carried out in the Unit.	
do.	18 3/18	✓	A.D.M.S. visited the Divisional Rest Station. Nothing special to note	
do	19 3/18	✓	1st Lieut. R. VINYARD. M.O.R.C. (U.S.A) reported his arrival for duty from No XI General Hospital (ROUEN) + taken on the strength. At 10 a.m. received orders to prepare at once to admit at least 150 slightly "gassed" cases: these were all accomodated by 5pm	
do.	20 3/18	✓	Visited the A.D.M.S. in morning: in afternoon had the usual bi-weekly pay-day. Lieut. + Q.M. R. WILSON. R.H. rejoined from leave.	Ferguson. Lieut. Col. R.A.M.C.
do	21 3/18	✓	Intermittent shelling of the Camp + neighbourhood all day: many huts perforated but no casualties amongst patients or staff. During the day we dealt with 41 cases of wounded men from the neighbourhood.	
do.	22 3/18	✓	Continued bombing + shelling of the whole area during the night + morning; the latter getting especially severe during the afternoon. Several shells landed in or near	

T2134. Wt. W708–776. 500000. 4/15. Sir J. C. & S.

Instructions regarding War Diaries and Intelligence Summaries are contained in F. S. Regs., Part II. and the Staff Manual respectively. Title pages will be prepared in manuscript.

Army Form C. 2118.

WAR DIARY
or
~~INTELLIGENCE SUMMARY.~~
(Erase heading not required.)

Place	Date	Hour	Summary of Events and Information	Remarks and references to Appendices
Barastre. 22/3/18 (Contd).		✓	the camp, but only a few casualties occurred of which only one man had to be sent away viz:- No:- S/3452. Pte. SOUTHGATE F.G. = G.S. wound of buttock: several officers + men of the unit received trivial wounds + remained at duty. One horse killed in the stables during the day. At 3 p.m. orders received for Major. ANDERSON. D.S.O. to relieve Major POWER R.A.M.C. (148th Fd. Amb) at ROYAULCOURT for temporary duty: this move was carried out later in the evening. The unit was placed under orders to move in 1½ hours if necessary as the situation looked serious: all possible patients evacuated by car to the C.C. Station.	J. Jagger Lieut-Col Commandg 100th (R.N.) Field Ambulance
do	23 3/18	✓.	Early in the morning orders were received to evacuate the Rest Station at once + to move to a bivouac area near LES BOEUFS: unit marched off at 11. a.m. having previously got rid of all patients + cleared all the equipment. Arrived at LES BOEUFS about 4 pm. + bivouaced for the night; several patients + stragglers picked up during the day + either sent on or attached to the unit. Visited the A.D.M.S at 6 pm.	
LES BOEUFS	24 3/18	✓	Fairly quiet night: at 7 a.m. I went by motor ambulance round GUILLEMONT + GINCHY area to look for a possible site for a Corps Main Dressing Station — no suitable place found owing to lack of water + it was obvious that troops were retiring on all sides	

T2134. Wt. W708—776. 500000. 4/15. Sir J. C. & S.

Instructions regarding War Diaries and Intelligence Summaries are contained in F. S. Regs., Part II. and the Staff Manual respectively. Title pages will be prepared in manuscript.

WAR DIARY
or
~~INTELLIGENCE SUMMARY.~~
(Erase heading not required.)

Army Form C. 2118.

Place	Date	Hour	Summary of Events and Information	Remarks and references to Appendices
MEAULTE.	24 3/18	✓	-ported this to ADMS on my return at 9 a.m. The Unit moved off at 10 a.m. & moved via GINCHY, CONTALMAISON, FRICOURT, to BECORDEL where we halted for two hours to feed & water. Later moved on to the "TANK Camp" at LE CARCAILLOT outside MEAULTE where we bivouaced for the night. Men & horses marched well; many stragglers picked up & disposed of in various ways during the days march on the crowded roads.	
BOUZINCOURT to LEALVILLERS	25 3/18	✓	Heavy bombing of whole district round ALBERT during the night. At 10am. the march was continued through MEAULTE, DERNANCOURT, ALBERT to BOUZINCOURT where we arrived about 1pm. & went into bivouacs. At 6pm further orders ~~where~~ were received to continue the march to LEALVILLERS; this was carried out & the unit went into billets in the village about 10-30pm after a slow & tedious march on crowded roads. No men fell out & all horses in good condition.	
LEALVILLERS.	26 3/18	✓	The Unit remained at LEALVILLERS throughout the day. Major ANDERSON D.S.O. M.C. rejoined from temporary duty with the 148th Fld. Amb: Major POWER R.A.M.C. rejoined No 148. Field Ambulance.	[signature] Lieut.-Col. Commanding. 150th (N.R.) Fld Amb

Instructions regarding War Diaries and Intelligence Summaries are contained in F. S. Regs., Part II. and the Staff Manual respectively. Title pages will be prepared in manuscript.

WAR DIARY
or
~~INTELLIGENCE SUMMARY.~~
(Erase heading not required.)

Army Form C. 2118.

Place	Date	Hour	Summary of Events and Information	Remarks and references to Appendices
LEALVILLERS.	27 3/18	✓	The Unit remained at LEALVILLERS throughout the day but under orders to move at one hours notice. About 5pm. orders were received for all transport, less Motor Ambulances etc required for collection of casualties to proceed to a bivouac area N.W. of PUCHEVILLERS – they moved off at 7pm accompanied by Capt. SCALES. R.A.M.C.: Lieut TAYLOR R.A.M.C. & the Interpreter. Lieut VINYARD. M.O.R.C. (U.S.A.) accompanied this party. The tent & bearer divisions remained behind. At 8p.m. Majors Anderson & Young went up to the 190th Bgde Hdqrs at SENLIS to ascertain the position & to evacuate any casualties: They returned at 1a.m. & reported that everything was satisfactory & all cases evacuated.	
"	28 3/18.	✓	Unit remained in bivouacs. Reconnoitred CLAIRFAYE FARM with the D.A.D.M.S. during the day with a view to starting a Corps Dressing Station if necessary. Quiet day & nothing special to note – rain started about 4p.m. The bearers that have recently been attached to No. 148 Fld. Amb. rejoined during the day.	
"	29 3/18	✓	No change. The A.D.M.S. visited the Unit & went round CLAIRFAYE which was found to be packed with troops. Major Young. R.A.M.C. visited the 190th Bgde & saw the "daily sick" of the 1/28th (Artists) Rifles. LIEUT. VINYARD. M.O.R.C. (U.S.A). attached for duty to the 1/28th (Artists) Rifles & struck off our strength – vice Capt. DOW. R.A.M.C. Killed at YTRES.	
"	30 3/18	✓	Quiet night & day though some shelling & bombing at intervals. Heavy rain during the night. The u/m officers joined the Unit:– 1/1st Lieuts. M. GREER: K.G. OGLESBY: R.S. O'NEAL M.Os R.C (U.S.A.). Lieuts GREER and O'NEAL sent up to the transport lines for accommodation.	Ferguson Lieut.-Col. Commanding 106th (RN) Fld Amb

A5834 Wt. W4973/M687 750,000 8/16 D. D. & L. Ltd. Forms/C.2118/13.

Instructions regarding War Diaries and Intelligence Summaries are contained in F. S. Regs., Part II. and the Staff Manual respectively. Title pages will be prepared in manuscript.

WAR DIARY
or
~~INTELLIGENCE SUMMARY.~~

(*Erase heading not required.*)

Army Form C. 2118.

Place	Date	Hour	Summary of Events and Information	Remarks and references to Appendices
LEALVILLERS	31/3/18	—	Visited the transport lines at PUCHEVILLERS + found everything correct but they have a very exposed bivouac. Received orders to take over some "Nissen" huts at CLAIRFAYE but on visiting the place, found it still full of troops of the 2nd + Anzac Division: arranged with the OCs of units to take over certain huts as soon as they are evacuated. More rain during the day. The u/m men have been officially reported as "missing" since the 24th inst – they had been attached to No. 148. Field Ambulance for some time + got lost during the retirement:- No:- 3/4070. Pte. A HALTON. " :- 3/4012. " J.W. HALL M.M. " :- S/3648. " G.S. CLARKE. " :- S./3138. " F. KENYON. " :- 3./3654. " W. FORSTER. " :- S./3775. " H. BARTON. The unit is 48 of all ranks ~~the~~ under strength but the remainder of the unit (horses, transport, equipment) is in good order. 31/3/18 Geo. S. Ferguson Lieut - Col R.A.M.C Commanding 150th Field Ambulance	[illegible] Lieut. Col. Commanding 150th Fld Amb

A5834 Wt. W4973/M687 750,000 8/16 D. D. & L. Ltd. Forms/C.2118/13.

Apr. 1918.

140/2900

150th Field Ambulance.

"CONFIDENTIAL" 16

Headquarters.
150th (RN) Field Ambulance.
1st. May 1918.

WAR DIARY OF

150th. (R.N.) FIELD AMBULANCE.

FROM

1st. APRIL 1918.

TO

30th. APRIL 1918.

Volume XXIII

To A.G's Office,
3rd. Echelon.

Lieut-Col. R.A.M.C.
Commanding 150th (RN) Field Ambulance.

Instructions regarding War Diaries and Intelligence Summaries are contained in F. S. Regs., Part II. and the Staff Manual respectively. Title pages will be prepared in manuscript.

WAR DIARY
or
INTELLIGENCE SUMMARY.
(Erase heading not required.)

Army Form C. 2118.

150th (R.N.) FIELD AMBULANCE
No. ______
Date ______

April 1918. Page 1. Vol 24

Place	Date	Hour	Summary of Events and Information	Remarks and references to Appendices
LEALVILLERS	April 1st	✓	All un-employed men went for a route-march under Major Young R.A.M.C. Stores drawn from the B.R. Cross Society by Lieut. WILSON R.M.	
"	2nd	✓	Visited the transport lines at PUCHEVILLERS. In evening received verbal orders to prepare to move into huts at CLAIRFAYE; visited the O.C. of units already in possession + arranged accordingly.	
CLAIRFAYE	3rd	✓	The Unit marched to the Aerodrome at CLAIRFAYE + took over the huts (less 12. occupied by the R.E.). The horse transport under Capt SCALES R.A.M.C. marched from PUCHEVILLERS + arrived about 5 p.m. ample accommodation. In afternoon, the 190th Brigade took over a sector of the line from the 6th Brigade (2nd Division) + I received orders to take over the "collecting" from the front line; this entailed the following movements viz:- Major ANDERSON D.S.O. M.C and 40 other ranks to ENGLEBELMER where an advanced Dressing Station was opened + relay-posts taken over at MESNIL and MARTINSART. Capt. SCALES R.A.M.C. and Lieut OGLESBY M.O.R.C. (USA) accompanied this party. Major Young R.A.M.C. and LIEUT. GREER M.O.R.C. (U.S.A.) and 26 O.Ranks went up to HEDAUVILLE and opened up an advanced Dressing Station in an empty farm. Motor ambulance cars attached to both places.	
"	4th	✓	A quiet night; heavy rain. Visited the A.D.Stn. at HEDAUVILLE + sent up various stores. Lieut TAYLOR R.A.M.C. proceeded to HEDAUVILLE for duty. No. 148. (R.N) Fld. Amb. arrived + took over all spare huts for a "gas" centre.	
"	5th	✓	Heavy rain during the night + some shelling of surrounding areas. Both A.D. Stns very busy. Sent up 12 O.Ranks to HEDAUVILLE for "relief" duty. Three M.T. re-inforcements reported for duty. Lt O'NEILL M.O. (R.C) U.S.A. visited the A.D.Stns at ENGLEBELMER + HEDAUVILLE.	
"	6th	✓	Numerous casualties during the night in front line but all successfully disposed of. Further re-inforcements sent up to HEDAUVILLE to relieve other bearers. The A.D.M.S. visited the Unit. No:- S/3317. Pte W. SMITH. Killed and No:- S/4289. Pte E. GREGORY severely wounded whilst on duty near ENGLEBELMER. No 149. (R.N) Fld Ambulance moved into the aerodrome.	

[signature]
Lieut. Col. R.A.M.C.
O.C. 150th (R.N). Field Ambulance

Instructions regarding War Diaries and Intelligence Summaries are contained in F. S. Regs., Part II. and the Staff Manual respectively. Title pages will be prepared in manuscript.

WAR DIARY
or
~~INTELLIGENCE SUMMARY.~~
(Erase heading not required.)

Army Form C. 2118.

Page 2

Place	Date	Hour	Summary of Events and Information	Remarks and references to Appendices
QAIRFAYE.	April 7th	✓	Heavy rain again. Nothing special to note. Twenty-two N.C.O.s. & men returned from the A.D.Stn	
"	8th	✓	Visited A.D.Stns. at ENGLEBELMER + HEDAUVILLE. Roads in bad condition after the recent rain. Everything in good working order.	
"	9th	✓	Received 34. N.C.Os. + men as re-inforcements. Lieut. O'NEILL. M.O.R.C. (U.S.A.) relieved Capt. SCALES R.A.M.C. at ENGLEBELMER.	
"	10th	✓	Visited the M.O. i/c. units of 190th Brigade + also interviewed the Commanding Officers. Nothing special to note + everything working satisfactorily.	
"	11th	✓	Visited both A.D. Stations + arranged for further reliefs. The D.D.M.S. visited the unit also A.D.M.S. of 35th Division. Lieut. TAYLOR, R.A.M.C. rejoined from HEDAUVILLE	
"	12th	✓	Weather improving + roads drying up. Advanced party of 51st Field Ambulance arrived + went into camp. The following men reported as having been killed owing to the collapse of a small dug-out No: S/4274. Pte. A. BLACK (Medical Unit) + No. S/184031. Pte R.W. ASHFORD (A.S.C. att): death due to suffocation in both cases.	
"	13th	✓	Unit engaged in packing up + ~~to~~ handing over: nothing special to note	
"	14th	✓	Funeral of Ptes. BLACK + ASHFORD. Usual routine work going on.	
"	15th	✓	No 52. Field Ambulance arrived + took over the A.D.Stns. at Englebelmer + Hedauville – also relay posts at MARTINSART + LE MESNIL: most of the Nissen huts at CLAIRFAYE were handed over + this unit moved into a camp pitched near the Transport "hangar". Relief completed by 5pm + all men rejoined from advanced positions. Some barns in LEALVILLERS were also taken over + held by a party of men in case they might be required.	
"	16th	✓	Visited Doullens. One N.C.O. and 3. O.Ranks reported their arrival for duty. Usual routine work carried out + all daily sick collected from the 190th Brigade at ACHEUX.	Pearson Lt Col RAMC OC 150th (RN) Fd Amb

A5834 Wt. W4973/M687 750,000 8/16 D. D. & L. Ltd. Forms/C.2118/13.

Instructions regarding War Diaries and Intelligence Summaries are contained in F. S. Regs., Part II. and the Staff Manual respectively. Title pages will be prepared in manuscript.

WAR DIARY
or
~~INTELLIGENCE SUMMARY.~~
(Erase heading not required.)

Army Form C. 2118.

Page 3.

Place	Date	Hour	Summary of Events and Information	Remarks and references to Appendices
CLAIRFAYE.	April 17th	✓	Visited all M.O. i/c of Units in 190th Brigade at the Medical Inspection Rooms. Inspected Kits of recently joined re-inforcements	
"	18th	✓	Board of inspection of Medical & Surgical Equipment, held on charge of units of 190th Brigade, by Major Young R.A.M.C. and Lieut Wilson R.M.; reports forwarded to A.D.M.S.	
"	19th	✓	Nothing special to note; evacuated 1. Riding and 1. H.D. horse for Veterinary reasons.	
"	20th	✓	Inspection of all S.B. Respirators & drill. Usual routine work carried out	
"	21st	✓	Lieuts GREER and OGLESBY (M.O. R.C. USA) sent to No 107. Fld. Amb. for temporary duty by orders from A.D.M.S. Church parades as usual. At 8pm received orders to move to LA.VICOGNE.	
ON LINE of MARCH.	22nd	✓	The Unit paraded at 11 a.m. and marched to LA.VICOGNE (15 miles): usual billeting parties sent on ahead. Good accommodation & everyone settled in by 6 p.m.	
LA VICOGNE	23rd	✓	Nothing special to note – men employed in cleaning out barns for reception of sick etc.	
"	24th	✓	Route march for all un-employed N.C.Os & men under Lieut. O'NEILL M.O.R.C. Staff Capt 190th Bgde visited the unit.	
"	25th	✓	Usual routine – visited 1/1st ARTISTS Rifles and 7th R. FUSILIERS at TALMAS. At 4 p.m. received orders for one "tent sub-division" and two "bearer sub-divisions" to accompany the 190th Bgde. to the reserve area at TOUTENCOURT.	
"	26th	✓	Reveille at 3.15 a.m. "B" tent sub-division and "B" & "C" bearers sub divisions paraded at 4-30 a.m. under Major ANDERSON DSO & Capt SCALES R.A.M.C. & marched to the Prisoners of War Camp outside Toutencourt & occupied huts. Visited Bgde. H.Q.s during the morning & also our own personnel. About 6pm the "bearer sub-division of "C" section rejoined Headquarters as the alarm was over.	
	27th	✓	Remainder of "B" & "C" Sections returned to LAVICOGNE during the day. Medical Board held on Capt ROSE (OC of No 44 U.P. Indian Labour Company)	
	28th	✓	Usual Church parades. nothing special to note	
	29th	✓	Unit paraded at 10 a.m. – inspection of S.B. Respirators etc. Inspected section equipment & marked off various articles for return to Store as not required.	[signature] Lt Col RAMC O.C. 1/3rd (R.N.) Fld Amb.

A5834. Wt. W4973/M687 750,000 8/16 D. D. & L. Ltd. Forms/C.2118/13.

Instructions regarding War Diaries and Intelligence Summaries are contained in F. S. Regs., Part II. and the Staff Manual respectively. Title pages will be prepared in manuscript.

WAR DIARY
or
~~INTELLIGENCE SUMMARY.~~
(Erase heading not required.)

Army Form C. 2118.

Page 4.

Place	Date	Hour	Summary of Events and Information	Remarks and references to Appendices
LAVICOGNE	April 30th	–	Usual daily parades. Heavy rain during the day. All horses in good condition & personnel of officers, N.C.O.s, & men nearly up to "Establishment". Nothing special to note.	[initials]

[signature] Ferguson
Lieut. Col.
Commanding. 150th (R.N.) Field Ambulance
63rd Division.

A5834 Wt. W4973/M687 750,000 8/16 D. D. & L. Ltd. Forms/C.2118/13.

May 1918.

No. 150 (A.A.) F.A.

140/2983.

"CONFIDENTIAL"

14

Headquarters,
150th(RN) Field Ambulance,
1st June 1918.

WAR DIARY OF

150th. (R.N.) FIELD AMBULANCE.

FROM

1st May 1918.

TO

31st May 1918.

[illegible signature]

Lieut-Col.,R.A.M.C.,

Commanding 150th (R.N.) Field Ambulance.

TO A.G's OFFICE.

3rd ECHELON.

Instructions regarding War Diaries and Intelligence Summaries are contained in F. S. Regs., Part II. and the Staff Manual respectively. Title pages will be prepared in manuscript.

WAR DIARY
or
~~INTELLIGENCE~~ SUMMARY.
(Erase heading not required.)

May 1918.

Army Form C. 2118.

150th (R.N.) FIELD AMBULANCE No. ___ Date ___

Page I.

Vol 24

Place	Date	~~Hour~~	Summary of Events and Information	Remarks and references to Appendices
LAVICOGNE	MAY.	1st.	Nothing special to note. General parade for all sections in "Skeleton order". In afternoon I visited LE MENAGE to arrange about the accomodation in the new area. The G.O.C. 63rd Division inspected the Unit in the evening.	
"	"	2nd.	Marching order parade & route march.	
"	"	3rd.	Warning orders to move to LE MENAGE received also notice that the Division would relieve the 17th Divn. in the line on night of 6th–7th inst. Capt. SCALES. R.A.M.C. awarded the Military Cross.	
"	"	4th.	Major Young. R.A.M.C., Capt SCALES. M.C., & Lieut. TAYLOR R.A.M.C. with a proportion of N.C.O.s & men of 'A' & 'C' sections proceeded to LE MENAGE to take over the billets allotted to the Unit and to open up a new Divisional Rest Station. Special "marching order" parade for all specially employed men etc.	
"	"	5th.	Lieut. VINYARD. M.O.R.C. (U.S.A.) rejoined Hdqrs. from duty with 1st/1st Artist Rifles. at 8 a.m. the Unit (less "B" section & transport of Section) moved to the new billeting area at LE MENAGE. The "B" section under Major Anderson. D.S.O. M.C; Lieuts' O'NEILL; & Lt. VINYARD U.S.A. remain at LE VICOGNE in order to continue the running of the Divisional "Scabies" Station.	
LE MENAGE.	"	6th.	Lieuts OGLESBY and GREER M.O.R.C (U.S.A) rejoined from duty with 107th Fld. Amb. Usual duties	
"	"	7th.	Nothing special to note: patients began to arrive at the new Divisional Rest Station in evening.	
"	"	8th.	"B" section & the "Scabies Station" moved from LAVICOGNE to the Aerodrome at CLAIRFAYE & re-opened in the huts recently occupied by the Unit	
"	"	9th.	Nothing special to report	
"	"	10th.	" " "	
"	"	11th.	Lieut. OGLESBY U.S.A. detailed & left for duty with "B" section at CLAIRFAYE.	[signature] Lieut-Colonel, R.A.M.C. Commanding, 150th Field Ambulance, 63rd (R.N.) Division.

Instructions regarding War Diaries and Intelligence Summaries are contained in F. S. Regs., Part II. and the Staff Manual respectively. Title pages will be prepared in manuscript.

WAR DIARY
or
~~INTELLIGENCE SUMMARY.~~
(Erase heading not required.)

Army Form C. 2118.

Page 2

Place	Date	Hour	Summary of Events and Information	Remarks and references to Appendices
LE MENAGE	MAY 12th	✓	Lieut. VINYARD M.O.R.C. (U.S.A.) placed on the sick list. Nothing special to note.	
" "	13th	✓	Very heavy rain during the past 36 hours: work at the D.R.Stn. going on steadily but delayed owing to lack of wood etc.	
" "	14th	✓	Major ANDERSON D.S.O. M.C. handed over command of "B" Section & the "Scabies Station" at CLAIRFAYE to Lieut. O'NEILL M.O.R.C. (U.S.A.) & reported his departure to join the 15th Division as D.A.D.M.S.	
" "	15th	✓	The D.A.D.M.S. visited the Divn. Rest Station. Sgt-Major ASHTON R.M. (W.O. i/c Horse Transport) struck off the strength of the Unit & handed over his duties to Sgt Major CANHAM (R.M.).	
" "	16th	✓	Capt SCALES M.C. R.A.M.C. proceeded to CLAIRFAYE & took over command of "B" Section & the SCABIES Station. The D.D.M.S. 5th Corps inspected the Divn. Rest Station	
" "	17th	✓	Lieut VINYARD M.O.R.C. (USA) rejoined Hdqrs. from Hospital. Lieut O'NEILL M.O.R.C. (U.S.A.) rejoined Hdqrs from "B" Section.	
" "	18th	✓	Nothing special to note.	
" "	19th	✓		
" "	20th	✓	Sgt Major BULL R.A.M.C. struck off the strength on departure for England: Sgt Major BARNES R.M. took over the duties of Regimental Sgt Major. Lieut. VINYARD M.O.R.C. (USA) sent to No. 3 General Hospital for further treatment.	
" "	21st	✓	Bearer Sub-division at CLAIRFAYE increased by 42 N.C.O.s & men by degrees. Nothing else to note	
" "	22nd	✓		
" "	23rd	✓		
" "	24th	✓	Usual routine work: Officers Rest Station opened on 25th inst.	
" "	25th	✓		

[signature] Lieut-Colonel, R.A.M.C. Commanding, 150th Field Ambulance, 63rd (R.N.) Division.

Army Form C. 2118.

WAR DIARY
or
~~INTELLIGENCE SUMMARY.~~
(Erase heading not required.)

Instructions regarding War Diaries and Intelligence Summaries are contained in F. S. Regs., Part II. and the Staff Manual respectively. Title pages will be prepared in manuscript.

Page 3

Place	Date	Hour	Summary of Events and Information	Remarks and references to Appendices
LEMENAGE.	MAY 26th	✓	Nothing special to note	
"	27th	✓	Lieut. TAYLOR R.A.M.C. proceeded to England on expiration of contract	
"	28th	✓	The A.A. & Q.M.G. inspected the D.R.Stn. otherwise nothing special happened.	
"	29th	✓	The G.O.C. 63rd (R.N.) Divn inspected the D.R.Stn. in company with the A.D.M.S	
"	30th	✓	Warning orders for move to TOUTENCOURT received.	
"	31st	✓	Lt. VINYARD. M.O.R.C. (USA) rejoined from No. 3 General Hospital. Nothing else special to note	

[signature]
Lieut-Colonel, R. A. M. C.
Commanding,
150th Field Ambulance,
63rd (R.N.) Division.

Lieut-Colonel, R. A. M. C.
Commanding,
150th Field Ambulance,
63rd (R.N.) Division.

A5834 Wt. W4973/M687 750,000 8/16 D. D. & L. Ltd. Forms/C.2118/13.

June 1918

160/30 ...

150th F. A.

"CONFIDENTIAL" 14

Headquarters,
150th (R.N.) Field Ambulance.
1st July 1918.

WAR DIARY OF

150th. (R.N.) FIELD AMBULANCE.

FROM

1st June 1918

To

30th June 1918.

To A.G's OFFICE,

3rd ECHELON.

[signature]

Lieut-Col.,R.A.M.C.,

Commanding 150th (R.N.) Field Ambulance.

Instructions regarding War Diaries and Intelligence Summaries are contained in F. S. Regs., Part II. and the Staff Manual respectively. Title pages will be prepared in manuscript.

WAR DIARY
or
INTELLIGENCE SUMMARY.
(Erase heading not required.)

JUNE. 1918

Page I

150th (R.N.) FIELD AMBULANCE
No. ______
Date ______

Army Form C. 2118.

N 26

Place	Date	Hour	Summary of Events and Information	Remarks and references to Appendices
LA. MENAGE (CRAMONT)		June 1st	The D.D.M.S. VI Corps inspected the Unit. Major Scales M.C. R.A.M.C. came over from CLAIRFAYE.	
"	2nd, 3rd, 4th		Nothing special to note. Average number of cases under treatment = 180.	
"	5th	—	The O.C. 149th Fd Ambulance visited the Unit to arrange about "taking over" in near future. Visited the O.C. 'Wings' 63rd (R.N.) Division — baths at CRAMONT now in good working order.	
TOUTENCOURT	6th	—	The Headquarters etc of Unit moved from LA MENAGE to the Aerodrome near the Wood at TOUTENCOURT. One large "Hangar" + several huts taken over + a "Scabies Station" started. The OC + 'B' Section already in possession after moving from CLAIRFAYE	
"	7th	—	A.D.M.S. visited the Camp. Usual routine work + generally settling down. Received warning orders to be prepared to take over the W.W.C. Post from the 36th Fd Amb.	
"	8th	—	Visited A.D.M.S.: also the three battalions of the 190th Bgde. camped in TOUTENCOURT WOOD.	
"	9th	—	Nothing special to note except that orders were received to be prepared to move at 9 hours notice.	
"	10th	—	Lieut. O'NEAL. M.O.R.C. (U.S.A.) and O.R. proceeded to CLAIRFAYE to be prepared to take over the W.W.C. Post from 36th Fd. Amb. Major YOUNG. R.A.M.C. + Lieut VINYARD. M.O.R.C. proceeded to the W.W.C.P. at PUCHEVILLERS + to be prepared to take over from the 12th Division. Medical Board held on N.493782. Gnr. JACKSON. R.F.A.	
"	11th	—	Lecture by Adviser in Pathology: nothing of interest to note	
"	12th	—	St.-Sgt. Booth. R.M. promoted to rank of Q.M. Sgt. The W.W.B.S. moved to Raincheval + taken over from 12th Division.	
"	13th	—	Nothing special to note. Unit under one hours order to move between 6 a.m. + 10 p.m.	

[signature] Lieut-Col. R.A.M.C. O.C. 150th (R.N.) Field Ambulance

A5834 Wt. W4973/M687 750,000 8/16 D. D. & L. Ltd. Forms/C.2118/13.

Army Form C. 2118.

WAR DIARY
or
~~INTELLIGENCE SUMMARY~~.
(Erase heading not required.)

Instructions regarding War Diaries and Intelligence Summaries are contained in F. S. Regs., Part II. and the Staff Manual respectively. Title pages will be prepared in manuscript.

JUNE. 1918. Page. 2.

Place	Date	Hour	Summary of Events and Information	Remarks and references to Appendices
TOUTENCOURT	June 14th	—	Nothing Special to note. No 3066 Cpl. WILSON J.H. taken on strength from 148th Fld. Amb.	
"	15th	—	Lieut GREER. M.O.R.C. detatched for temporary duty with 93rd. Bgde. R.F.A.	
"	16th	—	Nothing special to note.	
"	17th	—	Handed over the W.W.C.P. at CLAIRFAYE + RAINCHEVAL to the 17th Div. (51st Fld Amb). Officers + personnel rejoined Hdqrs.	
"	18th 19th 20th		Nothing special to note.	
"	21st	—	Lieut. VINYARD. M.O.R.C. detatched for temporary duty with 7th Royal Fusiliers. Orders to move to RAINCHEVAL (N.18.d. central) + to take over the W.W.C. Post received.	
"	22nd	—	Unit packing up prior to "move"; a large number of sick sent in from 190th Bgde. + Corps Troops. 190th Bgde moved to ACHEUX. Lieut. O'NEAL. M.O.R.C. with an Advance party went to the Main W.W.C.P. at RAINCHEVAL (N.18.d. Central). Visited O.C. 51st Fld. Amb. + discussed details of handing over + taking over.	
RAINCHEVAL.	23rd	—	The Unit moved to the W.W.C. Post near RAINCHEVAL and "took over from the 51st Fld. Amb. The Field Ambulance Site at TOUTENCOURT ("Aerodrome") handed over to the O.C. 53rd Field Ambulance (17th Division). Major SCALES. M.C. R.A.M.C. attached to 148th (R.N.). Fld. Amb. for temporary duty	
"	24th 25th 26 27th 28th 29th		Nothing of interest to note. Men busily employed erecting huts etc + enlarging the camp for the needs of a Corps Main Dressing Station. The number of "influenza" cases coming in has diminished during the past few days + the old cases are now convalescent.	
	30th	✓	Lieut. VINYARD. M.O.R.C. (U.S.A). rejoined Hdqrs. from temporary duty with 7th R. Fusiliers	[signature] Lieut.-Col. R.A.M.C. O.C. 150th (R.N.) Field Ambulance

[signature] J. E. Ferguson
Lieut-Colonel, R.A.M.C.
Commanding,
150th Field Ambulance,
63rd (R.N.) Division.

A5834 Wt. W4973/M687 750,000 8/16 D. D. & L. Ltd. Forms/C.2118/13.

July 1918.

140/3131

150th F. A.

"CONFIDENTIAL"

14

Headquarters,
150th. (RN) Field Ambulance
1st. August 1918

WAR DIARY OF

150th. (R.N.) FIELD AMBULANCE

FROM

1st.JULY 1918

TO

31st.JULY 1918

W. F. Grant

To A.G's Office,
3rd. Echelon.

Major, R.A.M.C.,
O.C. 150th. (R.N.) Field Ambulance

150th (R.N.)
FIELD AMBULANCE
No.
Date.

Instructions regarding War Diaries and Intelligence Summaries are contained in F. S. Regs., Part II. and the Staff Manual respectively. Title pages will be prepared in manuscript.

150th (R.N.) FIELD AMBULANCE
No.
Date

WAR DIARY
or
INTELLIGENCE SUMMARY.
(Erase heading not required.)

Army Form C. 2118.

Vol 27

Place	Date	Hour	Summary of Events and Information	Remarks and references to Appendices
			July	
RAINCHEVAL	1st	—	Local raid carried out during the night in 5th Corps Area; about 180 patients passed through the W. W. D. Centre. D.D.M.S. Vth Corps visited the Unit.	
	2nd	—	Nothing special to note.	
	3rd		Handed over Command of the Unit to Major Young. R.A.M.C.	
			Major	Lt Col RAMC
	3rd		Took over temporary Command of unit from Lt Col S. S. Ferguson Raine. Lieut-Col. RAMC who was evacuated sick to 3rd Canadian Stationary Hospital.	
	4th		A D M S inspected the Camp.	
	5th		G.O.C. division inspected the Camp.	
	6th		Nothing special to report. Aord Band played in Camp from 4 to 7 p.m.	
	7th		A D M S & D A D V S inspect Camp, & horse lines	
			1st Lt L Lipshitz M.R.C. U.S. taken on strength	
	8th		1st Lt R Vingord M R C U S struck off strength on going to O.C Casual Officers Depot S.O.S.	
	9th		Nothing to report.	
	10th		D.D.M.S. V Corp inspected Camp, & ordered all patients to be cleared to C.C.S. & D.R.S.	

A5834 Wt. W4973/M687 750,000 8/16 D. D. & L. Ltd. Forms/C.2118/13.

Instructions regarding War Diaries and Intelligence Summaries are contained in F. S. Regs., Part II. and the Staff Manual respectively. Title pages will be prepared in manuscript.

WAR DIARY
or
~~INTELLIGENCE SUMMARY.~~
(*Erase heading not required.*)

Army Form C. 2118.

Place	Date	Hour	Summary of Events and Information	Remarks and references to Appendices
	13th		Evacuation of own Brigade from forward area taken over.	H.J.
	15th		Seven O.R. to ENGLEBELMER Collecting Post for duty under O.C. 148 Fd Amb	H.J.
			five O.R. to O.27.b.8.9. Sheet 57.D as holding Party	H.J.
	25th		Personnel in forward area relieved by 63rd Fd. Amb. & rejoined Hd Qtrs. 148 Fd Amb. accomodated for the night	H.J.
	26th		1 Section 148 Fd Amb. remains at N18 D central Sheet 57 D	H.J.
	27		Orders received at midnight to be prepared to move to Assembly positions at short notice (Practice).	H.J.
	28th		Orders received to move to MARIEUX on the 29th	H.J.
H.24.d.9.7 Sheet 57d.	29th		Moved to MARIEUX & took over site of Fd Amb. from 3/2 West Lancs Fd Amb. at H.24 d. 9.7. Sheet 57.D. Transferred to IV Corps.	H.J.
	31st		Handed over Command of unit to Major M.F. Grant. RAMC. H.Young Major RAMC	H.J.
		3pm	MAJ. M.F. GRANT. RAMC assumed command of the F. Amb. in accordance with Third Army. A/A/13549. d/26/7/18 + IV Corps. A/84/9/96 d/27/7/18. W.F. Grant Major RAMC O.C. 150. F Amb.	

A5834 Wt. W4973/M687 750,000 8/16 D. D. & L. Ltd. Forms/C.2118/13.

CONFIDENTIAL.

Aug 1918 21

Headquarters,
150th (R.N.) Field Ambulance
1st Sep 1918.

140/3200.

WAR DIARY OF
150th (R.N.) FIELD AMBULANCE
FROM
1st AUGUST 1918.
To
31st AUGUST 1918.

To A.G's OFFICE,
3rd ECHELON.

W.F. Grant
Lieut-Col., R.A.M.C,
Commanding 150th (R.N.) Field Ambulance.

Instructions regarding War Diaries and Intelligence Summaries are contained in F. S. Regs., Part II. and the Staff Manual respectively. Title pages will be prepared in manuscript.

159th (R.N.) FIELD AMBULANCE
No.
Date

WAR DIARY
or
~~INTELLIGENCE SUMMARY.~~
(Erase heading not required.)

Army Form C. 2118.

VR 28 I

Place	Date	Hour	Summary of Events and Information	Remarks and references to Appendices
MARIEUX	1.8.18		Weather fine and hot.	
		11 am	A.D.M.S. visited the unit, & stated that a move would probably be made to BEAUQUESNE on 3/8/18	
		11.30 am	A.A.Q.M.G. 63rd Div. visited unit.	
		4.30 pm	O.C. proceeded to BEAUQUESNE & interviewed Town Major about billets. Saw billets satisfactory for hospital, unit, also horse lines. Received instructions to transfer patients of this Div. to Corps Rest Stn on 2/8/18 by M.A.C. cars.	
			Admitted (noon to noon) 32. Evacuated 32. Discharged 38.	
		5 pm	Lt. O'NEAL, M.O.R.C. proceeded to 1/R.M.L.I. for temporary duty in accordance with A.D.M.S. instns.	[illegible]
			1 O.R. joined from 149th F.Amb.	
"	2.8.18		Weather wet & mild.	
			Admitted Sick 14, Wounded 9 (8 gassed cases admitted & evacuated by V. Corps Gas centre)	
			Evacuated Sick 14 Wounded 9 (as above)	
			Transferred to 148 F Amb 27. To 65 F.Amb. (Corps Scabies Stn) 12. To duty 6.	[illegible]
"	3.8.18		Wet morning. Cleared later. Mild.	
		6 pm	D.D.M.S. IV Corps visited unit.	
			Admitted 44 Evacuated 14 To Corps Rest Stn 22. To duty 17	[illegible]
	4.8.18		Weather fine	
		5 pm	O.C. proceeded to BEAUQUESNE to interview TOWN MAJOR re billets.	
		6.30 pm	Received orders to march to BEAUQUESNE after dark on night of 4th/5th leaving rear party to look after sick. Maj. SCALES, 17 O.R. to BEAUQUESNE as advanced party.	
		8.45.	Paraded unit – less Maj. YOUNG & 37 O.R., rear party – & marched off.	

A5834 Wt. W4973/M687 750,000 8/16 D. D. & L. Ltd. Forms/C.2118/13.

Instructions regarding War Diaries and Intelligence Summaries are contained in F. S. Regs., Part II. and the Staff Manual respectively. Title pages will be prepared in manuscript.

WAR DIARY
or
~~INTELLIGENCE SUMMARY.~~
(Erase heading not required.)

Army Form C. 2118.

2

Place	Date	Hour	Summary of Events and Information	Remarks and references to Appendices
BEAUQUESNE	4.8.18	11.10pm	Arrived. Billeted men in CINEMA HALL, taken over for hospital purposes. Transport parked at end of village. Admitted 25 Evacuated 7. To C.R.S 40. To Scabies Stn 3. To duty 6	MSG
" "	5.8.18		Weather wet.	
			NCOs & men distributed to billets. CINEMA HALL arranged as hospital. Waggons parked on site near billets	
		11.30am	1 NCO & 5 men sent to O.C. rear party as reliefs.	MSG
		6.30pm	12 O.R. reported from MARIEUX	
" "	6.8.18		Weather showery.	
		10. noon	Maj. YOUNG returned to Hqrs. reported that he had handed over patients, buildings & stores to O.C. 2/2 W. RIDING F.Amb.	
		1pm	Remainder of party from MARIEUX rejoined.	MSG
" "	7.8.18		Weather fine & hot. Routine. Admission 16. Evac. To CCS 5 DRS 4. Duty 1	
" "	8.8.18		Weather warm & cloudy. Showers.	MSG
		12 noon	Orders received at noon to be prepared to move at 1 hours notice	
		12.45pm	" " to move early in afternoon	
		5pm	Received orders to accompany 190th Bgde to vicinity of BEAUCOURT. (SHEET 62D. B.12 central)	
		7pm	Marched off, via RAINCHEVAL, TOUTENCOURT & CONTAY.	MSG
BEAUCOURT Sur L'HALLUE.	9.8.18	1 am	Arrived & camped in field about 62 D, B 12, 4 9.	
		10am	Collected sick from 190th Bgde & in accordance with ADMS instructions, transferred CCS cases to No. 36 F.Amb. MONTIGNY & other cases to No. 31 F.Amb. BEAUCOURT. 16 cases transferred	MSG

A5834 Wt. W4973/M687 750,000 8/16 D. D. & L. Ltd. Forms/C.2118/13.

Instructions regarding War Diaries and Intelligence Summaries are contained in F. S. Regs., Part II. and the Staff Manual respectively. Title pages will be prepared in manuscript.

WAR DIARY

or

~~INTELLIGENCE SUMMARY.~~

(*Erase heading not required.*)

Army Form C. 2118.

Place	Date	Hour	Summary of Events and Information	Remarks and references to Appendices
BEAUCOURT.	10.8.18.		Weather fine & hot.	
		10.30am	Drill parade for unit & American officers	
		11 am	A.D.M.S. visited the unit	
		12 noon	Health inspection.	
		4 pm	Lt R.S. O'NEAL, M.R.C. returned from duty with 1/R.M.L.I.	
		5 pm	Dug trenches as protection against bomb raids & arranged for horses to be scattered on ~~arrival~~ warning of enemy planes. Balance of men of unit to sleep by adjacent reserve trenches.	WSL
" "	11.8.18.		Weather fine & very hot. Routine.	
" "	12.8.18.		Weather very hot & thundery.	WSL
			Drill & box-respirator parades for troops.	
			Arrangements made for horses to be moved S. of the road where better protection exists & they are not so close to the men's lines.	
		6.30pm	A.A.Q.M.G. 63rd Div. visited the camp	WSL
	13.8.18.		Weather fine & hot.	
		10 am	Kit inspection	
		11 am	Moved camp to grounds of adjacent chateau where shade & better protection from observation exists. Men to sleep near trenches as before.	
		12 noon	4 O.R. to leave in U.K.	WSL
			G.O.C. 190th Inf. Bgde. visited the camp.	
		2 pm	Cricket match	

A5834 Wt. W4973/M687 750,000 8/16 D. D. & L. Ltd. Forms/C.2118/13.

Instructions regarding War Diaries and Intelligence Summaries are contained in F. S. Regs., Part II. and the Staff Manual respectively. Title pages will be prepared in manuscript.

WAR DIARY
or
~~INTELLIGENCE SUMMARY.~~
(Erase heading not required.)

Army Form C. 2118.
4.

Place	Date	Hour	Summary of Events and Information	Remarks and references to Appendices
BEAUCOURT.	14.8.18		Weather hot & fine.	
		9.30am	OC. proceeded with ADMS. to call on Divisional Staff	
		10am	Parade for fitting equipment	
		11.45am	Warned that Division was held in readiness to proceed to ~~the~~ IIIrd Army area.	MSG
		12 noon	2 OR on leave to UK. - 1. to Paris. One reinforcement joined	
		1pm	Packing up.	
		10pm.	Paraded & marched to FAMECHON, via HERISSART, PUCHEVILLERS & MARIEUX.	
FAMECHON	15.8.18	3.45am	Arrived & went into billets.	
		11.am	Warned verbally to proceed during the day to THIEVRES.	
		1.pm	Received orders from Bgde to proceed to THIEVRES	MSG.
		3pm.	Paraded & marched.	
THIEVRES		3.30pm	Arrived & billeted.	
			Weather very hot.	
" "	16.8.18		Weather fine & very hot.	
			General routine & settling down into billets. Cricket in afternoon	MSG.
" "	17.8.18.		Weather overcast; cooler; dusty.	
		11pm	3 OR. from leave to UK. Routine.	
		2pm	1st LT. K.G. OGLESBY. U.S. M.R.C. proceed for duty as M.O. to 63rd D.A.C. attached 2/R.I. Regt. under instruction from A.D.M.S. 63rd Div. in place of Capt. M. O'BRIEN. R.A.M.C. who is taken on the strength of this unit.	MSG.

A5834 Wt. W4973/M687 750,000 8/16 D. D. & L. Ltd. Forms/C.2118/13.

Instructions regarding War Diaries and Intelligence Summaries are contained in F. S. Regs., Part II. and the Staff Manual respectively. Title pages will be prepared in manuscript.

WAR DIARY
or
~~INTELLIGENCE SUMMARY.~~
(Erase heading not required.)

Army Form C. 2118.

5

Place	Date	Hour	Summary of Events and Information	Remarks and references to Appendices
THIÉVRES	18.8.18		Weather cloudy & cooler	
		11am	Church Parade – 60 present.	
			Took into use new organisation as shown in attached roll (Appendix I)	WSh. ×
		2.15pm	Cricket match	
" "	19.8.18		Weather cloudy. Fairly cool	
		10am	Squad drill for officers & O.R.	
		1pm	D.A.D.M.S. visited unit & stated that in view of possible operations, Dressing Station at SOUASTRE taken held by 37 Div. be visited	
		2pm	O.C. & O.C. Bearer Divn visited M.D.S. at SOUASTRE & ~~[illegible]~~ & A.D.S. at BIENVILLERS & FONQUEVILLERS.	
		5pm	To A.D.M.S. billet for information	WSh.
		5.30pm	To 190 Bgde for information	
THIÉVRES	20.8.18		Packed & prepared to march.	
	~~12.30am~~	12.30pm	Marched. Bearer Divn proceeded to SOUASTRE.	
PAS		2.30pm	Arrived. Men accommodated in unit tents. Horses in open.	
		10.30 am	O.C. called on A.D.M.S. & received instruction for operation. Arrangements made	
		2.30pm	O.C. proceeded to 190 Bgde HQrs for information, & to Bearer Division to make arrangements. Found 100 stretchers & 200 blankets at SOUASTRE to form dump. On to BIENVILLERS to arrange with O.C. 50th F.Amb. about M.D.S. at FONQUEVILLERS.	
		7.30pm	Returned & reported to A.D.M.S. Found 37 bandsmen had reported at SOUASTRE & 61 at PAS.	

Instructions regarding War Diaries and Intelligence Summaries are contained in F. S. Regs., Part II. and the Staff Manual respectively. Title pages will be prepared in manuscript.

WAR DIARY
or
INTELLIGENCE SUMMARY.
(Erase heading not required.)

Army Form C. 2118.

6

Place	Date	Hour	Summary of Events and Information	Remarks and references to Appendices
PAS.	20.8.18	9pm	Marched to FONQUEVILLERS. Bearer Div. to neighbourhood of ESSARTS. Some time lost in not being allowed to march to SOUASTRE & being obliged to follow unknown tracks.	
FONQUEVILLERS	21.8.18	12.30 am	Arrived. Billeted men in such billets as could be obtained. Found space for horses & transport.	
		6.30 am	Fixed a site for Main Dressing Station on W. side of road at N end of village, opposite A.D.S. of 37th Div. A barn (in bad repair) is available as a receiving room & another similar one as an evacuating ward. One Operating Tent for Walking cases & one for Serious cases. Bell Tents for Resuscitation Ward, Mortuary & overflow.	
		9am	Reported M.D.S. open to A.D.M.S., Brigades & 21 M.A.C.	
		9.30 am	O.C. proceeded to BUCQUOY to get in touch with Bearer Divn. Found it had not been possible to start an A.D.S. but a car post was formed in BUCQUOY. The roads east of this village are practically non-existent & cars cannot pass further except via ABLAINZEVILLE south of the Divl area. O.C. Bearer Divn. had not only got into touch with one unit of the Brigade. Bgde. Hqrs had no knowledge of the situation. Roads bad especially between FONQUEVILLERS & GOMMECOURT.	
		12.15 pm	O.C. returned to M.D.S. Found that no evacuation had taken place & the M.D.S. was uncomfortably full. Met A.D.M.S. who had already taken steps since 10 am to obtain cars.	
		12.30 pm	O.C. proceeded to SOUASTRE in a motor ambulance to get in touch with 21 M.A.C. or obtain assistance from N.Z. F. Amb at that place. Met D.D.M.S. IV Corps. who undertook to expedite the matter & proceeded to his office forthwith.	

A5834 Wt. W4973/M687 750,000 8/16 D. D. & L. Ltd. Forms/C.2118/13.

Instructions regarding War Diaries and Intelligence Summaries are contained in F. S. Regs., Part II. and the Staff Manual respectively. Title pages will be prepared in manuscript.

WAR DIARY
or
~~INTELLIGENCE SUMMARY.~~
(*Erase heading not required.*)

Army Form C. 2118.

7

Place	Date	Hour	Summary of Events and Information	Remarks and references to Appendices
FONQUEVILLERS	21.8.18	2.45 pm	DDGMS visited the unit & instructed O.C. to report on the difficulty in obtaining cars	
		2.50 pm	Several cars arrived. Evacuation good up to 5 pm, at which hour situation was well in hand.	
		5 pm	ADMS visited unit. Cases coming in smaller numbers, evacuation free.	
		6 pm	Numbers received Off 10 OR 273 exclusive of other Divns.	
		9.30 pm	O.C. proceeded to 190 Bgde Hqrs. to ascertain if all requirements were being filled & what the probable course of events would be on the next day. Visited A.D.S.	
			The day has been very hot. The number of patients dealt with between 6 am & 6 pm. were Officers 21, O.R. 353. (including Off. 1. OR. 3. P.O.W.). ~~Between~~ Cases came in steadily all night in rather less numbers.	
			The following officers were attached. Capt. F.O. CLARKE. RAMC & 1st LIEUT JACKSON, U.S. M.R.C. from 149 F. Amb., 1st LIEUT. R. PADDOCK, U.S. M.R.C. from 148. F. Amb., Capt H. STANGER. R.A.M.C., att/63rd M.G. Batt.	
			Chaplains. – Rev. B.C. ROBINSON (C. of E.), REV. P.A. O'SULLIVAN (R.C.) & Rev. R.F. PRIESTLEY (WES.). Several other chaplains assisted from time to time	
" "	22.8.18	12.30 am	O.C. returned from A.D.S. Found cases coming in steadily. Evacuation sufficient	[illegible]
		6 am	Cases admitted since 6 pm 21/8/18, Officers 11, O.R. 266. (including 5 P.O.W.) & 19 [illegible] cases)	
		8. am	Wired to 21 M.A.C. for cars to evacuate cases.	
			No. S/3328 Pte. GREEN HILL slightly wounded	
		10. am	A.D.M.S. visited M.D.S. O.C. 21 M.A.C. arrived & requested that his despatch rider be sent at every clock hour with numbers for evacuation to 1. N.Z. F.Amb. SOUASTRE to report there to representative of M.A.C.	

A5834 Wt. W4973/M687 750,000 8/16 D. D. & L. Ltd. Forms/C.2118/13.

Army Form C. 2118.

7

Instructions regarding War Diaries and Intelligence Summaries are contained in F. S. Regs., Part II. and the Staff Manual respectively. Title pages will be prepared in manuscript.

WAR DIARY
or
~~INTELLIGENCE SUMMARY.~~
(Erase heading not required.)

Place	Date	Hour	Summary of Events and Information	Remarks and references to Appendices
FONQUEVILLERS	22.8.18	noon	Extra (tarpaulin) shelter erected.	
		2.30pm	O.C. 48 F.Amb. called and asked for details of line of evacuation; arranged to meet O.C. at ADS	
		2.45pm	O.C. to A.D.S.; visited relay post + 190th Bgde. Hqrs; ascertained that evacuation was satisfactory, no operation was contemplated tonight + that Div would shortly be relieved.	
		5pm	Corps Commander + DDMS, IV Corps visited Dressing Station.	
		7pm	Returned.	
			Patients received from 6am to 6pm – Off 9 – OR 185 (Off 4, OR 140, 63rd Div), including 24 gassed cases. Cases came in steadily + MAC vehicles were plentiful – evacuation worked smoothly all along the line.	
			A.D.S. formed in BUSH TRENCH (F27, b. 10.2 – Sht. 57d); officers + O.R. of all three F.Ambs. are doing duty at this, which is a conjoint ADS; work + transport is considerably lightened. Three relay posts are established along road in L.4+5. Three RAPs in G.1.d + G.2.c.	WSG
			1st Lt. JACKSON U.S.M.R.C. (149 F.Amb. attached) ordered to report for duty to 2/R.I. Regt. in place of 1st Lt. OGLESBY, U.S.M.R.C. killed.	
			1 O.R. gassed (Pte. COLLINS, E.) + 1 H.T. (Pte CURRY) slightly wounded – to duty. Pte Ashton, killed.	
	23.8.18	12.30am	Received orders from ADMS to hand over relay + car posts to O.C. 50th F.Amb. Sent orders accordingly to O.C. Bearer Divn. after arranging this with O.C. 50th F.Amb. that posts should be shared with us for the present	
		10.30am	ADMS visited ADS.	
		12noon	Cases coming in slowly. Reviewed stores + arranged to collect requirements – shell dressings + suspensory – ADS requirements here.	
		1.30pm	Buried 1st Lt. K.G. OGLESBY at Sheet 57D, E27.a.8.3	

A5834 Wt. W4973/M687 750,000 8/16 D. D. & L. Ltd. Forms/C.2118/13.

Instructions regarding War Diaries and Intelligence Summaries are contained in F. S. Regs., Part II. and the Staff Manual respectively. Title pages will be prepared in manuscript.

WAR DIARY
or
~~INTELLIGENCE SUMMARY.~~
(*Erase heading not required.*)

Army Form C. 2118.

8.

Place	Date	Hour	Summary of Events and Information	Remarks and references to Appendices
FONQUEVILLERS	23/8/18	3 pm	A good many cases, mostly 37th Division, began to come in.	
		6 pm	O.C. proceeded to Adv. ~~D. St~~. Found about 400 cases, almost entirely of other Division had been dealt with & evacuated.	
			Personnel recalled from relay posts.	
			To 190th Bgde. Hqrs. Found this had moved.	
		9.15 pm	Returned.	
			Weather cooler – v. dusty. Quiet morning but a good deal of work in afternoon, mostly of other Division. Admissions 6 pm 22nd to 6 am 23rd – Off. 5. O.R. 142. 6 am 23rd to 6 pm 23rd – Off. 10. O.R. 166. (63rd Div. Off. 3. O.R. 22).	
			Two O.R. of this unit evacuated gassed; one wounded.	W.S.G.
" "	24/8/18	12 noon	A.D.M.S. visited the M.D.S. Warned O.C. that M.D.S. was likely to move today & that it should move in two halves, keeping the Dressing Station at FONQUEVILLERS open till the new one was ready to take in	
		1 pm	D.D.M.S. visited the M.D.S.	
		2 pm	O.C. visited A.D.S. & found it on the point of moving forward. Visited 190th Bgde Hqrs. Went to ACHIET LE PETIT & inspected site of new M.D.S. Returned to Hqrs. & arranged to move with half M.D.S. party & equipment.	
		7.30.	Marched with party & equipment as above.	
		10 pm	Arrived at L.12.c. central (W. of ACHIET LE PETIT).	

A5834 Wt. W4973/M687 750,000 8/16 D. D. & L. Ltd. Forms/C.2118/13.

Army Form C. 2118.

9.

Instructions regarding War Diaries and Intelligence Summaries are contained in F. S. Regs., Part II. and the Staff Manual respectively. Title pages will be prepared in manuscript.

WAR DIARY
or
INTELLIGENCE SUMMARY.
(Erase heading not required.)

Place	Date	Hour	Summary of Events and Information	Remarks and references to Appendices
ACHIET LE PETIT	25.8.18	1.30 am	Opened. Wired to ADMS, 188, 189 & 190 Bgdes & to 21 MAC. Directed O/C M.D.S. at FONQUEVILLERS to close & join main body.	
		5 am	Rear Party rejoined.	
		6. am	Wounded began to arrive.	
		10.30 am	ADMS visited the M.D.S.. Wounded arriving quickly. M.A.C. cars scanty.	
		1.30 pm	AAQMG, 63rd Div., called & promised to have a dust-screen placed along the road & also to supply a motor water tank	
		3pm	O.C. proceeded to A.D.S. at G.28.c.10.10. which had been established at 6.30 a.m. This is simply a car post in a field: also used by 149 F.Amb. There are 4 relay posts in connection with it - one at either end of LOUPART WOOD, one in front of the wood & one further forward, manned by NCOs & men of 149 & 150 F.Amb. O.C. visited 3 posts; found the men very footsore & arranged for clean socks to be issued. Visited 190th Bgde. HQrs. & learned that a fresh offensive was contemplated tomorrow morning.	
		6pm	O.C. returned to M.D.S. Found M.D.S. crowded with lying cases & a great scarcity of MAC cars. Walking cases had been got away fairly satisfactorily in empty Supply lorries. Found party of 14/WORCESTERS erecting dust shelter along the road.	
		6.45 pm	DDMS, IV Corps, visited M.D.S. & was informed that only 23 MAC cars had been received during the day & that there were over 70 stretcher cases awaiting evacuation.	
		7pm	M.A.C. cars began to arrive in sufficient quantities & were loaded.	
		9pm	Heavy thunderstorm.	
		10pm	All British stretcher cases evacuated. Some German prisoners remaining.	
			The day was hot, but with a good breeze. The following cases were admitted between 6 am	

A5834 Wt. W4973/M687 750,000 8/16 D. D. & L. Ltd. Forms/C.2118/13.

Instructions regarding War Diaries and Intelligence Summaries are contained in F. S. Regs., Part II. and the Staff Manual respectively. Title pages will be prepared in manuscript.

WAR DIARY
or
~~INTELLIGENCE SUMMARY.~~
(Erase heading not required.)

Army Form C. 2118.

10

Place	Date	Hour	Summary of Events and Information	Remarks and references to Appendices
			+ 6 pm. Officers 32 (4 P.O.W.) O.R. 619 (78 P.O.W.). 19 Officers + 452 O.R. belonged to 63rd Div.	
			Owing to the scarcity of M.A.C. cars, evacuation was not satisfactory; owing to insufficient shelter (no buildings being available) a large number of wounded were obliged to lie out in the sun.	
			Received a few Thomas' splints + slings from O.C. 21 M.A.C. who called during the evening	
ACHIET LE PETIT.	26.8.18	9.20 am	O.C. M.A.C. called to enquire what assistance was needed; the M.D.S. was practically clear.	
		10. am	10 Bandsmen, Anson Bn., arrived + were sent to A.D.S. for duty there + in nearest posts.	
		2.30 pm	O.C. Bearer Division reported personally that all was clear at the A.D.S. + RAPs + that everything was quiet	
		11 am	Indented on M.A.C. for 100 blankets + 50 stretchers.	
		4.30 pm	A.A.Q.M.G. 63rd Div. called. Motor water tank arrived. Drew material for building additional shelters	
		4.40 pm	D.D.M.S. IV Corps visited M.D.S.	
			Admitted between 6 pm. 25/8/18 + 6 am 26/8/18 Officers 5. O.R. 141. Between 6 am + 6 pm. 26/8/18 Off 7. O.R. 141.	
			Weather colder; slight rain in morning fine later.	
		8 pm	15 Bandsmen of ANSON Bn. reported + were sent to A.D.S. for duty.	
" "	27.8.18		Preceding night was quiet, only 31 cases being received.	
		9.30 am	O.C. M.A.C. called to enquire what assistance was required	
		11.30 am	A.D.M.S. visited M.D.S. + informed O.C. that Division was likely to be relieved tonight + that M.D.S. would be retained. T/Surgeon J.R. BARROW-CLOUGH R.N. + 4 O.R. reported for duty.	
			Evacuated walking cases to PUISIEUX by returning Ammunition lorries + sent ~~2~~ 2. N.C.Os + 4 men to PUISIEUX for duty, in accordance with orders.	
		1.30 pm	Representative of 21 M.A.C. called + was informed that casualties were expected later in the day.	
		1.45 pm	O.C. proceeded to A.D.S. Visited H.Q. 190 Bgde + learned that an attack was in preparation for about 6 pm; that wounded were satisfactorily cleared. Visited relay posts + R.A.Ps.	
		6.30 pm	Returned	

A5834 Wt. W4973/M687 750,000 8/16 D. D. & L. Ltd. Forms/C.2118/13.

Instructions regarding War Diaries and Intelligence Summaries are contained in F. S. Regs., Part II. and the Staff Manual respectively. Title pages will be prepared in manuscript.

WAR DIARY
or
~~INTELLIGENCE SUMMARY.~~
(Erase heading not required.)

Army Form C. 2118.

11

Place	Date	Hour	Summary of Events and Information	Remarks and references to Appendices
ACHIET LE PETIT	27.8.18	7.30 pm	D.D.M.S. IV Corps visited M.D.S. enquired about evacuation &c.	
			Admissions ~~since~~ between 6 am & 6 pm. Off 6 OR 155.	
			The weather was cooler; rain in afternoon & evening; cold.	
			The morning was quiet, but patients arrived steadily during the afternoon. Evacuation was satisfactory.	
			Commenced erection of fresh shelters	
			O.C. 1/1 E. LANCS F. Amb. (42nd Div.) called at A.D.S. to enquire about the line & posts.	W.S.G.
"	28.8.18	4.15 am	Line of 190th Inf. Bgde. reported cleared of casualties.	
		5.30 pm	M.D.S. clear of cases	
		9.30 pm	Relief of A.D.S. & posts completed.	
		10.30 am	A.D.S. party reported. Issued with clean clothing.	
		11. am	A.D.M.S. visited M.D.S. & arranged that F. Amb. should collect sick from their own Brigades & that all C.C.S. & D.R.S. cases should be collected at M.D.S. ~~[illegible]~~ for evacuation. Each F. Amb. to attach one motor ambulance to 150th F. Amb. for the purpose.	
		11.15 am	O.C. 21. M.A.C. called. A.D.M.S. arranged with him to attach 2 cars to M.D.S. for evacuation.	
		4.15 pm	D.D.M.S. IV Corps visited M.D.S. & discussed the question of Walking Wounded evacuation	
		5 pm	Sick arrived & were evacuated	
		6 pm	Attached bandsmen were returned to their units - exc. Band of M.G. Bn. which had left at 11.30 am	
			Patients admitted between 6 pm 27th & 6 am 28th. - Off 6 & O.R. 217.	
			The weather was cold & showery.	W.S.G.

Army Form C. 2118.

12

Instructions regarding War Diaries and Intelligence Summaries are contained in F. S. Regs., Part II. and the Staff Manual respectively. Title pages will be prepared in manuscript.

WAR DIARY
or
~~INTELLIGENCE SUMMARY.~~
(Erase heading not required.)

Place	Date	Hour	Summary of Events and Information	Remarks and references to Appendices
ACHIET LE PETIT	29.8.18		Weather fine but cloudy. Cold N wind	
			Routine. Collected & evacuated sick of Division & neighbouring troops to D.R.S. & C.C.S.	
		6.30 pm	D.D.M.S. IV Corps visited ~~the~~ M.D.S.	
		8 pm	Despatched 1 Sgt. H.P.R. to A.P.M. PARIS as escort for prisoner.	WJG
			Some rain in night	
" "	30.8.18		Routine	
		11.30 am	D.A.D.M.S. called & said that there was a possibility of the Division going into the line again shortly & O.C. went with D.A.D.M.S. to select site of M.D.S. Suitable site found at 57c. Sq. H 31 a. 3.6, E of GREVILLERS with a few sheds; good evacuation via GREVILLERS & by ALBERT–BAPAUME Rd	
		2 pm	Representative of O.C. 21 M.A.C. called & had situation explained to him	
		4 pm	Warned to be in readiness to march to AYETTE (XVII Corps)	
			Commenced packing & arranged a dump of surplus stretchers & material. Requested O.C. 21 M.A.C. to collect, as other F. Amb. of other Division had moved	
		10 pm ~~9.30 pm~~	Marched with 190 Bgde. Left dump of surplus stores at site of old M.D.S.	
			Weather fine but cold wind	WJG
BOIRY STE RICTRUDE	31.8.18	1.30 am	Arrived & bivouacked at Sht. 51 B. Sq. S.8.b.1.1. Rain	
			Collected sick & evacuated to C.R.S. at GOUY EN ARTOIS & C.C.S. BAC DU SUD	
		6 pm	Received maps & operation orders.	
			Weather cold & cloudy. Wind.	

W J Grant

A5834 Wt. W4973/M687 750,000 8/16 D. D. & L. Ltd. Forms/C.2118/13.

APPENDIX to 150th. (RN) Field Ambulance Order No.0811 dated 19-8-18

TENT DIVISION

Major H. Young R.A.M.C. Captain M. O'Brien R.A.M.C.
Sgt.Major Barnes R.M.

S.Sgt.Fitton R.)
Pte.Buxton W.) Orderly Room
Pte.Woodhead W.)

Q.M.S. Booth D. Steward

Sgt.Swain E.E.)
Cpl.Evens F.C.) Pack Stores

A/Cpl.Burton J.)
Pte.Lawton Hd.) Stores

Sgt.Crowston A. General Duties

Sgt.Tong W.)
Sgt.Dun W.C.) Dispensers

S.Sgt.Duckworth E.E.)
Sgt.Leake R.) Nursing

Sgt.Hulme S.)
Pte.Gibson S.) Clerks

Sgt.Findley W.)
Cpl.Entwistle J.) Cooks
Pte.Heap J.)
Pte.Harkness A.E)

Pte.Cuthbert)
Pte.Hargreaves) Water Carts

LCpl.Hodson W,)
Pte.Burn J.) Sanitary

Pte.Ferriday E.)
Pte.Slater H.) Sergts.Mess

LCpl.Wright W.)
Pte.Shanks F.) Officers Mess
Pte.Ingham W.) &
Pte.Knowles J.C.) Batmen
Pte.Woodhouse A.)
Pte.Rayner F.)

Pte.Morris P. Postman

Pte.Ashton J. Despatch Rider

Pte.May J. Tailor

Pte.Wood F. Cobbler

LCpl.Swallow C.)
Pte.Rawstron H.) Evacuations

Pte.Venus L. Divl.Train

Nursing Orderlies :-
Pte.Dickie M.L.
Pte.Penny R.T.
Pte.Taylor A.
Pte.Somerville J.
Pte.Richardson S.
Pte.Brown W.
Pte.Tallantire S.V.
Pte.Phillips C.G.
Pte.Moseley P.
Pte.Salisbury J.V.
Pte.Curley J.
Pte.Castle T.C.
Pte.Brooks W.T.
Pte.Penkett W.
Pte.Sykes C.A.

BEARER DIVISION

Major C. Scales M.C, R.A.M.C. 1st.Lieut. R.S. O'Neal U.S.M.R.C.
1st. Lieut. L. Lipshitz U.S.M.R.C.
Staff Sgt. Childs H.

At ADS

Sgt. O'Connor T. (Nursing)
Cpl.Wooding J. (Pack Stores, Rations, etc.)
Pte.Makin J. (Clerk)
Pte.Ward A. (Clerk)
Pte.Constantine H.B. (Water Cart)
Pte.Smith H. (Nursing Orderly)
Pte.Sills A. (do.)
Pte.Dean J. (do.)
Pte.Cowie F. (do.)
Pte.Litherland A. (do.)
Cpl.Hodgson J. (Cook)
Pte.Nutter E. (Cook)
Pte.Mordue J. (Batman)
Pte.Holroyd F.T. (Sanitary)

Wagon Orderlies :-
Pte.Armstrong J.T.
Pte.Holt T.
Pte.Chisholm J.R.

BEARER DIVISION (Contd.)

Section 1

Staff Sgt. Childs H.

Cpl.Tomlin E.S.
Pte.Williams T.
Pte.Cardy H.H.
Pte.Baxendale J.
Pte.Minnikin A.
Pte.Collins E.
Pte.Greenhill W.
Pte.Butler P.
Pte.Hunter J.C.
Pte.Kirk D.F.
Pte.Lamb F.
Pte.Fletcher H.

Cpl.Wilson J.M.
Pte.Moxon Hd.
Pte.Bradley L.
Pte.Bushell J.R.
Pte.Fletcher J.W.
Pte.Curtis J.
Pte.Yerrell J.W.
Pte.Green A.H.
Pte.Paxton R.
Pte.Law J.
Pte.Marr S.N.
Pte.Leaver F.

LCpl.Constantine A.
Pte.Moxon Hy.
Pte.Clarkson R.M.
Pte.Radcliffe J.
Pte.Gresty H.S.
Pte.Craven C.
Pte.Barrett J.F.
Pte.White R.
Pte.Newby W.
Pte.Worrall H.
Pte.Broome G.

Section 2

Sgt.Brien C.P.

Cpl.Compston R.
Pte.Ackroyd A.
Pte.Vose C.
Pte.Hawley L.
Pte.Hodgson G.W.
Pte.Harrop W.E.
Pte.Redpath T.
Pte.Beal J.C.
Pte.Robinson F.
Pte.Riddle J.
Pte.Hindle H.
Pte.Wild J.

LCpl.Lawton R.
Pte.Ainscough M.
Pte.Bateson J.
Pte.Gazey A.H.
Pte.Brown G.R.
Pte.Coop J.
Pte.Brooks J.
Pte.Kirkbride H.
Pte.Wiggans H.
Pte.Moore S.T.
Pte.Salisbury T.E.

Pte.Almond J.
Pte.Garside A.
Pte.Murphy F.
Pte.Lawton Ht.
Pte.Mitchell S.
Pte.Bowden J.
Pte.Taylor H.B.
Pte.Chambers N.
Pte.Morton E.
Pte.Robinson J.T.
Pte.Iles A.C.G.

Section 3

Sgt.Clewes W.

Cpl.Beaty H.F.
Pte.James F.W.
Pte.Nicholl J.W.
Pte.Wilcock T.
Pte.Kay A.D.
Pte.Fletcher H.
Pte.Mills G.A.
Pte.Henderson R.G.
Pte.Robinson W.N.
Pte.Penkethman A.
Pte.Hall J.
Pte.Mack W.

LCpl.Hampson J.
Pte.Grimshaw J.
Pte.Bateman H.F.
Pte.Christian C.J.
Pte.Parkinson E.
Pte.Mills E.
Pte.Thelwall F.B.
Pte.Hoyle J.J.
Pte.Russon W.J.
Pte.Gardener A.
Pte.Hilton R.

LCpl.Spence F.A.
Pte.Grey J.A.
Pte.Bedford P.
Pte.Marren M.
Pte.Sargeant S.A.
Pte.Butterworth W.
Pte.Andrew H.
Pte.Barton J.W.
Pte.Houghton J.D.R.
Pte.Hepplestone S.
Pte.Parr H.

"CONFIDENTIAL"

19

Headquarters,
150th(RN) Field Ambulance.
1st October 1918.

WAR DIARY OF

150th (R.N.) FIELD AMBULANCE

FROM

1st SEPTEMBER 1918

TO

30th SEPTEMBER 1918.

W A Grant

To A.G's Office,
3rd Echelon.

Lieut-Col.,R.A.M.C.,
Commanding 150th (R.N.) Field Ambulance.

Instructions regarding War Diaries and Intelligence Summaries are contained in F. S. Regs., Part II. and the Staff Manual respectively. Title pages will be prepared in manuscript.

150th (R.N.) FIELD AMBULANCE
No. ______
Date ______

WAR DIARY
or
~~INTELLIGENCE SUMMARY.~~
(Erase heading not required.)

Army Form C. 2118.

I

VR 29

Place	Date	Hour	Summary of Events and Information	Remarks and references to Appendices
BOIRY STE RICTRUDE	1/9/18	11 am	O.C. + Bearer Officer proceeded to CROISILLES + FONTAINE to see A.D.S. of 57th Divn. Called at XVII Corps Main Dressing Stn. near HENIN to arrange where to send Tent Subdivn. as instructed	
		2.30 pm	Returned. 140 bandsmen, attached for duty - not to be used in front of A.D.S. - reported	
			Received orders to march about 5 pm	
		3 pm	To 190th Bde. H.Q. - conference of C.Os.	
		4.50 pm	Marched to Sht. 57 B S.7.8 central	
		8 pm	Arrived + bivouacked. Considerable enemy bombing activity.	W.S.L.
		9.30 pm	Sent 1st Lieut. O'Mead + Paddock, with 18 O.R. to Corps M.D.S. 5 O.R. reported from leave. Weather fine, cold wind.	
Nr HENIN SUR COJEUL.	2/9/18	7.30 am	Sent 2 squads of bearers to each unit of the Brigade. Applied to Corps M.D.S. for 50 stretchers	
		8 am	Proceeded with A.D.S. party to CROISILLES, leaving H.Q. + remainder of A.D.S. party, bandsmen (less 50), Transport (less Motor Ambulances, 2 limbers + 1 watercart) under Lt + Qmr WILSON at HENIN	
		10 am	Arrived CROISILLES. O.C. proceeded to FONTAINE to ascertain situation. Met D.A.D.M.S. Found roads + paths impassable + unsuited for evacuation but ascertained there was a good road to BULLECOURT.	
		11 am	Marched to HENDECOURT via BULLECOURT	
		1 pm	Arrived HENDECOURT + erected A.D.S. in tents at V.11 b 2.2 on bad ground - shell holes - but avoided Heavy Shelling	
		2.30 pm	Reported A.D.S. open + established car post at V.13 on CAGNICOURT road. Some difficulty in evacuating owing to car shortage + failure to obtain assistance from 15 M.A.C. in spite of several requests	
		5 pm	One lorry arrived	
		7.30 pm	Obtained lorries working an ammunition for walking cases.	

Instructions regarding War Diaries and Intelligence Summaries are contained in F. S. Regs., Part II. and the Staff Manual respectively. Title pages will be prepared in manuscript.

WAR DIARY
or
~~INTELLIGENCE SUMMARY.~~
(*Erase heading not required.*)

Army Form C. 2118.

2

Place	Date	Hour	Summary of Events and Information	Remarks and references to Appendices
HENDECOURT	2.9.18	9.30 pm	A.D.S. practically clear.	
		10 pm	Rather a rush of wounded – mostly Germans.	
		12 pm	Two motor lorries received from 15 M.A.C.	
			Weather fine; rather cool. Some showers.	WSL
			190th Infy. Bgde. were in reserve; bearers not engaged.	
" "	~~3.9.18~~		Increased A.D.S. party by 2 N.C.Os. for night duty & sent for additional lamps & tents.	
			MAJ. ROBERTSON, 1st LT. BROWN (U.S. MRC) & Capt HUNTER (att C.R.E.) were attached to A.D.S. for duty.	
			1st Lt BROWN was sent to Corps M.D.S. for duty in relief of 1st Lt PADDOCK, detailed for duty with a Bn.	
			Indented (at 4.45 pm) on Corps M.D.S. for 100 blankets.	
" "	3.9.18	1. am	9 cases remaining.	
		2.30 am	1 car received from M.A.C. – A.D.S. Cleared.	
		10.30 am	O.C. proceeded to Hqrs 190 Bgde & ascertained that a forward movement was intended.	
		1.45 pm	O.C. to CAGNICOURT to reconnoitre a site for A.D.S. Found suitable ground for tents at V.5.c.1.8.	
		12.30 pm	A.A.Q.M.G. called. Arranged with D.A.D.M.S. to send T/Surgeon BARROW-CLOUGH to Corps M.D.S. in relief of 1st Lt R. S. O'NEAL, U.S. MRC. (struck off strength & posted to HOOD Bn.)	
		5.00 pm	Moved half A.D.S. to CAGNICOURT.	
CAGNICOURT		6.15 pm	Arrived & found selected site occupied by artillery. Found good accommodation with dug-out & cellar at chateau (V.15.a.8.5)	
		9 pm	Reported A.D.S. open. Arranged for Rear Hqrs. to move to HENDECOURT.	WSL
			190th Infy. Bgde. not in action	

Instructions regarding War Diaries and Intelligence Summaries are contained in F. S. Regs., Part II. and the Staff Manual respectively. Title pages will be prepared in manuscript.

WAR DIARY
or
~~INTELLIGENCE SUMMARY.~~
(Erase heading not required.)

Army Form C. 2118.

3

Place	Date	Hour	Summary of Events and Information	Remarks and references to Appendices
CAGNICOURT	4.9.18	1.30 am	Remainder of ADS part reported from HENDECOURT. ADS is in the area of the Canadian Corps + a large proportion of the admissions are Canadian – about half. Sick + wounded coming in slowly.	
		2.30 pm	A.D.S. practically clear	
		3.30 pm	O.C. to Rear H.Q.	
		4 pm	190th Infy. Bgde. moved up into line in support. Bearers accompanied Bgde.	
		6.30 pm	O.C. to HINDENBURG SUPPORT LINE to get in touch with Brigade + Bearers. Found Bgde. H.Q. had moved back. Found bearer officer + decided that nothing further arrangements could be made tonight as arrangements were uncertain.	
		11.45 pm	Returned	
			Applied during the day to D.D.M.S. for get [illegible] cleared of other troops raised for hospital purposes only. Informed that it was not in Corps area.	
			Weather fine – warmer. Sick 26 Wounded 69 – about half (63rd Div) – evacuated between 6am + 6pm by the [illegible]	
CAGNICOURT	5.9.18	6 am	Weather warm. Conditions quiet.	
		12 noon	A.A.Q.M.G. visited A.D.S. 112 cases (5 gassed – mostly slight) received since 6 pm on 4th.	
		12.30 pm	O.C. visited posts. Arranged for a car post at D.12.a. (just west of MOEUVRES) with evacuating post cutting out Foxhole(?). R.A.P. of 7/R Fusiliers is a considerable distance from the road + involves a long carry. Evacuation via DROUVILLE.	
		7 pm	O.C. returned. Informed that Walking Wounded portion of Corps M.D.S. had moved to [illegible] of [illegible]COURT by 5th	
			The night was quiet. 28 admissions (14 sick).	
CAGNICOURT	6.9.18	9.30 am	Bearer Officer proceeded to reduce posts. Reported that 7/R Fus. had closed in to their left, which greatly simplifies evacuation.	

A5834 Wt. W4973/M687 750,000 8/16 D. D. & L. Ltd. Forms/C.2118/13.

Instructions regarding War Diaries and Intelligence Summaries are contained in F. S. Regs., Part II. and the Staff Manual respectively. Title pages will be prepared in manuscript.

WAR DIARY
or
~~INTELLIGENCE SUMMARY.~~
(Erase heading not required.)

Army Form C. 2118.

4

Place	Date	Hour	Summary of Events and Information	Remarks and references to Appendices
CAGNICOURT	6.9.18	12.30 pm	2 M.A.C. cars in the [illegible]	
		1.30 pm	Heavy thunderstorm. Roads very heavy & muddy.	
		2.30 pm	O.C. called at 190th Infy. Bgde. Hqrs. & learnt that the Divn. expected to be relieved on the following night. To QUEANT to reconnoitre site for alternative A.D.S.	
		7 pm	2 officers of 57th Div. called to arrange about taking over	
		9 pm	Village [illegible] - one [illegible] near A.D.S. - [illegible]	
			The condition of the road between CAGNICOURT & HENDECOURT was so bad that evacuation was suspended.	[illegible]
			22 wounded & 10 sick admitted during the night. (to 6 am 7th)	
CAGNICOURT	7.9.18		Weather hot & thundery. Very few admissions during the morning. A.D.S. [illegible] [illegible] [illegible] [illegible] [illegible] [illegible]	
		5.30 pm	2/2 Wessex F. Amb. arrived to take over the car [illegible] post	
		7.30 pm	As the 2/2 W. LANCS F. AMB. had not arrived, O.C. 2/2 WESSEX F. Amb. took over A.D.S.	
		7.30 pm	[illegible]	[illegible]
		10 pm	Arrived at U.19, near CROISILLES; [illegible]	
CROISILLES	8.9.18		Cloudy, [illegible]	
		11 am	O.C. to 190th Infy. Bgde. Hqrs.; ascertained that move would be made tonight to [illegible] at BOYELLES	
		1 pm	Transport (less Motor Amb. [illegible]) [illegible]	
		3.30 pm	Heavy rain	
		4.30 pm	O.C. to BOYELLES by car to reconnoitre road. Called at [illegible] A.D.S. & ascertained that Tent Sub. [illegible] there has been recalled [illegible]	

A5834 Wt. W4973/M687 750,000 8/16 D. D. & L. Ltd. Forms/C.2118/13.

Instructions regarding War Diaries and Intelligence Summaries are contained in F. S. Regs., Part II. and the Staff Manual respectively. Title pages will be prepared in manuscript.

WAR DIARY
or
~~INTELLIGENCE SUMMARY.~~
(Erase heading not required.)

Army Form C. 2118.

5

Place	Date	Hour	Summary of Events and Information	Remarks and references to Appendices
CROISILLES	8.9.18	6pm	3 motor ambulances left for BAILLEULVAL with instructions for them to meet Brigade [illegible] at LAHERLIERE at 7 am on 9th	[illegible]
CROISILLES	9.9.18	1.30 am	Parades [illegible] V. heavy going. Rain. Picked up [illegible] for [illegible] on [illegible]	
BOYELLES		2.30 am	Arrived	
		5 am	[illegible]	
LAHERLIERE		10.30 am	Detrained [illegible]	
BAILLEULVAL		1.30 pm	Arrived & took over [illegible] Div. [illegible] in Sandbagged Nissen Hut	[illegible]
		4pm	Received orders to move to BLAIREVILLE	
		5.30pm	At [illegible] ADMS [illegible] learnt that it was desired to [illegible] F Amb site at BLAIREVILLE [illegible]	
BAILLEULVAL	10.9.18	10 am	Capt. Hunter RAMC [illegible] CRE. Heavy rain.	
		10.30	Paraded [illegible]	
BLAIREVILLE		1pm	Arrived. Took over F Amb site close to [illegible]	
			New Sunbeam Motor Amb (No.19) received	[illegible]
"	11.9.18		Weather showery. Routine. Bathing, [illegible]	[illegible]
"	12.9.18		Weather wet. Heavy showers	
		12 noon	G.O.C. 63 (RN) Div. [illegible] the [illegible]	
		1pm	[illegible] 190 Bde [illegible] 1 2 [illegible] each Inf. Bde in accordance with [illegible] orders [illegible]	
		3pm	Sent [illegible] [illegible] Div. [illegible]	[illegible]

A5834 Wt. W4973/M687 750,000 8/16 D. D. & L. Ltd. Forms/C.2118/13.

Instructions regarding War Diaries and Intelligence Summaries are contained in F. S. Regs., Part II. and the Staff Manual respectively. Title pages will be prepared in manuscript.

WAR DIARY
or
~~INTELLIGENCE SUMMARY.~~
(Erase heading not required.)

Army Form C. 2118.

7.

Place	Date	Hour	Summary of Events and Information	Remarks and references to Appendices
ST. LEGER.	21.9.18		Weather cold. Succession of heavy showers in morning. Finer later. Routine	WSL
" "	22.9.18.		Weather fine in morning - rain in afternoon & evening. Cold. Routine	
" "	23.9.18		Weather cloudy, some rain in morning - fine later. Routine. Squad drill.	WSL
" "	24.9.18		Weather fine. Routine	WSL
		4 pm	O.C. called on ADMS + 190 Bdge Hqrs. with reference to active operation	WSL.
" "	25.9.18		Weather showery to fine. Routine. One officer in car to reconnoitre new area.	
		3 pm	O.C. visited 190th Bgde Hqrs. for information.	WSL
" "	26.9.18	12.30 pm	Maj. Scales + 65 O.R. (Bearers) proceeded to join 190th Infy. Bgde. at concentration area (Sht. 57 C Sq. D.14.	
		1 pm	Remainder of unit marched	
LOUVERVAL.		4.30 pm	Arrived & camped at J.9.b. Weather fine	WSL
" "	27.9.18.	5.20 am	Zero hour. Bearers follow Brigade.	
		7 am	O.C. with Surg. BARROW-CLOUGH, a small Collecting Stn. party & all cars & horsed ambulances forward up BAPAUME-CAMBRAI Rd. as far as K.1.b. On reconnoitring, 3 large craters were found forward of this point & the road was impassable for cars; road also swept by machine guns. Therefore found suitable place in road & down to canal bed. In canal bed, information received that enemy still held LEOPOLD AVENUE, parallel with canal. Worked back by trenches to MOEUVRES to find Bearer Officer. Found 4/BEDFORD R.A.P. west of village & learnt that Brigade had advanced. Found 3 passages over canal. Found a relay post across canal, about E.15.c.6.0. Found R.A.Ps & Bgde. Hqrs in HINDENBURG LINE. Ascertained that Bgde. had taken its first objective & were well on with 2nd phase	

A7092 Wt. W128 9/M1293 750,000. 1/17. D. D & L. Ltd. Forms/C2118/14.

Instructions regarding War Diaries and Intelligence Summaries are contained in F. S. Regs., Part II. and the Staff Manual respectively. Title pages will be prepared in manuscript.

WAR DIARY
or
~~INTELLIGENCE SUMMARY.~~
(*Erase heading not required.*)

Army Form C. 2118.

6

Place	Date	Hour	Summary of Events and Information	Remarks and references to Appendices
BLAIREVILLE	13.9.18		Weather showery, with bright intervals. General Routine & cleaning up. Scabies inspection & Respirator Drill.	
		5pm	Meeting of unit to discuss suggestion for subscription to Prisoners of War Fund. WSL	
" "	14.9.18		Weather fine & cloudy. Routine. Divl. Race Meeting - 30 O.R. attended. WSL	
" "	15.9.18		Weather fine & warm	
		6pm	Orders received for move at 8.30 am tomorrow. WSL	
" "	16.9.18	8.30am	Marched to Sheet 57.C. Sq. B.8.b.8.5 (near ST. LEGER). Arranged for motor ambulance to move behind Brigade	
ST. LEGER		12 noon	Arrived. Camp consists of a trench with bivouacs & shallow dugouts. Erected tents for patients, Treatment Room, some of the personnel & the Orderly Room. Good revetted horse lines. WSL	
			Weather fine & warm.	
		7.30pm	Surgeon J.R. BARROW-CLOUGH left for temporary duty at No 38 CCS, in accordance with instructions of ADMS	
" "	17.9.18	2.30am	Very heavy gale & thunderstorm. Tents blown down & trenches flooded. Day spent in cleaning up & erecting shelters. WSL	
" "	18.9.18		Weather mild & cloudy. Routine.	
" "	19.9.18		WSL Weather fine but cloudy - cold S.W. gale. Sports for men in afternoon. T/Surgeon BARROW-CLOUGH rejoined from 38 CCS. 1st LIEUT. LIPSHITZ, U.S. M.O.R.C. rejoined from 149 F Amb. (att/3 CCS) & proceeded to 38 CCS in relief. WSL	
" "	20.9.18	8.30am	The Tent subdivision (less officers) sent to XVII Corps Main Dressing Stn., under orders of ADMS, 63rd Div. Weather cold & showery: bright intervals. Routine. WSL	

A5834 Wt. W4973/M687 750,000 8/16 D. D. & L. Ltd. Forms/C.2118/13.

Army Form C. 2118.

8.

Instructions regarding War Diaries and Intelligence Summaries are contained in F. S. Regs., Part II. and the Staff Manual respectively. Title pages will be prepared in manuscript.

WAR DIARY
or
~~INTELLIGENCE SUMMARY.~~
(*Erase heading not required.*)

Place	Date	Hour	Summary of Events and Information	Remarks and references to Appendices
LOUVERVAL.	27.9.18		On return met Surg. BARROW-CLOUGH & learnt that Bearer Officer had been to cars on road & arranged for him to proceed with 12 bearers to ARTISTS' RIFLES R.A.P. to reinforce, & that car were coming up road from MOEUVRES to K.I.a. Returned of this road & sent remaining cars to bridge in E.15.c. via MOEUVRES. Up to about noon, casualties had been evacuated through organisation of 52nd Div.	
		5 pm	O.C. visited relay posts. Found cars up as far as bridge & evacuation working smoothly. Visited Bgde. H.Q. (which had moved up) & learnt that the next line had been taken. Brigade might move at short notice tomorrow. Arranged for Surg. BARROW-CLOUGH to proceed to 1/RMLI as M.O. i/c to replace a casualty. Found cars could proceed as far as E.16.c. & arranged accordingly. Weather fine. Road very congested & in bad repair.	
LOUVERVAL.	28.9.18		Weather wet & stormy.	[initials]
		11 am	Sent mounted messenger to report if BAPAUME-CAMBRAI Rd. open. Reported passable for traffic.	
		1 pm	O.C. proceeded to ~~[illegible]~~ A.D.S. (Factory on CAMBRAI Rd) & learnt that the Divn was moving up to attack east of CANTAING. Met O.C. Bearers & arranged for them to proceed.	
		4 pm	Car post established at L.3.a. on road W. of CANTAING, in conjunction with other Ambulance of the Divn.	
		6 pm	Found 190th Bgde. H.Q. & learnt that it was advancing in support to F.29.b. Arranged to establish relay posts towards F.29.b. Weather wet in the morning. Fine afternoon & evening.	[initials]

A7092 Wt. W128 9/M1293 750,000. 1/17. D. D & L. Ltd. Forms/C2118/14.

Instructions regarding War Diaries and Intelligence Summaries are contained in F. S. Regs., Part II. and the Staff Manual respectively. Title pages will be prepared in manuscript.

WAR DIARY
or
~~INTELLIGENCE SUMMARY.~~
(*Erase heading not required.*)

Place	Date	Hour	Summary of Events and Information
LOUVERVAL	29.9.18	~~[illegible]~~	Weather fine in morning wet later. Cold from W.
		10 am	Moved up to E.27.c.7.7
		11.30 am	OC to Car post & Bgde Hqrs. Learnt that two Bgdes were moving forward – 190th Bgde [illegible]
			Car post shelled. 1 Ford car hit but no serious damage.
		3.30 pm	Car post moved to F.28.d.5.9 established (jointly with other Amb's of Div) in last house E of CANTAING
		6.30 pm	OC to Bgde Hqrs. Found Bgde moving in support to F.30.a. & probably advancing. [illegible]
			Arranged to retain car post & send a relay to the Lock at 29 b.7.5.
BAPAUME-CAMBRAI Rd	30.9.18		Weather wet & windy. Cloudy [illegible] all day.
		~~[illegible]~~ 7 am	Car post established at F.29.a.6.7 with relay post at Lock F.29.b.5.7 & Mill F.30.a.6.4
			Previous car post retained as walking wounded post.
		10.15	Cases coming through steadily. Cars used for stretcher cases – horsed ambulance for walking wounded
		10.45	To Bgde Hqrs. Learnt that no progress was being made, casualties considerable, fresh attack
			planned at 1 pm. Aid posts in shell holes about 100 yds in advance of Mill. Good track
			but exposed to MG fire. 3 casualties among bearers – slightly wounded. Heavy shelling [illegible]
		3.30 pm	OC returned to Bgde Hqrs. Learnt that position would be consolidated & fresh attack unlikely.

W. J. F. Grant Lt Col
OC 150th (RN) F Amb

Oct 1918

140/3027

150 d. 7. a

23

159th (R.N.) FIELD AMBULANCE
No. ______
Date ______

Army Form C. 2118.

Vol 30 I

Instructions regarding War Diaries and Intelligence Summaries are contained in F. S. Regs., Part II. and the Staff Manual respectively. Title pages will be prepared in manuscript.

WAR DIARY
or
INTELLIGENCE SUMMARY.
(Erase heading not required.)

Place	Date	Hour	Summary of Events and Information	Remarks and references to Appendices
BAPAUME–CAMBRAI Rd. 57C Sq. E 25 c 7 7	1.10.18		Weather fine & cold, following a wet night.	
		10.30 am	O.C. proceeded to F 28 c. H.Qrs. Found that few casualties had occurred during the night; that relays posts &c were working smoothly. Ascertained that Div. was being relieved during the night. Arranged disposal of bearers on relief.	
		22 hrs	R.A.Ps reported clear. Bearers assisted to evacuate wounded of 52nd Div. & then withdrew to L 2.	[initials]
" "	2.10.18		Weather fine in morning; rain later.	
		14 hrs	Bearers (less 1 NCO & 4 men, holding party for dug-out at L2) returned to H.Qrs.	
		15 hrs	Brigade sick cleared & sent to XVII C.M.D.S.	[initials]
" "	3.10.18		Weather fine. Routine.	[initials]
" "	4.10.18		Weather fine, rather cold. Routine.	
		13.30	O.C. proceeded to 190th Bgde. H.Qrs. & was informed that the Div. would move – personnel by train, transport by road – on 6th or 7th to 1st Army area, & would remain in rest in the meantime.	[initials]
" "	5.10.18		Weather fine – cold wind. Routine & [illegible] of Tents. Warning order received for move to ~~[illegible]~~ 1st Army Area.	[initials]
" "	6.10.18	01.00	Clocks put back 1 hour, to normal time.	
		11.00	Warned that move was cancelled & Div. about to take the line again. Sent 3 squads to each Bn. of 190th Infy. Bgde. & Maj. Scales to Bgde. H.Qrs for orders & information.	
		12.30	Capt. A. HENDRY. RAMC & T/Lt. J.M. SHERIDAN. RAMC. arrived.	
		1330	O.C. & Maj. YOUNG to ARRAS (at A.D.S.) & to Bgde. H.Qrs. to enquire about arrangements & recce in trenches. Ascertained Bgde. would form up at 16 hrs. tomorrow. It was decided that A.D.S. would be at MARCOING. Arranged accordingly.	[initials]

159th (R.N.) FIELD AMBULANCE
No.
Date

Army Form C. 2118.

2.

Instructions regarding War Diaries and Intelligence Summaries are contained in F. S. Regs., Part II. and the Staff Manual respectively. Title pages will be prepared in manuscript.

WAR DIARY

or

~~INTELLIGENCE SUMMARY.~~

(Erase heading not required.)

Place	Date	Hour	Summary of Events and Information	Remarks and references to Appendices
57c Sq E28a7.7	7/10/18	8 hrs	Bearer Officer & party left to reconnoitre line. LT. SHERIDAN & 2 clerks detached to 148 F.Amb. for temp duty	
		9 hrs	One officer & 20 O.R. to ANNEUX to take over accommodation at A.D.S.	
		10 hrs	Hqrs & main party marched to ANNEUX	
ANNEUX		10.45	Arrived. 148 F.Amb. had not yet marched out.	
		12	O.C. to 190 Bde. Hqrs. Ascertained Bde moving at 17 hrs & arranged for bearers to go independently.	
		11.	MAJ. SCALES detailed to temporary duty at XVII C.M.D.S. Under orders A.D.M.S. received orders to arrange an entraining point for light Ry near FACTORY (BAPAUME-CAMBRAI Rd) for walking wounded. Sent 1 N.C.O., 4 men, 1 operating tent, 1 Soyer's stove & medical comforts.	
		15.15	O.C. visited entraining point & found preparation well forward	
		16.	Informed that A.D.S. would be at NOYELLES & a car post in RUMILLY (G.15.a.5.0).	
		16.30	Bearer officer & bearers (36) with 3 cars marched to RUMILLY.	
			Weather fine. Heavy shower at 16.30.	[initials]
	8.10.18	4.30.	Zero hour. 190th Infy Bde advanced in support. R.A.Ps in dug-outs in sunken rd (57.B. Sq. G.9.d).	
		8.30.	R.A.Ps advanced to G.5 & 11. Bearer post established at G.9.8, carrying to Car Post at G.15.a.	
			O.C. & Bearer Officer visited 190th Bde. Hqrs & R.A.P. & established a relay post at G.10.d. in a shell-hole.	
		19 hrs	Orders received that 24th Div. would relieve; bearers to be withdrawn on relief.	
		23.50	Support Bde. of 24th Div. assembled behind RUMILLY & relay posts not required. Bearers withdrawn & returned to ANNEUX by car.	
			Casualties in 190th Bde v. few; no difficulties in evacuation. Casualties in unit - 7 O.R. mostly due to shell fire, which was very heavy at times.	
			Weather fine	[initials]

Instructions regarding War Diaries and Intelligence Summaries are contained in F. S. Regs., Part II. and the Staff Manual respectively. Title pages will be prepared in manuscript.

150th (R.N.) FIELD AMBULANCE
No.
Date

WAR DIARY
or
~~INTELLIGENCE SUMMARY.~~
(Erase heading not required.)

Army Form C. 2118.
3.

Place	Date	Hour	Summary of Events and Information	Remarks and references to Appendices
ANNEUX	9.10.18	10.30.	Marched back to 57.C Sq. E28.C. in accordance with A.D.M.S. instruction	
		15.30	Marched to MORCHIES I.18.6.C. with Bgde. Arrived in dark. Shelters + tents.	
		13. hrs	20 O.R. Reinforcements received	
			Weather fine but cold.	W.S.L.
MORCHIES	10. hrs		O.C. proceeded on leave to U.K. handed over to ~~T/~~Major H. YOUNG.	H.Y.
	11th	16.00	Unit left MORCHIES 1600 hours marched to VAULX VRAUCOURT, entrained at 1715 hours + moved off at 1800 hours. Arrived St. POL 0600 hours Oct 12th + marched to BELVAL	H.Y.
BELVAL	12th		at BELVAL Map Ref. M 23 d 0.5 Sheet 44.	H.Y.
	13th		A/Sgt EVENS awarded Military Medal.	H.Y.
	14th	14.00	Lt. LIPSHITZ M.R.C. + one tent subdivision complete with equipment proceeded by road to VIII Corp Rest Station for temporary duty.	
		1500	Capt HENDRY Transferred to HOOD Batt. + Struck off strength	
		18.00	T. Capt CATHCART taken on strength. new Ford car received from 63 Div MT Coy	H.Y.
	16th	10.00	Three men proceeded 1st Army Rest Camp.	H.Y.
	18th	10.20	Major SCALES, M.C. proceeded on leave to ENGLAND	H.Y.
	21st	21.00	T/Surgeon PRATT J. taken on strength.	
	22nd	0800	Left BELVAL 0800 hours + marched to VILLERS-SIR-SIMON. I 5 a. 3.7 (Sheet 51C) arrived 1330 hours.	H.Y.
VILLERS-SIR-SIMON	23	14.00	Lieut SHERIDAN, + one tent subdivision with one car of 148 (RN) Fd Amb one car 149 + two car 150th (RN) Fd Amb. proceeded to ECOLE NORMAL DOUAI for duty with French Civilians	H.Y.

Instructions regarding War Diaries and Intelligence Summaries are contained in F. S. Regs., Part II. and the Staff Manual respectively. Title pages will be prepared in manuscript.

150th (R.N.) FIELD AMBULANCE
No. ____
Date ____

WAR DIARY
or
~~INTELLIGENCE SUMMARY.~~
(Erase heading not required.)

Army Form C. 2118.

Place	Date	Hour	Summary of Events and Information	Remarks and references to Appendices
VILLERS-SIR-SIMON.	Oct 24th	14.00	Surgn. PRATT R.N. detailed for temporary duty with HAWKE Battn	A.Y.
do.	25th	12.00	Routine duties.	A.Y.
	26th	14.00	Handed over command to Lt-Col. W.T. Grant,	A.Y.
" "	27.		Weather wet. Church parades. Routine.	
" "	28.		Weather fine & bright. Routine parades & fatigues. 63 OR. to Divisional Cinema. Sent in fr. 225 40 as contribution of unit to Divisional Comforts Fund.	W.T.G.
" "	29		Weather fine - overcast. OC visited detachment at DOUAI Pay. Usual parades & fatigues	W.T.G.
" "	30.		Weather fine. Physical drill & fatigues. Divisional football league match against F. Ambulance v. Anson Bn. in afternoon. Lost 0-1.	W.T.G.
		9 hrs	Major H. Young departed on leave to U.K.	W.T.G.
" "	31		Weather damp & showery.	
		10 hrs	O.C. proceeded to area FLERS-AUBY-COURCELLES, (near DOUAI) to reconnoitre for hospital site to treat as many Influenza cases as possible. Found suitable site at Ecole des Garçons, at LE FORREST.	
		17 hrs	Transport, less 2 limbers + 1 water cart, under LT WILSON. R.M. left for new area under Bgde. arrangements.	
		18 hrs	Capt. CATHCART, RAMC & 1st LT. LIPSHITZ M.C. USA. left for temporary duty with DRAKE Bn. & 4/BEDFORD R. respectively. Cross. Country run cancelled.	

W.T. Grant Lt Col RAMC
O.C. 150th (RN) F. Amb.

nov. 1918

140/3401

150^t. 7. a.

Instructions regarding War Diaries and Intelligence Summaries are contained in F. S. Regs., Part II. and the Staff Manual respectively. Title pages will be prepared in manuscript.

150th (R.N.) FIELD AMBULANCE
No. ______
Date ______

WAR DIARY
or
~~INTELLIGENCE~~ SUMMARY.
(Erase heading not required.)

150 Fd Amb

Army Form C. 2118.
1.

Place	Date	Hour	Summary of Events and Information	Remarks and references to Appendices
VILLERS-SIR-SIMON	1/11/18	7.10	Paraded & marched to LE HAMEAU. Strength 1 Officer, 134 O.R. Cars & remaining personnel to proceed by road, via ARRAS, DOUAI.	
		8.45.	Embussed & proceeded to HENIN-LIÉTARD, via SOUCHEZ & LENS.	
		10. hrs	Remainder of transport – 2 limbers & 1 water cart, marched to AGLAIN-ST NAZAIRE, to proceed the next day to new area.	
		12 hrs	Arrived HENIN-LIÉTARD.	
		13hrs	Marched, via COURCELLES & AUBY.	
LE FOREST.		16.15hrs	ARRIVED. Took over billets in "FRIEDRICKSTRASSE". Good accomodation for 120 patients in building (? late DETENTION BARRACK) behind MAIRIE. Stables for horses – orchard for vehicles	
		20.30hrs	Horse transport arrived.	
		17.30.	Capt E.O. Clarke RAMC. & 42 O.R. with 1 motor ambulance, 2 horsed Ambulance wagons, 1 G.S. wagon & 2 limbers arrived for temporary duty.	
			Weather fine & mild. New motor cycle received. 1 Reinforcement (M.T.) joined unit	
" "	2/11/18		Weather wet & mild. Day spent in cleaning up v. dirty accomodation – constructing latrines, incinerator etc.	
			Received instruction that T/Capt. J CATHCART was to report to 57th Divn for duty.	
			T/Capt J.V. COPE, M.C., RAMC relieved T/Capt. CATHCART as M.O. i/c DRAKE Bn. & was taken on the strength of this unit	
		16.30	Two limbers & one water cart, 2 NCOs 13 Ptes rejoined.	
			10 sick admitted during the day – 9 retained	

A7092 Wt. W128 9/M1293 750,000. 1/17. D. D & L. Ltd. Forms/C2118/14.

Instructions regarding War Diaries and Intelligence Summaries are contained in F. S. Regs., Part II. and the Staff Manual respectively. Title pages will be prepared in manuscript.

150th (R.N.) FIELD AMBULANCE
No. ____
Date ____

WAR DIARY
or
~~INTELLIGENCE SUMMARY.~~
(Erase heading not required.)

Army Form C. 2118.

2

Place	Date	Hour	Summary of Events and Information	Remarks and references to Appendices
LE FOREST.	3/11/18		Weather wet. Clearing up continued. 14 admissions (6 Influenza).	
		17 hrs.	Warned verbally that move would probably take place on 5th inst. & that all ambulance transport would probably be required to evacuate Div. Rest Station, now moving up	[initials]
			2 Reinforcements received	
~ ~	4/11/18	5.30 hrs	Reveillé. Packed wagons due to march at 10 hrs	
		10 hrs.	Horsed transport (less 2 limbers & water-cart) under Lt WILSON, R.M. proceeded with 190th Bgde. Transport to MASTAING - to proceed to THIANT the next day.	
		8 hrs	Lt. SHERIDAN reports from civil hospital, DOUAI, returned.	
		10 hrs	1 car sent to report for duty to ADMS - leaving two cars available.	
			Evacuated sick - including civilians - to BREDIERE; (23 CCS) till about 19 hrs - roads congested.	
		17 hrs	LT SHERIDAN left for temporary duty as M.O. i/c 14/WORCESTER R.	
		20 hrs.	Warned to proceed tomorrow by ~~bus~~ bus to THIANT.	[initials]
			Weather fine & cold.	
~ ~	5/11/18	7.20 hrs	Paraded & marched to COURCELLES - arrived 8.30 hrs.	
		11 hrs	Embussed	
THIANT.		16.20.	Arrived. Billeted chiefly in old factory. No hospital accommodation.	
		21 hrs	Visited 190th Bgde. Hqrs. & ascertained that move would be made to SAULTAIN early tomorrow.	
			Rained heavily all day.	[initials]
~	6/11/18	7 hrs	Paraded & marched to SAULTAIN	
SAULTAIN		13 hrs	Arrived after trying march. Roads frequently blocked by traffic - road blown up in places. Town very crowded & with difficulty obtained two barns for personnel & one small room for officers. No hospital accommodation but MDS of 56th Div. in the town who took cases.	

Instructions regarding War Diaries and Intelligence Summaries are contained in F. S. Regs., Part II, and the Staff Manual respectively. Title pages will be prepared in manuscript.

150th (R.N.) FIELD AMBULANCE
No. ______
Date ______

WAR DIARY
or
~~INTELLIGENCE SUMMARY.~~
(Erase heading not required.)

Army Form C. 2118.

3

Place	Date	Hour	Summary of Events and Information	Remarks and references to Appendices
SAULTAIN		21 h	Received orders to open M.D.S tomorrow at SEBOURQUIAUX tomorrow & to get in touch with O.C. 2/3 LONDON F. AMB. ~~who~~ (M.D.S. of 56th Divn) who would receive cases pending opening of 63rd Divn. M.D.S.	
		22 h	Visited O.C. M.D.S 56th Divn & arranged to send Tent Sub divn to assist him	
			Very wet all day.	
" "	7/11/18	07.30	Paraded & marched to SEBOUQUIAUX. O.C. went ahead in Ford car to select site. Unit (less 21 N.C.O. & men to 56th Dn. M.D.S.) ~~followed~~ followed	
SEBOUQUIAUX			O.C. found one bridge into village blown up but footbridge available for men on foot. Found O.C. 149 F Amb running A.D.S. at only suitable site & unable to advance as forward roads were not practicable for cars. O.C. proceeded to SEBOURG to look for alternative sites for M.D.S. Found town out of Divn area & full of troops. Found alternative route to SEBOUQUIAUX. Decided in consultation with O.C. 149 F Amb & DADMS to open as M.D.S as soon as M.A.C cars could be obtained, means having been found for horsed transport to get forward.	
		15 h	Notified 42 M.A.C. that M.D.S. was open & took over site from 149 F Amb. Maj. Scales & 65 bearers proceeded to ANGRE with 190 Inf. Bde.	
		1830	3 cars from M.A.C arrived. Reported to A.D.M.S that M.D.S was open.	
			No further cars received & own cars were out till late. 6 stretcher cases & 33 walking cases remained all night & using most of the available accommodation, there being civilians still on the premises & portion of other units whom it was not possible to displace. CAPTS. ILES & CURTIS. R.A.M.C. joined for temporary duty, also SURG. GILLESPIE. R.N.	
			Weather dull & damp but no rain	
	8/11/18	0900 ~~h~~	~~3 cars from M.A.C.~~ Few wounded but a fair number of sick admitted. A few gassed cases & later some Trench Feet.	
		1000 h	Ascertained that O.C. 148 F Amb. had found a route ~~way~~ practicable for cars & proposed to move forward & re-establish M.D.S. at the Convent, ANGRE.	
		1300 h	3 cars from M.A.C. Used own cars in addition. Asked for lorries from M.A.C. to evacuate walking cases	

A7092 Wt. W128 9/M1293 750,000. 1/17. D. D & L. Ltd. Forms/C2118/14.

Instructions regarding War Diaries and Intelligence Summaries are contained in F. S. Regs., Part II. and the Staff Manual respectively. Title pages will be prepared in manuscript.

150th (R.N.) FIELD AMBULANCE
No. ______
Date ______

WAR DIARY
or
~~INTELLIGENCE SUMMARY.~~
(Erase heading not required.)

Army Form C. 2118.

4

Place	Date	Hour	Summary of Events and Information	Remarks and references to Appendices
SEBOURQUIAUX	8/11/18		Received notice that Capt. COPE had been evacuated sick & Capt. NEILSON would join the unit as relief as M.O. i/c ARTISTS RIFLES.	
		1500h	Capt. BROWN. M.Corps. U.S.A. reported for temporary duty. Surg. GILLESPIE rejoined 148 F. Amb.	
		2030h	Received information from Bearer Officer of location of R.A.Ps & F. Amb Relay posts (Sheet 45 Sq. T 24, T30 & T28). Also a request for horsed ambulances on account of the ~~distance~~ length of the carry; this could not be complied with as all the horses had been working & were unfit for further work. Bearer Officer hopes to open a Collecting Post at T30.c.5.0 shortly.	his
			57 patients unevacuated retained for the night – about 50% sick. Unable to obtain M.A.C. cars for evacuation. Received information from O.C. 148 F. Amb. that he had opened M.D.S. & was prepared to clear patients as soon as M.A.C. cars reported for duty, necessitating transfer of bottom [illegible] M.G.C. & R.E. No means of sending these officers of the unit. Weather – dull & showery – very muddy.	
	9/11/18	0800h	Received orders to move forward to AUDREGNIES (Sh 45. Sq. T 19) as soon as clear with a view to forming A.D.S. further forward.	
		1000	5 cars from No 2 M.A.C. collected patients except 16, whom it was arranged should be evacuated during the day.	
		1015	Under orders from G.H.Q., Capt. CURTIS left for U.K. to report at War Office.	
		1020	3 Horsed Ambulances with 1 water cart & one limber (stores & rations) left for AUDREGNIES to clear cases from Bearer Post to M.D.S.	
		1130h	Marched to AUDREGNIES. Parts of the road v. deep in mud & others mined – very difficult for transport.	
AUDREGNIES		1500	Left small party to look after sick till evacuated. Arrived, but not able to get into touch with Brigade or ADMS till after dark. Billeted & fed personnel.	
		1630	Horsed transport arrived.	
		1730h	Visit ADMS & arranged to move to SARS LA BRUYERE early tomorrow. Weather fine & bright.	[illegible]

A5834 Wt. W4973/M687 750,000 8/16 D. D. & L. Ltd. Forms/C.2118/13.

Instructions regarding War Diaries and Intelligence Summaries are contained in F. S. Regs., Part II. and the Staff Manual respectively. Title pages will be prepared in manuscript.

150th (R.N.)
FIELD AMBULANCE
No.
Date

WAR DIARY
or
~~INTELLIGENCE SUMMARY.~~
(Erase heading not required.)

Army Form C. 2118.

5

Place	Date	Hour	Summary of Events and Information	Remarks and references to Appendices
AUDREGNIES	10/11/18	0730	Marched	
SARS LA BRUYÈRE		1145	Arrived. Found 149 F Amb occupying School & about to march out with their Brigade.	
		1205	The DADMS & OC 149 F Amb consulted. Decided to form a joint car post at SARS where patients could be transferred from horsed Ambulances to cars, roads forward not being good enough for motor transport. Motor transport to evacuate back to AUDREGNIES.	
			Sent Capt BROWN USA to rejoin 151st Amb.	
		1515 ~~1400~~	Marched to BOUGNIES – delayed by Brigade in front. Road very bad in places & many checks.	
BOUGNIES		2000h	Arrived. Village very full of troops. Billeted. Met Bearer Officer [illegible] for next day's work. Ascertained that cars could get up via FRAMERIES.	
		2100	Sent despatch rider to SARS with order for all cars to rejoin as soon as possible tomorrow	
			CAPT NEILSON RAMC from 1st/1/ARTISTS' RIFLES joined Bearer Officer for duty during the day.	
	11/11/18	0630	Reconnoitred village & arranged to take over Chateau, the only suitable place for ADS, though large, still crowded with RFA who could not be billeted elsewhere.	
		0930	DADMS arrived & brought information that hostilities would cease at 1100 hrs. Arranged to return part of SARS car post.	
		1030	Opened in chateau. Sent horsed ambulances to ACQUILLIES where Bearer Officer had established a post.	
		1130	One car arrived.	
		1200	Began to admit patients.	
		1600h	Informed that 25 cases, 188 Bde, where at Bearer Post at NOUVELLES arranged to clear them.	
		1900	Posts at ACQUILLIES & NOUVELLES [illegible] closed. Cars evacuating to SARS	

A5834 Wt. W4973/M687 750,000 8/16 D. D. & L. Ltd. Forms/C.2118/13.

Instructions regarding War Diaries and Intelligence Summaries are contained in F. S. Regs., Part II. and the Staff Manual respectively. Title pages will be prepared in manuscript.

150th (R.N.) FIELD AMBULANCE
No.
Date

WAR DIARY
or
~~INTELLIGENCE SUMMARY.~~
(Erase heading not required.)

Army Form C. 2118.

6

Place	Date	Hour	Summary of Events and Information	Remarks and references to Appendices
BOUGNIES	11/11/18		Weather fine. Scotch mist later.	[illegible]
— " —	12/11/18	0245	Message from NCO at SARS that 62 walking cases + 12 stretcher cases remained there & MAC cars [illegible] clearing. Arranged to send rations & assistance at daylight	
			Received wire from ADMS to proceed to ACQUILLIES	
		0930	8 MAC cars arrived & cleared the Ambulance. Brought information that post at SARS was clear	
		1030	Mobile Bearers & [illegible] attached to Bns.	
		1050	ADS clear of patients	
		1300	Sick arrived from Brigade	
		1400	Capt ILES rejoined 63rd MGC	
		1650	Lt SHERIDAN rejoined on relief as MO i/c 14/WORCESTERS.	
			Weather fine & bright. Frost at night	[illegible]
— " —	13/11/18		Cleaning up house & site, left in very dirty condition	
		1100	ADMS visited Ambulance & informed OC that cases likely to be well in [illegible] days would be retained, cases would be received from other Ambulances of the Div for evacuation.	
		1430	T/CAPT NEILSON returned to 145 F.Amb. Surg PRATT RN appointed to HOOD Bn struck off the strength of the Ambulance, relieving CAPT HENDRY who returned & was taken on the strength	
			About 40 cases admitted & retained pending arrival of MAC cars	
			Weather fine & bright	[illegible]

Instructions regarding War Diaries and Intelligence Summaries are contained in F. S. Regs., Part II. and the Staff Manual respectively. Title pages will be prepared in manuscript.

150th (R.N.) FIELD AMBULANCE No. Date

WAR DIARY
or
~~INTELLIGENCE SUMMARY.~~
(Erase heading not required.)

Army Form C. 2118.

7

Place	Date	Hour	Summary of Events and Information	Remarks and references to Appendices
DOUGNIES	14.11.18		Weather fine, bright cold. Over 50 cases retained owing to scarcity of cars. General cleaning up continued.	
		1700h	7 MAC cars arrived but had no petrol & were unable to evacuate.	
		1300h	SURGEON-LIEUT. BOYD. R.N. reported his arrival.	[initials]
" "	15.11.18		Weather bright cold.	
			3 MAC cars withdrawn by O.C. 42 MAC. Cleaning re continued.	
			Admitted 47 (incl. 20 cases of Influenza), Evacuated 57 (incl. 20 Influenza). Remaining 28 (15 Influenza)	[initials]
" "	16.11.18		Weather bright, frosty, cold. Considerable congestion of hosp. relieved by notification of a C.C.S. being opened at MONS, to which serious cases were evacuated, instead of to VALENCIENNES.	
		1500h	A.D.M.S. 63rd (R.N.) Div. inspected the unit & bade it farewell on leaving the Divn.	
			Admitted 46 (13 Influenza) Evacuated 43 (15 Influenza) Remaining 29 (12 Influenza)	
		2100	Maj. YOUNG returned from leave	[initials]
" "	17.11.18		Weather dull cold.	
		1100h	Capt. A. HENDRY left for duty with 4th Divn.	
		1500h	O.C. visited No. 1 CCS to enquire what cases could be received & ascertained that only very severe cases could be taken owing to lack of space & expectation of receiving a large number of prisoners of war.	
			Admitted. Officers 3, (1 Influenza) O.R. 38 (19 Influenza) Evacuated, Officers 2 O.R. 38 (21 Influenza) To Duty, O.R. 2. Remaining. Off. 2. O.R. 27 (9 Influenza)	[initials]

A5834 Wt. W4973/M687 750,000 8/16 D. D. & L. Ltd. Forms/C.2118/13.

Instructions regarding War Diaries and Intelligence Summaries are contained in F. S. Regs., Part II. and the Staff Manual respectively. Title pages will be prepared in manuscript.

150th (R.N.) FIELD AMBULANCE
No. ______
Date ______

WAR DIARY
or
~~INTELLIGENCE SUMMARY.~~
(Erase heading not required.)

Army Form C. 2118.

8.

Place	Date	Hour	Summary of Events and Information	Remarks and references to Appendices
BOUGNIES	18.11.18	0830	Capt. SHERIDAN left for temporary duty with 63rd Div. Reception Camp DOUAI.	MSh
		1400	Inter-section football match.	
			Weather cold. Sleet & later rain.	
			Admitted 55 (25 Influenza) Evacuated 42, (17 Influenza) Duty 2.	MSh
" "	19.11.18		Weather dull & damp - warmer	
		1100	ADMS, 63rd (RN) Div. visited the Ambulance.	
		1400	Intersection football match	
			Admissions 41 (21 Influenza) Evacuated 33 (20 Influenza). To Duty - Nil. Remaining 107 (26 Influenza - 10 with fever above 103°).	MSh
" "	20.11.18		Routine.	
		1400	Intersection football match.	
		1800	Weather damp & foggy. Concert in conjunction with 1/7 Middlesex R.	
			Admitted 40 (20 Influenza). Evacuated 37 (22 Influenza). To duty - Nil. Remaining 50 (19 Influenza). 5 cases with high temperature.	MSh
" "	21.11.18		Routine.	
			Weather bright & frosty.	
			Admitted 43 (21 Influenza) Evacuated 50 (20 Influenza) To duty 5. Remaining 38 (19 Influenza).	MSh
" "	22.11.18		Routine. Football matches. Weather bright & frosty	
			Admitted 27 (8 Influenza). Evacuated 10 (8 Influenza) To duty 4. Remaining 49 (19 Influenza).	MSh

Instructions regarding War Diaries and Intelligence Summaries are contained in F. S. Regs., Part II. and the Staff Manual respectively. Title pages will be prepared in manuscript.

150th (R.N.) FIELD AMBULANCE
No. ____
Date ____

WAR DIARY
or
~~INTELLIGENCE SUMMARY.~~
(Erase heading not required.)

Army Form C. 2118.

9.

Place	Date	Hour	Summary of Events and Information	Remarks and references to Appendices
BOUGNIES	23.XI.18		Routine. Football matches. Concert in evening. Weather bright & frosty.	
			M.A.C. cars failed to return from journey yesterday; consequent inability to evacuate led to excessive numbers remaining in hospital – 71 at 1700 hrs.	
			Admitted 38 (16 Influenza). Evacuated 16 (11 Influenza). Duty 2. Remaining 71 (24 Influenza)	[initials]
– –	24.XI.18		Routine. Football match in afternoon. Weather bright; frost.	
			Two MAC arrived – 1 from 149 F.Amb. (in accordance with ADMS' instructions)	
			Admitted 20 (8 Influenza). Evac. 40 (11 Influenza) Duty 4. Remained 46.	[initials]
		1530 hrs	O.C. 2/3 LONDON F.Amb. called to see premises prior to taking over.	
			~~Admitted 20 (8 Influenza) Evac. 40 (11 Influenza) To duty 4. Remain~~	[initials]
" –	25.XI.18	0900	Received orders to march to ERQUENNES with 190th Bgde. Group tomorrow at 1000 hrs.	
			Routine. Packing up.	
		1230	Advanced party from 2/3 LONDON F.Amb. arrived	
		1330	Maj. Young & small party left for ERQUENNES as advanced party	
			Received orders to return MAC cars to their unit.	
		1400 hrs	Lecture by Lt. [illegible] WILSON. R.M. on "Argentina.	[initials]
			Admitted 34 (8 Influenza) Evac. 38 (6 Influenza) To duty 19 (12 Influenza) Remain 33 (11 Influenza	
– –	26.XI.18	1000	Marched via GENLY - SARS LA BRUYERE - BLAUGIES - ATHIS to ERQUENNES, handing over 27 cases to detachment of 2/3 LONDON. F. AMB. with ration equipment, to be replaced by that unit at ERQUENNES as arranged. Received loan of 1 G.S. wagon & 1 limber from 63rd Div. A.C. to assist in move	

A5834 Wt. W4973/M687 750,000 8/16 D. D. & L. Ltd. Forms/C.2118/13.

Instructions regarding War Diaries and Intelligence Summaries are contained in F. S. Regs., Part II. and the Staff Manual respectively. Title pages will be prepared in manuscript.

150th (R.N.) FIELD AMBULANCE
No. ______
Date ______

WAR DIARY
or
~~INTELLIGENCE SUMMARY.~~
(Erase heading not required.)

Army Form C. 2118.

10

Place	Date	Hour	Summary of Events and Information	Remarks and references to Appendices
ERQUENNES	26.XI.18	1515	Arrived & took over sick accommodation in convent; billets & receiving room in town.	
		1530	A.D.M.S. 63rd Div. visited the unit. Heard that 2/3 LONDON F.AMB. were not going to BOUGNIES as arranged. A.D.M.S. left for BOUGNIES to enquire into state of affairs there.	M.S.G.
			1 Car from 149 (RN) F.Amb. arrived for duty.	
"	27.XI.18	0700	Sent 1 car & 3 horsed ambulances to evacuate 28 patients left at BOUGNIES, on transfer to 2/3 LONDON F.AMB.	
			Fitted up accommodation in CONVENT & two rooms in the town. Called upon to collect sick from a good many Artillery units in neighbourhood & accident cases from AUDREGNIES. Evacuated with remaining cars. A second car arrived from 149 F.Amb. to assist in evacuating. Weather dull. One car reported broken springs.	M.S.G.
			Admitted 38 (2 civilian, 19 Influenza) Evacuated 42 (2 civilian, 21 Influenza) To duty 13 Remaining 49 (31 Infl.)	
"	28.XI.18		Wet day. Routine. Reconnoitred town for extra accommodation; all places suitable for hospital use already occupied.	M.S.G.
			Admitted 23 (13 Influenza) Evac. 29 (17 Influenza) To duty 3 Remaining 37 (26 Influenza)	
"	29.XI.18		Routine.	
		0945	A.D.M.S. 63rd (RN) Div. visited the unit & arranged that the two cars of 149 (RN) F.Amb. should be returned, the car of this unit rejoining from his office.	
		1400	Lecture on procedure for voting at Parliamentary Election. Weather dull: no rain	
			Admitted 22 (12 Influenza) Evacuated 25 (19 Influenza) To Duty 8 (5 Influenza) Remaining 26 (15 Influenza)	M.S.G.

A5834 Wt. W4973/M687 750,000 8/16 D. D. & L. Ltd. Forms/C.2118/13.

Instructions regarding War Diaries and Intelligence Summaries are contained in F. S. Regs., Part II. and the Staff Manual respectively. Title pages will be prepared in manuscript.

WAR DIARY
or
~~WAR DIARY~~ INTELLIGENCE ~~SUMMARY~~.

(Erase heading not required.)

Army Form C. 2118.

11.

Place	Date	Hour	Summary of Events and Information	Remarks and references to Appendices
ERQUENNES	30.XI.18		Routine. Football match. Weather dull; bright intervals Education Committee appointed & room obtained for lectures Admitted 19 (Influenza 10) Evacuated 17 (Influenza 10) Duty 4 Remaining 24 (Influenza 13) W. F. Grant. Lieut-Colonel, R.A.M.C. Commanding, 150th Field Ambulance.	I. List of Instructors II. Timetable of Classes attached

A5834 Wt. W4973/M687 750,000 8/16 D. D. & L. Ltd. Forms/C.2118/13.

List of Instructors. attached to War Diary for Nov./18.

I

Lieut J. Wilson R.M. .... Spanish
Bookkeeping
Commercial Correspondence & Office Management.

Staff Sergeant Childs ..... French

Staff Sergeant Duckworth .... Arithmetic
Elem. Maths.
English History
European History
Expansion of the British Empire.
Geography Commercial

Sergeant Holme .... Mathematics, Pure & applied
Citizenship.

L. Cpl. Hampson .... Cotton Spinning

Pte Terrell .... Shorthand

" Brocklehurst .... English Language & literature

" Taylor .... Arithmetic Higher Commercial
Music.

" Moseley .... Drawing, Art & Design

Attached to War Diary for Nov. /18 II

150th (R.N.) FIELD AMBULANCE
No.
Date

150th (R.N.) Field Ambce

TIME TABLE

DAY	SUBJECT	SUBJECT			SUBJECT		
	1115 – 1215	1345 – 1445	1445 – 1545	1545 – 1645	1800 – 1900	1900 – 2000	2000 – 2100
MONDAY			ARITHMETIC	MATHS. PURE & APPLIED.	SPANISH EXPANSION OF ENGLAND	MUSIC	PRIVATE STUDY
TUESDAY		SHORTHAND	HIGHER. COMMERCIAL ARITHMETIC.	ENGLISH	FRENCH	ELEMENTARY MATHS	COTTON SPINNING.
WEDNESDAY	EUROPEAN HISTORY	GAMES & SPORTS ROOM OPEN FOR PTE STUDY			BOOK KEEPING	ENGLISH HISTORY	PRIVATE STUDY
THURSDAY		COMMERCIAL CORRESPONDENCE	BOOK KEEPING.	MATHS PURE & APPLIED	SPANISH GEOGRAPHY	ENGLISH LANGUAGE & LITERATURE	PRIVATE STUDY.
FRIDAY		ARITHMETIC	CITIZENSHIP	SHORTHAND	FRENCH	DRAWING ART & DESIGN	COTTON SPINNING
SATURDAY	HIGHER COMMERCIAL ARITHMETIC.	GAMES, SPORTS & PASSES ROOM OPEN FOR PRIVATE STUDY					
SUNDAY	ROOM OPEN FOR PRIVATE STUDY						

28/11/18.

Dec 1918

40/3481

No 150 F.A

Instructions regarding War Diaries and Intelligence Summaries are contained in F. S. Regs., Part II. and the Staff Manual respectively. Title pages will be prepared in manuscript.

150th (R.N.) FIELD AMBULANCE
No.
Date

WAR DIARY
or
~~INTELLIGENCE SUMMARY.~~
(Erase heading not required.)

Army Form C. 2118.

I

18 32

Place	Date	Hour	Summary of Events and Information	Remarks and references to Appendices
ERQUENNES	1.XII.18.		Routine Weather dull & cold	
		1400	CO's parade.	
			Admitted 15 (6 Influenza) Evac. 16 (3 Influenza). Remaining 23	W.S.A.
"	2.XII.18.		Routine. Hockey match. Weather dull & cold.	
			Admitted 16 (Influenza 9) Evacuated 7 (Influenza 5) To duty 2 (Influenza 1) Remaining 30 (Influenza 19).	W.S.A.
"	3.XII.18.	0930	Paraded with 3 officers & 81 O.R. for practice inspection by Army Commander. Two Brigade Groups present	
		1130	Returned. ADMS. 63rd (RN) Div. visited the unit.	
			Weather cold & wet.	
			Admissions 17 (Influenza 7) Evacuated 15 (Influenza 9) Duty 4 (Influenza 3) Remaining 28 (Influenza 14)	W.S.A.
"	4.XII.18	0900	Inspection by 1st Army Commander cancelled on account of bad weather	
		1100	Billet Inspection	
			Admitted 17 (Influenza 8). Evac. 11 (Influenza 3) Duty 5 (Influenza 3) Remaining 27 (Influenza 16)	W.S.A.
			Weather wet & cold.	
"	5.XII.18		Routine. Football match. Commenced disinfecting blankets at Divl. Laundry.	
		1330hrs	Inspection of Transport.	
		1600	Surg. Lt. BOYD R.N. rejoined from detached duty at MONS. (No.1. CCS).	
			Weather cold, dull with bright intervals	
			Admitted 14 (Influenza 4) Evac. 11 (Influenza 7) Duty 11 (Influenza 7). Remained 23 (Infl. 8)	W.S.A.
"	6.XII.18		Routine Football match – Brigade League. Use of baths of N.Z. Tunnelling Coy. obtained for the daily – 30 men	
			Admitted 14 (Influenza 4). Evac 10 (Influenza 1) Duty 9 (Influenza 5) Remaining 18 (Influenza 6)	W.S.A.
"	7.XII.18		Routine. 77 O.R. to FOLLIES. Weather dull – bright intervals	
			Admitted 10 (Influenza 4) Evac 4 (Influenza 4) Duty 4 (Influenza 3). Remaining 20 (Influenza 8)	W.S.A.

Instructions regarding War Diaries and Intelligence Summaries are contained in F. S. Regs., Part II. and the Staff Manual respectively. Title pages will be prepared in manuscript.

150th (R.N.) FIELD AMBULANCE
No. ____
Date ____

WAR DIARY
or
~~INTELLIGENCE SUMMARY.~~
(Erase heading not required.)

Army Form C. 2118.

2

Place	Date	Hour	Summary of Events and Information	Remarks and references to Appendices
ERQUENNES	8.XII.18		Routine. Weather fine & bright.	
			Admitted 10 (Influenza 5) Evac 3 (Influenza 2) Duty 5 (Influenza 3) Remaining 22 (Influenza 8)	[initials]
" "	9.XII.18		Routine. Brigade League Football match. Weather fine & bright.	
		1330	C.O's parade.	
		1130	O.C., having been instructed to supervise sanitation in the Brigade area, visited 4/Bedford R. lines & inspected sanitary arrangements with the M.O. i/c Bn.	
			Admitted 16 (Influenza 11) Evac 10 (Influenza 5) Duty 5 (Influenza 3) Remaining 23 (Influenza 12)	[initials]
" "	10.XII.18	0030	Lt & Qm. J. WILSON R.M. proceeded on leave to U.K.	
		1400	O.C. visited 1/1 Artists Rifles to supervise sanitation.	
			Weather wet.	
			Admitted 11 (Influenza 6) Evac 8 (Influenza 3) Duty 5 (Influenza 1) Remaining 21 (Influenza 14).	[initials]
" "	11.XII.18	1000	6 Coalminers left for Concentration Camp on demobilization	
		1030	Maj. SCALES, M.C., 1st Lt. LIPSHITZ, & 41 O.R. left by lorries for temporary duty at No. 6. C.C.S. MONTIGNY, under orders from D.D.M.S. 8th CORPS.	
		1400	O.C. inspected Refilling Point of 190th Bgde area, under instruction from A.D.M.S.	
			Weather wet.	
			Admitted Officers 2, O.R. 20, civilian 2. (Influenza 9) Evacuated Officers 2, O.R. 7, civilian 2, (Influenza 6) Duty 3 Influenza 2. Remaining 27 (Influenza 15)	[initials]
" "	12.XII.18	0845	Two coalminers left for demobilization.	
			Routine. Wet day.	
		1430	O.C. reconnoitred MONTIGNY AU ROC for suitable accomodation. Roads v. bad - unsuitable for motor transport	

A5834 Wt. W4973/M687 750,000 8/16 D. D. & L. Ltd. Forms/C.2118/13.

Instructions regarding War Diaries and Intelligence Summaries are contained in F. S. Regs., Part II. and the Staff Manual respectively. Title pages will be prepared in manuscript.

150th (R.N.) FIELD AMBULANCE
No. ____
Date ____

WAR DIARY
or
INTELLIGENCE SUMMARY.
(*Erase heading not required.*)

Army Form C. 2118.

3

Place	Date	Hour	Summary of Events and Information	Remarks and references to Appendices
ERQUENNES	12.XII.18		Admitted OR 18, civilian 2 (Influenza 11). Evac. O.R. 12, civilian 2 (Influenza 4). Duty 7 (Influenza 5). To 149 F Amb 1. Remaining 28 (Influenza 18.	[illegible]
" "	13.XII.18		Routine. Dull weather with some rain	
		13.15h	Kit inspection	
		17.30	Pay.	
			Admitted 14 (Influenza 5). Evac 11. (Influenza 7) Duty 6 (Influenza 5). Remaining 25 (Influenza 11).	
" "	14.XII.18		Routine. Weather dull, fine intervals. Brigade League Football match	
		1100h	ADMS 63rd Div inspected the Ambulance.	[illegible]
		1145	O.C. visited AUTREPPE, MONTIGNY SUR ROC, GUSSIGNIES to ascertain if better accommodation existed. None found; roads v. bad.	
			Admitted 12 (Influenza 6) Evac. 12 (Influenza 3) Duty 2. (Influenza 1) Remaining 23 (Influenza 13)	[illegible]
" "	15.XII.18		Routine. Church Parade. Weather fine. Billet inspection.	
			Admitted 7 (Influenza 6) Evac 3 (Influenza 1) Duty 7 (Influenza 4). Remained 20 (Influenza 14)	[illegible]
" "	16.XII.18		Routine. C.O.'s inspection. Weather dull.	
		1540h	O.C. visited 7/R. Fusiliers inspected sanitary arrangements.	
			Admitted 9 (5 Influenza). Evac. 4 (2 Influenza). Duty 3 (2 Influenza). Remaining 21 (14 Influenza).	
" "	17.XII.18		Routine. Weather fine; colder. Belgian Interpreter Sgt. L. GUNST. reported his arrival	
			Admitted 8 (2 Influenza) Evac 2 Duty 5 (5 Influenza) Remaining 22 (Influenza 10)	[illegible]
" "	18.XII.18		Routine. Billet inspection. Weather wet.	

A5834 Wt. W4973/M687 750,000 8/16 D. D. & L. Ltd. Forms/C.2118/13.

Instructions regarding War Diaries and Intelligence Summaries are contained in F. S. Regs., Part II. and the Staff Manual respectively. Title pages will be prepared in manuscript.

150th (R.N.) FIELD AMBULANCE
No. ______
Date ______

WAR DIARY
or
~~INTELLIGENCE~~ SUMMARY.
(Erase heading not required.)

Army Form C. 2118.

4

Place	Date	Hour	Summary of Events and Information	Remarks and references to Appendices
ERQUENNES	18.XII.18		Admitted 8 (Influenza 4) Evacuated 5 Duty 3 (Influenza 1) Remaining 22 (Influenza 13)	MFG
" "	19.XII.18		Routine. Football match (Brigade League) Tug of war practise	
		1100h	ADMS visited the Ambulance	
			Weather fine & cold.	MFG
" "	20.XII.18		Routine. Tug of war v. 14/WORCESTER R. Weather dull & cold	
		1100h	DDMS XIII Corps inspected the arrangements of the F. Ambulance	
		1500h	Maj (a/Lt Col.) M.F. Grant, RAMC handed over command of the 150th (RN) F.Amb. to Capt. (a/Maj) G.F. ALLISON RAMC	
			M.F. Grant Lt Col	
	20 XII.18		Took over command of 150 (R.N.) Field Ambulance from Lt. Col. M.F. GRANT RAMC.	GFA
	21.XII.18		Routine	GFA
	22.XII.18		Routine	GFA
	23.XII.18		By order of ADMS I visited BOUSSU to inspect the orphanage with a view to taking it over as a site for the Ambulance when Brigade moves to that area. Did not think the orphanage suitable. The house of Burgomaster in St. GHISLAN more suitable. ~~reported~~	GFA

A5834 Wt. W4973/M687 750,000 8/16 D. D. & L. Ltd. Forms/C.2118/13.

Instructions regarding War Diaries and Intelligence Summaries are contained in F. S. Regs., Part II. and the Staff Manual respectively. Title pages will be prepared in manuscript.

150th (R.N.) FIELD AMBULANCE
No.
Date

WAR DIARY
or
~~INTELLIGENCE SUMMARY.~~
(*Erase heading not required.*)

Army Form C. 2118.

Place	Date	Hour	Summary of Events and Information	Remarks and references to Appendices
In the Field	24.12.18		Visited AUTREPPE & inspected 112 Labour Bn	
			Reported to A.D.M.S. the result of my visit to BOUSSU & St. GHISLAN.	G.F.A.
	25.12.18		The Brig. General visited Unit	G.F.A.
	26.12.18		Routine	G.F.A.
	27.12.18		Routine	G.F.A.
	28.12.18		Final of Brigade Football League. The Ambulance won by 3 goals to one	G.F.A.
			Four men (Miners) left for VIII Corps Concentration Camp for Demobilisation	
	29.12.18		Four men (Miners) left for VIII Corps Concentration Camp for Demobilisation	G.F.A.
	30.12.18		Inspected the cooking & Sanitary arrangement of the ARTISTS Bn	G.F.A.
	31.12.18		Routine	G.F.A.

G. F. Awson
Major RAMC
O.C. 150 (R.N.) Field Ambulance

A5834 Wt. W4973/M687 750,000 8/16 D. D. & L. Ltd. Forms/C.2118/13.

63rd DIV

Box 2985

Jan. 1919 / 1

140/3490.

No. 150. F. A.

Instructions regarding War Diaries and Intelligence Summaries are contained in F. S. Regs., Part II. and the Staff Manual respectively. Title pages will be prepared in manuscript.

WAR DIARY
or
INTELLIGENCE SUMMARY.
(Erase heading not required.)

Army Form C. 2118.

150 Fd Amb

Vol 33

Place	Date	Hour	Summary of Events and Information	Remarks and references to Appendices
In the Field	1/1/19		Brigadier General visited the unit	E.T.A.
	2/1/19		Two miners were sent to VIII Corps concentration camp for Demobilization	E.T.A.
	3/1/19		Routine	E.T.A.
	4/1/19		Routine	E.T.A.
	5/1/19		Surgeon Lt. Boyd RN was struck off the strength of the unit to D.R.A.R.E. Bn	E.T.A.
			Lieut Wilson returned from leave	E.T.A.
	6/1/19		Three miners were sent to VIII Corps concentration Camp for Demobilization	E.T.A.
	7/1/19		The unit moves with the 190 Inf. Bde to St GHISLAIN Map Ref. O15 b central (Sheet 45)	E.T.A.
	8/1/19		ADMS inspected unit and Hospital	E.T.A.
	9/1/19		Routine	E.T.A.
	10/1/19		Routine	E.T.A.
	11/1/19		Three teachers one student and one miner were sent to VIII Corps concentration Camp for Demobilization	E.T.A.
			The horses of the Unit were inspected by DADVS at BOUSSU	E.T.A.

A5834 Wt. W4973/M687 750,000 8/16 D. D. & L. Ltd. Forms/C.2118/13.

Instructions regarding War Diaries and Intelligence Summaries are contained in F. S. Regs., Part II. and the Staff Manual respectively. Title pages will be prepared in manuscript.

WAR DIARY
or
INTELLIGENCE SUMMARY.
(*Erase heading not required.*)

Army Form C. 2118.

Place	Date	Hour	Summary of Events and Information	Remarks and references to Appendices
In the Field	23/1/19		Routine	
	24/1/19		Routine	
	25/1/19		The Brigadier-General visited the unit, he inspected the Hospital and men's quarters. GFA	
	26/1/19		Routine.	
	27/1/19		Routine	
	28/1/19		I inspected the sanitation of QUIVERAIN. It is much cleaner but not satisfactory yet. GFA.	
	29/1/19		Routine	
	30/1/19		Routine	
	31/1/19		Routine	

G F Allison
Lieut Col RAMC
O.C. 150 (R.N.) Field Amb.

SECRET and
CONFIDENTIAL.

V O L U M E   XXXIII.

W A R   D I A R Y .

of

150(ROYAL NAVAL) FIELD AMBULANCE.

for

period

1st. February 1919.

to

28th. February 1919.

(inclusive)

==*=*=*=*=*=*=*=*=*=*=*=*=*=*=*=*

Army Form C. 2118.

Instructions regarding War Diaries and Intelligence Summaries are contained in F. S. Regs., Part II. and the Staff Manual respectively. Title pages will be prepared in manuscript.

WAR DIARY
or
INTELLIGENCE SUMMARY.
(Erase heading not required.)

Place	Date	Hour	Summary of Events and Information	Remarks and references to Appendices
In the Field	12/1/19		Two reinforcements reported for R.A.S.C. M.T. and were taken on the strength of unit. G.A.H.	
	13/1/19		Six men were sent to VIII Corps Concentration Camp for Demobilization G.A.H.	
	14/1/19		Routine	
	15/1/19		I inspected the sanitary condition of Boussu and found them satisfactory G.A.H.	
	16/1/19		Routine	
	17/1/19		Routine	
	18/1/19		Routine	
	19/1/19		Routine	
	20/1/19		I inspected the Sanitation of HORNU and found everything quite satisfactory G.A.H.	
	21/1/19		Six men were sent yesterday and six this morning to VIII Corps Concentration Camp. for Demobilization G.A.H.	
	22/1/19		Five men were demobilized. G.A.H.	

A5834 Wt. W4973/M687 750,000 8/16 D. D. & L. Ltd. Forms/C.2118/13.

Instructions regarding War Diaries and Intelligence Summaries are contained in F. S. Regs., Part II. and the Staff Manual respectively. Title pages will be prepared in manuscript.

WAR DIARY
or
INTELLIGENCE SUMMARY.
(*Erase heading not required.*)

Army Form C. 2118.

130th (RN) Fd. Ambce

Place	Date	Hour	Summary of Events and Information	Remarks and references to Appendices
In the Field	1/2/19		Routine G.A.A.	
	2/2/19		Routine G.A.A.	
	3/2/19		Four men proceeded to VIII Corps Concentration Camp for demobilization G.A.A.	
	4/2/19		One man " " " " " G.A.A.	
	5/2/19		Two reinforcements reported for duty from Base and were taken on the strength accordingly. G.A.A.	
	6/2/19		Routine G.A.A.	
	7/2/19		Three men reported to the VIII Corps Con. Camp for demobilization G.A.A.	
	8/2/19		No 49819 Pte R. Collins 2nd Bedford Regt. died in Ambulance G.A.A.	
	9/2/19		Inspected the Sanitation of QUIVERAIN. G.A.A.	
	10/2/19		Three men proceeded to VIII Corps Con. Camp for demobilization G.A.A.	
	11/2/19		Two " demobilized. G.A.A.	

A7092 Wt. W128.9/M1293 750,000. 1/17. D. D & L. Ltd. Forms/C2118/14.

Army Form C. 2118.

Instructions regarding War Diaries and Intelligence Summaries are contained in F. S. Regs., Part II. and the Staff Manual respectively. Title pages will be prepared in manuscript.

WAR DIARY
or
INTELLIGENCE SUMMARY.
(*Erase heading not required.*)

Place	Date	Hour	Summary of Events and Information	Remarks and references to Appendices
In the Field	12/2/19		One other rank was evacuated sick to No 6 C.C.S. SAA	
	13/2/19		Major SCALES returned from No 6 C.C.S. for duty on the 12th inst. SAA	
	14/2/19		Major SCALES reported to ADMS. to act as DADMS. SAA	
	15/2/19		Capt Sheridan was granted special leave to England. SAA	
	16/2/19		Routine	
	17/2/19		I inspected sanitation of BOUSSU. A number of Diphtheria SAA cases were reported among civilians but I could get no SAA confirmation. SAA	
	18/2/19		Routine.	
	19/2/19		Six men were demobilized, and one man demobilized while on leave SAA Lieut SUNNES reported for duty from 1/48 (R.N.) Field Amb. SAA	
	20/2/19		Routine. SAA	

Instructions regarding War Diaries and Intelligence Summaries are contained in F. S. Regs., Part II. and the Staff Manual respectively. Title pages will be prepared in manuscript.

WAR DIARY
or
INTELLIGENCE SUMMARY.
(Erase heading not required.)

Army Form C. 2118.

Place	Date	Hour	Summary of Events and Information	Remarks and references to Appendices
In the Field	21/2/19		Major Scales was posted to 149 (R.N.) Field Amb. for duty. G.F.A.	
	22/2/19		Routine G.F.A.	
	23/2/19		Four men were sent to VIII Corps concentration Camp for demobilization G.F.A.	
	24/2/19		Pte MARLAND was evacuated sick. G.F.A.	
	25/2/19		Routine G.F.A.	
	26/2/19		Routine G.F.A.	
	27/2/19		Five men were demobilized G.F.A.	
	28/2/19		Four other ranks proceeded to VIII Corps Con. Camp for demobilization G.F.A.	

G. F. Allison
Lieut Col. RAMC
O.C. 150 (R.N.) Field Ambulance

A7092 Wt. W128 9/M1293 750,000. 1/17. D. D & L. Ltd. Forms/C2118/14.

150th. (R.N.) Field Ambulance,
St. Ghislain.

Mar. 1919

WAR DIARY

of

the

150th. (R.N.) FIELD AMBULANCE.

From

1st. March 1919.

To

31st. March 1919.

144/3551

Jos Wilson Lieut RN
for
Lieut. Col., M.C., R.A.M.C.
O.C., 150th. (R.N.) Field Ambulance.

Army Form C. 2118.

Instructions regarding War Diaries and Intelligence Summaries are contained in F. S. Regs., Part II. and the Staff Manual respectively. Title pages will be prepared in manuscript.

WAR DIARY
or
INTELLIGENCE SUMMARY.
(Erase heading not required.)

Place	Date	Hour	Summary of Events and Information	Remarks and references to Appendices
In the Field	1/3/19		The Brigadier visited the Hospital GAA	
	2/3/19		Lt. Sumner M.C. USA was posted to 148 (R.N.) Field Amb by order of A.D.M.S. GAA	
	3/3/19		ADMS inspected Hospital GAA	
	4/3/19		Routine	
	5/3/19		Routine	
	6/3/19		Routine	
	7/3/19		PTE BATESON RM was transferred from No 4 to No 1 Coy DIV TRAIN GAA CAPT W P NELSON RAMC was taken on the strength of this unit GAA	
	8/3/19 to 17/3/19		Routine	
	18/3/19		CAPT W.P. NELSON RAMC proceeded to 77 Army Bde R.F.A. by order of ADMS and was struck of the strength of this unit. GAA CAPT W. G WATTS MC USA was taken on the strength of this unit from 77 Army Bde RFA. GAA	
	19/3/19 to 22/3/19		Routine	
	23/3/19		By order of ADMS. Capt LIPSHITZ proceeded to 62 CCS. for temporary duty R.N.D. was reduced to cadres midday 23/3/19 GAA	
	24/3/19 to 27/3/19		Routine	

A5834 Wt. W4973/M687 750,000 8/16 D. D. & L. Ltd. Forms/C.2118/13.

Instructions regarding War Diaries and Intelligence Summaries are contained in F. S. Regs., Part II. and the Staff Manual respectively. Title pages will be prepared in manuscript.

WAR DIARY
or
INTELLIGENCE SUMMARY.
(Erase heading not required.)

Army Form C. 2118.

Place	Date	Hour	Summary of Events and Information	Remarks and references to Appendices
28/3/19 Mille Fuels	28/3/19		Capt. LIPSHITZ MC USA was demobilised from 42 CCS	
			By order of ADMS Capt SHERIDAN proceeded to BOULOGNE to report to ADMS and was struck off the strength of this unit from that date	
			Surgeon SHAW RN was taken on the strength of this unit from HA ANSON Bn	
	29/3/19 to 30/3/19		Routine	

G. F. Allison MC
Lt Col RAMC
OC 150 (RN) Field Ambulance

A5834 Wt. W4973/M687 750,000 8/16 D. D. & L. Ltd. Forms/C.2118/13.

SECRET &
CONFIDENTIAL.

150th. (RN) Field Ambulance.

4th. May 1919.

=*=*=*=*=*=*=*=*=

V O L U M E XXXV

W A R D I A R Y.

of

150th. (R.N.) Field Ambulance, for period

1st. APRIL 1919.

to

30th. April 1919

(inclusive)

April 1919

4/5/19.

G. Allison

Lieut. Col. R.A.M.C.
O.C., 150th. (RN) Field Ambulance.

Army Form C. 2118.

WAR DIARY
or
INTELLIGENCE SUMMARY.
(Erase heading not required.)

Instructions regarding War Diaries and Intelligence Summaries are contained in F. S. Regs., Part II. and the Staff Manual respectively. Title pages will be prepared in manuscript.

Place	Date	Hour	Summary of Events and Information	Remarks and references to Appendices
In the Field	1/4/19 to 6/4/19		Routine	[illegible]
			Routine	[illegible]
	7/4/19		Major Young RAMC. returned from English leave	[illegible]
	8/4/19		Routine	
	9/4/19 to 15/4/19		Routine	
			Routine	
	16/4/19		Surgeon Lieut. Boyd R.N. joined this unit from the Drake Bn	[illegible]
	17/4/19 to 21/4/19		Routine	[illegible]
	22/4/19		All cars but one were withdrawn from this Ambulance	[illegible]
	23/4/19		Routine	[illegible]
	24/4/19		Major Young RAMC. proceeded to England for demobilization	[illegible]

A5834 Wt. W4973/M687 750,000 8/16 D. D. & L. Ltd. Forms/C.2118/13.

Army Form C. 2118.

WAR DIARY
or
INTELLIGENCE SUMMARY.
(Erase heading not required.)

Instructions regarding War Diaries and Intelligence Summaries are contained in F. S. Regs., Part II. and the Staff Manual respectively. Title pages will be prepared in manuscript.

Place	Date	Hour	Summary of Events and Information	Remarks and references to Appendices
[illegible]	24/4/19		Surgeon Shaw R.N. proceeded to Admiralty for duty	[illegible]
	25/4/19		Capt. G. F. Watt O.C.M.S.A. reported A.E.F. on 15/4/19.	[illegible]
	26/4/19 to 30/4/19		Routine	[illegible]

G. F. [illegible]
Lieut-Col. R.A.M.C.
O.C. 150 (R.N.) Field Amb.

A5834 Wt. W4973/M687 750,000 8/16 D. D. & L. Ltd. Forms/C.2118/13.

May 1919

1x8135-60

No 150 Field Ambulance

Instructions regarding War Diaries and Intelligence Summaries are contained in F. S. Regs., Part II. and the Staff Manual respectively. Title pages will be prepared in manuscript.

WAR DIARY
or
INTELLIGENCE SUMMARY.
(Erase heading not required.)

Army Form C. 2118.

150 3rd Amb Cancel

Place	Date	Hour	Summary of Events and Information	Remarks and references to Appendices
In the Field	1/5/19		Routine	
	2/5/19		Routine	
	3/5/19		Routine	
	4/5/19		No 5/4375 Pte M.L. DICKIE promoted to L/Sergt. Pte A MAIJAH 5/3417 to L/Cpl. No 4210 Pte T.C. CASTLE to L/Cpl	
	5/5/19		Lieut & QM Wilson proceeded on … to England on leave	
	6/5/19		Routine	
	7/5/19		Orders received for Capt. A/Lt. Col to proceed to No 1 C.C.S.	
	8/5/19		Routine	
	9/5/19		Routine	
	10/5/19		Handed over 150 (R.N.) Field Ambulance to Surgeon W.E. Boyd R.N.	

G F Allen
Lt. Col. R.A.M.C.

A5834 Wt. W4973/M687 750,000 8/16 D. D. & L. Ltd. Forms/C.2118/13.

98 37

Army Form C. 2118.

Instructions regarding War Diaries and Intelligence Summaries are contained in F. S. Regs., Part II. and the Staff Manual respectively. Title pages will be prepared in manuscript.

WAR DIARY
or
INTELLIGENCE SUMMARY.
(Erase heading not required.)

Place	Date	Hour	Summary of Events and Information	Remarks and references to Appendices
St. Ghislain Belgium	10.5.19		Took over Ambulance from Lt Col Allison who proceeded to 6 CCS.	
	11.5.19		Routine	
	12.5.19		Routine	
	13.5.19		Routine	
	14.5.19		Routine	
	15.5.19		Handed over Ambulance to Capt Wilson RAMC who had returned from leave.	
			W. E. Boyd Surg Lt RN. A/O.C. 150 (RN) Field Ambulance RND.	

A5834 Wt. W4973/M687 750,000 8/16 D. D. & L. Ltd. Forms/C.2118/13.

Instructions regarding War Diaries and Intelligence Summaries are contained in F. S. Regs., Part II. and the Staff Manual respectively. Title pages will be prepared in manuscript.

WAR DIARY
or
INTELLIGENCE SUMMARY.
(Erase heading not required.)

Army Form C. 2118.

Place	Date	Hour	Summary of Events and Information	Remarks and references to Appendices
St Ghislain Belgium	15/5/19		Took over command of Field Ambulance from Surgeon W E BOYD. R.N.	
			Routine	
	16/5/19		Routine	
	17/5/19		Routine.	
	18/5/19		Received warning telegram that Cadre of Unit would probably move on 20th or 21st.	
	19/5/19		Orders received from D HQ to move by first train on 21st. and S.M.O to close hospital and evacuate all cases to MONS direct.	
	20/5/19		Handed over balance of Imprest a/c to Field Cashier MONS.	
			Hospital closed down, all drugs & dressings sent to No 1 CCS at MONS.	
			Surgeon W E BOYD joined DRAKE Battn and proceeded with that Unit to Base.	
			Capt METCALFE R.A.M.C. took sick parade.	
			Jos Wilson Capt RAMC	

Instructions regarding War Diaries and Intelligence Summaries are contained in F. S. Regs., Part II. and the Staff Manual respectively. Title pages will be prepared in manuscript.

WAR DIARY
or
INTELLIGENCE SUMMARY.
(Erase heading not required.)

Army Form C. 2118.

Place	Date	Hour	Summary of Events and Information	Remarks and references to Appendices
St GHISLAIN. Belgium	21/5/19	0700.	Moved wagons to railhead by hand and commenced entraining them at 0900. finished at 0930.	
		1800	Marched off with Unit to railhead and entrained for Dunkirk.	
		1910	Train left ST. GHISLAIN with cadre of this Unit and 63rd (RN) Battn Machine Guns.	
DUNKIRK.	22/5/19.	0700.	Train arrived sidings at DUNKIRK.	
		1000.	Unit marched to cadre reception camp for baths &c	
		1630.	" " " " " departure camp No 3.	
			10 Wagons detrained during day	
-do-	23/5/19.	1000.	Imprest Account closed and clearance certificate signed. Remaining 4 wagons detrained, visited docks & inspected guard.	
		1900.	Orders received to detail working party for loading wagons into ship and for Unit to stand by to embark following day.	
-do-	24/5/19	1200.	All wagons shipped.	
		1630	Unit paraded and marched to ship S.S. "MOGILEFF."	
		1630	Unit embarked in S.S. "MOGILEFF."	
		1730	S.S. "MOGILEFF" sailed for Southampton.	

Jo Wilson
Capt RN

A5834 Wt. W4973/M687 750,000 8/16 D. D. & L. Ltd. Forms/C.2118/13.

Army Form C. 2118.

Instructions regarding War Diaries and Intelligence Summaries are contained in F. S. Regs., Part II. and the Staff Manual respectively. Title pages will be prepared in manuscript.

WAR DIARY
or
INTELLIGENCE SUMMARY.
(Erase heading not required.)

Place	Date	Hour	Summary of Events and Information	Remarks and references to Appendices
At Sea	25/5/19	0800	Sighted Beachy Head.	
		1200	Arrived at SOUTHAMPTON.	
SOUTHAMPTON		1300	Disembarked and marched to Rest Camp. All accomodated there for night	
– do –	26/5/19	0700	Unit paraded and marched to Docks to unload wagons from S.S. "MOGILEFF"	
		1100	All wagons unloaded and entrained.	
		1300	Train left Southampton for Aldershot.	
ALDERSHOT.		1600	Arrived at ALDERSHOT. Men & wagons detrained. Men attd No 1 Coy RAMC in McGRIGOR Barracks.	
do	27/5/19	–	All Ordnance, Medical & Veterinary Stores handed in	
– do –	28/5/19	1600	Men entrained for London.	
LONDON		2000	" accomodated at Y.M.CA HOSTEL. BELGRAVE Rd to await inspection by King.	

Jos Wilson
Capt RAVC

A5834 Wt. W4973/M687 750,000 8/16 D. D. & L. Ltd. Forms/C.2118/13.

www.ingramcontent.com/pod-product-compliance
Lightning Source LLC
Chambersburg PA
CBHW080901230426
43663CB00013B/2592
* 9 7 8 1 4 7 4 5 3 3 8 9 8 *